Dimensions of Ethical Thought

Dimensions of Ethical Thought

edited by

Anthony E. Hartle
and
John Kekes

PETER LANG
New York · Bern · Frankfurt am Main · Paris

Library of Congress Cataloging-in-Publication Data

Dimensions of ethical thought.

Bibliography: p.
1. Ethics. 2. Social ethics. I. Hartle, Anthony E.
II. Kekes, John.
BJ1012.D47 1988 170 87-17252
ISBN 0-8204-0590-6

CIP-Kurztitelaufnahme der Deutschen Bibliothek

Dimensions of ethical thought / ed. by Anthony
E. Hartle and John Kekes. – New York; Bern;
Frankfurt am Main; Paris: Lang, 1987.
ISBN 0-8204-0590-6

NE: Hartle, Anthony E. [Hrsg.]

Printed by Weihert-Druck GmbH, Darmstadt, West Germany

Contents

PART V HAPPINESS AND VIRTUES

Preface

The history of ethical thought is the history of human thinking about the nature of the good life, the justification of moral choices, and the resolution of moral disagreements. These are controversial matters about which reasonable and decent people can and do reach different conclusions. We believe, however, that the history of ethical thought contains a development; it is not merely a repository of conflicting moral theories, but an advance toward better answers to moral questions. The organization of this book is intended to reflect this belief.

We begin with the fundamental question, raised by egoism, of why reasonable people would accept moral restrictions on their conduct. The answer is that we all want to have a good life and morality is part of that life. One reason why this is so is that good lives for ourselves require a stable society in which everyone can try to live a good life and morality is the way in which this is achieved. The theoretical statement of this answer is utilitarianism, developed in Part I. But social stability may be protected by immoral means. Nonconsequentialist moral theories, discussed in Part II, aim to define a set of requirements which is the duty of everyone to observe, even if doing so would weaken social stability. In Part III, we examine contractarian theories whose purpose it is to identify the specific rights individuals have. These rights derive from universal characteristics of human nature and this is the reason why respecting them is a requirement of good lives and why our duty is to observe them. The moral theories discussed in the first three parts establish the social framework within which we can try to make good lives for ourselves. Thus, they aim to formulate social morality. But there is also need for personal morality to answer the question of what would make our lives good if the social conditions are hospitable to our development. In Parts IV and V, therefore, we turn to the questions of where social morality ends and personal morality begins and what character-traits we need to develop in ourselves to make it possible for us to live good lives. Personal morality is the domain of human freedom; within it we pursue individual ideals of good lives which may differ from person to person. But social morality is needed to define the limits we cannot trespass in pursuit of these ideals, because doing so would undermine the very possibility of the pursuit we are engaged in. The character-traits needed for good lives are the virtues. And we end our discussion by considering what these virtues are. Reasonable people would want to develop these virtues in themselves, because they are necessary components of good lives regardless of how these lives are conceived.

The readings we have selected are arranged so as to lead to a progressive development of social and personal morality and to a consideration of their connection. We suggest that the two are compatible and that their development can be best accomplished by recognizing the valuable contributions traditional moral theories make while recognizing and eliminating their problematic features.

The structure of each of the five parts is the same. We begin with an introduction to set the stage for the coming discussion. Then we present a problem case in the form of a moral dilemma. Reasonable and decent people may disagree about the requirements of morality in our hypothetical situations. After this, we present a classical and a contemporary reading. It is our hope that a thoughtful application of these readings to the problem cases will provide justifiable answers to what morality requires us to do.

Acknowledgments

The sources of the readings we have selected are as follows:

Plato, *Republic*, 357–362, tr. B. Jowett (London: Macmillan, 1892).

J.S. Mill, *Utilitarianism* (London: Frasier Magazine, 1861), selections from Chapters One, Two, and Four.

R.B. Brandt, "Some Merits of One Form of Rule-Utilitarianism," *University of Colorado Studies in Philosophy*, 3(1967), 39–65. We are grateful to the Colorado University Press for permission to reprint it.

I. Kant, *Fundamental Principles of the Metaphysics of Morals*, tr. T.K. Abbott, (London: Macmillan, 1873), selections.

W.D. Ross, "What Makes Right Acts Right?" *The Right and the Good*, Chapter Two (Oxford: Clarendon, 1930). We are grateful to Oxford University Press for permission to reprint it.

J. Locke, *Two Treatises of Government* (London: Corner, 1690), selections from Book II, Chapters Two, Three, Four, Five, Six, Seven, Eight, Nine, and Eleven.

J. Rawls, "Justice as Fairness," *The Journal of Philosophy* 54(1957), 653–662. We are grateful to the Editors of *The Journal of Philosophy* and to Professor John Rawls for persmission to reprint it.

D. Hume, *An Enquiry Concerning the Principles of Morals* (London: Cadell, 1977), selections from Sections One, Two, Three, Five, and Nine.

P.F. Strawson, "Social Morality and Individual Ideal," *Philosophy* 36(1961), 1–17. We are grateful to Cambridge University Press and to Sir Peter F. Strawson for permission to reprint it.

J.S. Mill, *On Liberty* (London: 1859), selections from Chapters One, Two, Three, and Four.

Aristotle, *Nicomachean Ethics*, tr. W.D. Ross (Oxford: Clarendon, 1925), selections from Books One, Two, Three, Five, Six, and Ten.

Omissions from the texts are indicated by ". . .", except when chapter or paragraph numbering of the original makes omissions obvious. Additions to the texts are enclosed in "[]"; these consist mainly of headings we have added for the sake of clarity.

Part I

The Common Good

Introduction

One primary concern of moral philosophy is with the justification of the choices we make. Most of the actions we choose to perform are guided by our preferences. Indeed, for most people most of the time, no consideration carries greater weight than their own interests and desires. This suggests that the justification of choices may simply be that they accord with the agent's preferences. But since preferences may be stupid, self-destructive, ignorant, or mutally exclusive, we need to ask what should guide us in evaluating preferences. A traditional answer is that our own welfare should guide us. We should prefer what seems on balance to be the best for us. This is the view of *egoism.*

The first reading in this section is a brief excerpt from one classic consideration of egoism, the famous dialogue of Plato (427–347 B.C.), *The Republic.* One of the participants in it, Glaucon, tells the story of Gyges who found himself suddenly able to pursue his own preferences without regard for anyone else. Glaucon puts forward the view that people in Gyges' position would generally choose to act so as to injure others if need be in order to get what they want.

The most important participant in the dialogue is Socrates, and he disagrees. He argues that our own welfare is inseparable from the welfare of others. Consequently, rational preferences do not ignore the preferences of others, but exist in harmony with them. According to Socrates, the task of moral philosophy is to harmonize rational preferences.

A systematic development of this view is *utilitarianism.* Utilitarians agree with egoists in claiming that the reasons for our choices derive from the benefits our actions are likely to produce, but the two positions differ significantly in response to the question of whose benefit matters. Utilitarians argue that rational and moral actions aim to produce the greatest happiness for the greatest number of people, and not just for ourselves.

The classic statement of utilitarianism is by John Stuart Mill (1806–1873), the author of the second reading in this section. He argues that each and every human being has equal intrinsic value. Consequently, the agent of an action has the same importance as anyone else. Thus it follows that an action is right in proportion to the degree it produces happiness for all concerned.

In the third reading, Richard Brandt presents a contemporary development of Mill's view, *rule utilitarianism.* He defends utilitarianism from some of the objections which have been made against Mill's formulation of it. According to Brandt, the moral rightness of actions depends on their conformity to rules which, were we all to follow them, would produce at least as much overall satisfaction as any other set of rules which could be adopted to guide conduct.

Thus the argument in this section progresses by beginning with the egoistic view that people tend to act on their preferences. It builds on Socrates' realization that people's preferences are interdependent. And it concludes with the utilitarian claim that reason and morality both require that in pursuing our preferences we should act for the common good. In the next section, we shall go on to consider whether this utilitarian claim is acceptable.

Problem Case: Morality and Egoism, Plato, *Republic*, Book II

. . .Glaucon, who is always the most pugnacious of men, wanted to have the battle out. So he said to me: Socrates, do you wish really to persuade us, or only to seem to have persuaded us, that to be just is always better than to be unjust?

I should wish really to persuade you, I replied, if I could.

Then you certainly have not succeeded. Let me ask you now:—How would you arrange goods—are there not some which we welcome for their own sakes, and independently of their consequences, as, for example, harmless pleasures and enjoyments, which delight us at the time, although nothing follows from them?

I agree in thinking that there is such a class, I replied.

Is there not also a second class of goods, such as knowledge, sight, health, which are desirable not only in themselves, but also for their results?

Certainly, I said.

And would you not recognize a third class, such as gymnastic, and the care of the sick, and the physician's art; also the various ways of money-making—these do us good but we regard them as disagreeable; and no one would choose them for their own sakes, but only for the sake of some reward or result which flows from them?

There is, I said, this third class also. But why do you ask?

Because I want to know in which of the three classes you would place justice?

In the highest class, I replied,—among those goods which he who would be happy desires both for their own sake and for the sake of their results.

Then the many are of another mind; they think that justice is to be reckoned in the troublesome class, among goods which are to be pursued for the sake of rewards and of reputation, but in themselves are disagreeable and rather to be avoided.

I know, I said, that this is their manner of thinking, and that this was the thesis which Thrasymachus was maintaining just now, when he censured justice and praised injustice. But I am too stupid to be convinced by him.

I wish, he said, that you would hear me as well as him, and then I shall see whether you and I agree. For Thrasymachus seems to me, like a snake, to have been charmed by your voice sooner than he ought to have been; but to my mind the nature of justice and injustice have not yet been made clear. Setting aside their rewards and results, I want to know what they are in themselves, and how they inwardly work in the soul. If you please, then, I will revive the argument of Thrasymachus. And first I will speak of the nature and origin of justice according to the common view of them. Secondly, I will show that all men who practise justice do so against their will, of necessity, but not as a good. And thirdly, I will argue that there is reason in this view, for the life of the unjust is after all better far than the life of the just—if what they say is true, Socrates, since I myself am not of their opinion. But still I acknowledge that I am perplexed when I hear the voices of Thrasymachus and myriads of others dinning in my ears; and, on the other hand, I have never yet heard the superiority of justice to injustice maintained by any one in a satisfactory way. I want to hear justice praised in respect of itself; then I shall be satisfied, and you are the person from whom I think that I am most likely to hear this, and therefore I will praise the unjust life to the utmost of my power, and my manner of speaking will indicate the manner in which I desire to hear you too praising justice and censuring injustice. Will you say whether you approve of my proposal?

Indeed I do; nor can I imagine any theme about which a man of sense would oftener wish to converse.

I am delighted, he replied, to hear you say so, and shall begin by speaking, as I proposed, of the nature and origin of justice.

They say that to do injustice is, by nature, good; to suffer injustice, evil; but that the evil is greater than the good. And so when men have both done and suffered injustice and have had experience of both, not being able to avoid the one and obtain the other, they think that they had better agree among themselves to have neither; hence there arise laws and mutual covenants; and that which is ordained by law is termed by them lawful and just. This they affirm to be the origin and nature of justice;—it is a mean or compromise, between the best of all, which is to do injustice and not be punished, and the worst of all, which is to suffer injustice without the power of retaliation; and justice, being at a middle point between the two, is tolerated not as a good, but as the lesser evil, and honoured by reason of the inability of men to do injustice. For no man who is worthy to be called a man would ever submit to such an agreement if he were able to resist; he would be mad if he did. Such is the received account, Socrates, of the nature and origin of justice.

Now that those who practise justice do so involuntarily and because they have not the power to be unjust will best appear if we imagine something of this kind: having given both to the just and the unjust power to do what they will, let us watch and see whither desire will lead them; then we shall discover in the very act the just and unjust man to be proceeding along the same road, following their interest, which all natures deem to be their good, and are only diverted into the path of justice by the force of law. The liberty which we are supposing may be most completely given to them in the form of such a power as is said to have been possessed by Gyges the ancestor of Croesus the Lydian. According to the tradition, Gyges was a shepherd in the service of the king of Lydia; there was a great storm, and an earthquake made an opening in the earth at the place where he was feeding his flock. Amazed at the sight, he descended into the opening, where, among other marvels, he beheld a hollow brazen horse, having doors, at which he stooping and looking in saw a dead body of stature, as appeared to him, more than human, and having nothing on but a gold ring; this he took from the finger of the dead and reascended. Now the shepherds met together, according to custom, that they might send their monthly report about the flocks to the king; into their assembly he came having the ring on his finger, and as he was sitting among them he chanced to turn the collet of the ring inside his hand, when instantly he became invisible to the rest of the company and they began to speak of him as if he were no longer present. He was astonished at this, and again touching the ring he turned the collet outwards and reappeared; he made several trials of the ring, and always with the same result—when he turned the collet inwards he became invisible, when outwards he reappeared. Whereupon he contrived to be chosen one of the messengers who were sent to the court; where as soon as he arrived he seduced the queen, and with her help conspired against the king and slew him, and took the kingdom. Suppose now that there were two such magic rings, and the just put on one of them and the unjust the other; no man can be imagined to be of such an iron nature that he would stand fast in justice. No man would keep his hands off what was not his own when he could safely take what he liked out of the market, or go into houses and lie with any one at his pleasure, or kill or release from prison whom he would, and in all respects be like a God among men. Then the actions of the just would be as the actions of the unjust; they would both come at last to the same point. And this we may truly affirm to be a great proof that a man is just, not willingly or because he thinks that justice is any good to him individually, but of necessity, for wherever any one thinks that he can safely be unjust, there he is unjust. For all men believe in their hearts that injustice is far more profitable to the individual than justice, and he who argues as I have been supposing, will say that they are right. If you could imagine any one obtaining this power of becoming invisible, and never doing any wrong or touching what was another's, he would be thought by the lookers-on to be a most wretched idiot, although they would praise him to another's faces, and keep up appearances with one another from a fear that they too might suffer injustice. Enough of this.

Now, if we are to form a real judgment of the life of the just and unjust, we must isolate them; there is no other way; and how is the isolation to be effected? I answer: Let the unjust man be entirely unjust, and the just man entirely just; nothing is to be taken away from either of them, and both are to be perfectly furnished for the work of their respective lives. First, let the unjust be like other distinguished masters of craft; like the skilful pilot or physician, who knows intuitively his own powers and keeps within their limits, and who, if he fails at any point, is able to recover himself. So let the unjust make his unjust attempts in the right way, and lie hidden if he means to be great in his injustice (he who is found out is nobody): for the highest reach of injustice is, to be deemed just when you are not. Therefore I say that in the perfectly unjust man we must assume the most perfect injustice; there is to be no deduction, but we must allow him, while doing the most unjust acts, to have acquired the greatest reputation for justice. If he has taken a false step he must be able to recover himself; he must be one who can speak with effect, if any of his deeds come to light, and who can force his way where force is required by his courage and strength, and command of money and friends. And at his side let us place the just man in his nobleness and simplicity, wishing, as Aeschylus says, to be and not to seem good. There must be no seeming, for if he seem to be just he will be honoured and rewarded, and then we shall not know whether he is just for the sake of justice or for the sake of honours and rewards; therefore, let him be clothed in justice only, and have no other covering; and he must be imagined in a state of life the opposite of the former. Let him be the best of men, and let him be thought the worst; then he will have been put to the proof; and we shall see whether he will be affected by the fear of infamy and its consequences. And let him continue thus to the hour of death; being just and seeming to be unjust. When both have reached the uttermost extreme, the one of justice and the other of injustice, let judgment be given which of them is the happier of the two.

Heavens! my dear Glaucon, I said, how energetically you polish them up for the decision, first one and then the other, as if they were two statues.

I do my best, he said. And now that we know what they are like there is no difficulty in tracing out the sort of life which awaits either of them.

This I will proceed to describe; but as you may think the description a little too coarse, I ask you to suppose, Socrates, that the words which follow are not mine.—Let me put them into the mouths of the eulogists of injustice: They will tell you that the just man who is thought unjust will be scourged, racked, bound—will have his eyes burnt out; and, at last, after suffering every kind of evil, he will be impaled: Then he will understand that he ought to seem only, and not to be, just; the words of Aeschylus may be more truly spoken of the unjust than of the just. For the unjust is pursuing a reality; he does not live with a view to appearances—he wants to be really unjust and not to seem only:—

> 'His mind has a soil deep and fertile,
> Out of which spring his prudent counsels.'[1]

In the first place, he is thought just, and therefore bears rule in the city; he can marry whom he will, and give in marriage to whom he will; also he can trade and deal where he likes, and always to his own advantage, because he has no misgivings about injustice; and at every contest, whether in public or private, he gets the better of his antagonists, and gains at their expense, and is rich, and out of his gains he can benefit his friends, and harm his enemies; moreover, he can offer sacrifices, and dedicate gifts to the gods abundantly and magnificently, and can honour the gods or any man whom he wants to honour in a far better style than the just, and therefore he is likely to be dearer than they are to the gods. And thus, Socrates, gods and men are said to unite in making the life of the unjust better than the life of the just. . . .

[1] Seven against Thebes, 574.

John Stuart Mill

Utilitarianism

General Remarks

There are few circumstances among those which make up the present condition of human knowledge more unlike what might have been expected, or more significant of the backward state in which speculation on the most important subjects still lingers, than the little progress which has been made in the decision of the controversy respecting the criterion of right and wrong. From the dawn of philosophy, the question concerning the *summum bonum*, or, what is the same thing, concerning the foundation of morality, has been accounted the main problem in speculative thought, has occupied the most gifted intellects and divided them into sects and schools carrying on a vigorous warfare against one another. And after more than two thousand years the same discussions continue, philosophers are still ranged under the same contending banners, and neither thinkers nor mankind at large seem nearer to being unanimous on the subject than when the youth Socrates listened to the old Protagoras and asserted (if Plato's dialogue be grounded on a real conversation) the theory of utilitarianism against the popular morality of the so-called sophist. . . .

To inquire how far the bad effects of his deficiency have been mitigated in practice, or to what extent the moral beliefs of mankind have been vitiated or made uncertain by the absence of any distinct recognition of an ultimate standard, would imply a complete survey and criticism of past and present ethical doctrine. It would, however, be easy to show that whatever steadiness of consistency these moral beliefs have attained has been mainly due to the tacit influence of a standard not recognized. Although the nonexistence of an acknowledged first principle has made ethics not so much a guide as a consecration of men's actual sentiments, still, as men's sentiments, both of favor and of aversion, are greatly influenced by what they suppose to be the effects of things upon their happiness, the principle of utility, or, as Bentham latterly called it, the greatest happiness principle, has had a large share in forming the moral doctrines even of those who most scornfully reject its authority. Nor is there any school of thought which refuses to admit that the influence of actions on happiness is a most material and even predominant consideration in many of the details of morals, however unwilling to acknowledge it as the fundamental principle of morality and the source of moral obligation. I might go much further and say that to all those *a priori* moralists who deem it necessary to argue at all, utilitarian arguments are indispensable. It is not my present purpose to criticize these thinkers; but I cannot help referring, for illustration, to a systematic treatise by one of the most illustrious of them, the *Metaphysics of Ethics* by Kant. This remarkable man, whose system of thought will long remain one of the landmarks in the history of philosophical speculation, does, in the treatise in question, lay down a universal first principle as the origin and ground of moral obligation; it is this: "So act that the rule on which thou actest would admit of being adopted as a law by all rational beings." But when he begins to deduce from this precept any of the actual duties of morality, he fails, almost grotesquely, to show that there would be any contradiction, any logical (not to say physical) impossibility, in the adoption by all rational beings of the most outrageously immoral rules of conduct. All he shows is that the *consequences* of their universal adoption would be such as no one would choose to incur.

On the present occasion, I shall, without further discussion of the other theories, attempt to contribute something toward the understanding and appreciation of the "utilitarian" or "happiness" theory, and toward such proof as it is susceptible of. It is evident that this cannot be proof in the ordinary and popular meaning of the term. Questions of ultimate ends are not amenable to direct proof. Whatever can be proved to be good must be so by being shown to be a means to something admitted to be good without proof. The medical art is proved to be good by its conducing to health; but how is it possible to prove that health is good? The art of music good, for the reason, among others, that it produces pleasure; but what proof is it possible to give that pleasure is good? If, then, it is asserted that there is a comprehensive formula, including all things which are in themselves good, and that whatever else is good is not so as an end but as a means, the formula may be accepted or rejected, but is not a subject of what is commonly understood by proof. We are not, however, to infer that its acceptance or rejection must depend on blind impulse or arbitrary choice. There is a larger meaning of the word "proof,' in which this question is as amenable to it as any other of the disputed questions of philosophy. The subject is within the cognizance of the rational faculty; and neither does that faculty deal with it solely in the way of intuition. Considerations may be presented capable of determining the intellect either to give or withhold its assent to the doctrine; and this is equivalent to proof.

We shall examine presently of what nature are these considerations; in what manner they apply to the case, and what rational grounds, therefore, can be given for accepting or rejecting the utilitarian formula. But it is a preliminary condition of rational acceptance or rejection that the formula should be correctly understood. I believe that the very imperfect notion ordinarily formed of its meaning is the chief obstacle which impedes its reception, and that, could it be cleared even from only the grosser misconceptions, the question would be greatly simplified and a large proportion of its difficulties removed. Before, therefore, I attempt to enter into the philosophical grounds which can be given for assenting to the utilitarian standard, I shall offer some illustrations of the doctrine itself, with the view of showing more clearly what it is, distinguishing it from what it is not, and disposing of such of the practical objections to it as either originate in, or are closely connected with, mistaken interpretations of its meaning. Having thus prepared the ground, I shall afterwards endeavor to throw such light as I can call upon the question considered as one of philosophical theory.

What Utilitarianism Is

The creed which accepts as the foundation of morals "utility" or the "greatest happiness principle" holds that actions are right in proportion as they tend to promote happiness; wrong as they tend to produce the reverse of happiness. By happiness is intended pleasure and the absence of pain; by unhappiness, pain and the privation of pleasure. To give a clear view of the moral standard set up by the theory, much more requires to be said; in particular, what things it includes in the ideas of pain and pleasure, and to what extent this is left an open question. But these supplementary explanations do not affect the theory of life on which this theory of morality is grounded—namely, that pleasure and freedom from pain are the only things desirable as ends; and that all desirable things (which are as numerous in the utilitarian as in any other scheme) are desirable either for pleasure inherent in themselves or as means to the promotion of pleasure and the prevention of pain.

Now such a theory of life excites in many minds, and among them in some of the most estimable in feeling and purpose, inveterate dislike. To suppose that life has (as they express it) no higher end than pleasure—no better and nobler object of desire and pursuit—they designate as utterly mean and groveling, as a doctrine worthy only of swine, to whom the followers of Epicurus were, at a very early period, contemptuously likened; and modern holders of the doctrine are occasionally made the subject of equally polite comparisons by its German, French, and English assailants.

When thus attacked, the Epicureans have always answered that it is not they, but their accusers, who represent human nature in a degrading light, since the accusation supposes human beings to be capable of no pleasures except those of which swine are capable. If this supposition were true, the charge could not be gainsaid, but would then be no longer an imputation; for if the sources of pleasure were precisely the same to human beings and to swine, the rule of life which is good enough for the one would be good enough for the other. The comparison of the Epicurean life to that of beasts is felt as degrading, precisely because a beast's pleasures do not satisfy a human being's conceptions of happiness. Human beings have faculties more elevated than the animal appetites and, when once made conscious of them, do not regard anything as happiness which does not include their gratification. I do not indeed, consider the Epicureans to have been by any means faultless in drawing out their scheme of consequences from the utilitarian principle. To do this in any sufficient manner, many Stoic, as well as Christian, elements require to be included. But there is no known Epicurean theory of life which does not assign to the pleasures of the intellect, of the feelings and imagination, and of the moral sentiments a much higher value as pleasures than to those of mere sensation. It must be admitted, however, that utilitarian writers in general have placed the superiority of mental over bodily pleasures chiefly in the greater permanency, safety, uncostliness, etc., of the former—that is, in their circumstantial advantages rather than in their intrinsic nature. And on all these points utilitarians have fully proved their case; but they might have taken the other and, as it may be called, higher ground with entire consistency. It is quite compatible with the principle of utility to recognize the fact that some kinds of pleasure are more desirable and more valuable than others. It would be absurd that, while in estimating all other things quality is considered as well as quantity, the estimation of pleasure should be supposed to depend on quantity alone.

If I am asked what I mean by difference of quality in pleasures, or what makes one pleasure more valuable than another, merely as a pleasure, except its being greater in amount, there is but one possible answer. Of two pleasures, if there be one to which all or almost all who have experience of both give a decided preference, irrespective of any feeling of moral obligation to prefer it, that is the more desirable pleasure. If one of the two is, by those who are competently acquainted with both, placed so far above the other that they prefer it, even though knowing it to be attended with a greater amount of discontent, and would not resign it for any quantity of the other pleasure which their nature is capable of, we are justified in ascribing to the preferred enjoyment a superiority in quality so far outweighing quantity as to render it, in comparison, of small account.

Now it is an unquestionable fact that those who are equally acquainted with and equally capable of appreciating and enjoying both do give a most marked preference to the manner of existence which employs their higher faculties. Few human creatures would consent to be changed into any of the lower animals for a promise of the fullest allowance of a beast's pleasures; no intelligent human being would consent to be a fool, no instructed person would be an ignoramus, no person of feeling and conscience would be selfish and base, even though they should be persuaded that the fool, the dunce, or the rascal is better satisfied with his lot than they are with theirs. They would not resign what they possess more than he for the most complete satisfaction of all the desires which they have in common with him. If they ever fancy they would, it is only in cases of unhappiness so extreme that to escape from it they would exchange their lot for almost any other, however undesirable in their own eyes. A being of higher faculties requires more to make him happy, is capable probably of more acute suffering, and certainly accessible to it at more points, than one of an inferior type; but in spite of these liabilities, he can never really wish to sink into what he feels to be a lower grade of existence. We may give what explanation we please of this unwillingness; we may attribute it to pride, a name which is given indiscriminately to some of the most and to some of the least estimable feelings of which mankind are capable; we may refer it to the love of liberty and personal independence, an appeal to which was with the Stoics one of the most effective means for the inculcation of it; to the love of power or to the love of excitement, both of which do really enter into and contribute to it; but its most appropriate appellation is a sense of dignity, which all human beings possess in one form or other, and in some, though by no means in exact, proportion to their higher faculties, and which is so essential a part of the happiness of those in whom it is strong that nothing which conflicts with it could be otherwise than momentarily an object of desire to them. Whoever supposes that this preference takes place at a sacrifice of happiness—that the superior being, in anything like equal circumstances, is not happier than the inferior—confounds the two very different ideas of happiness and content. It is indisputable that the being whose capacities of enjoyment are low has the greatest chance of having them fully satisfied; and a highly endowed being will always feel that any happiness which he can look for, as the world is constituted, is imperfect. But he can learn to bear its imperfections, if they are at all bearable; and they will not make him envy the being who is indeed unconscious of the imperfections, but only because he feels not at all the good which those imperfections qualify. It is better to be a human being dissatisfied than a pig satisfied; better to be Socrates dissatisfied than a fool satisfied. And if the fool, or the pig, are of a different opinion, it is because they only know their own side of the question. The other party to the comparison knows both sides.

It may be objected that many who are capable of the higher pleasures occasionally, under the influence of temptation, postpone them to the lower. But this is quite compatible with a full appreciation of the intrinsic superiority of the higher. Men often, from infirmity of character, make their election for the nearer good, though they know it to be the less valuable; and this no less when the choice is between two bodily pleasures than when it is between bodily and mental. They pursue sensual indulgences to the injury of health, though perfectly aware that health is the greater good. It may be further objected that many who begin with youthful enthusiasm for everything noble, as they advance in years, sink into indolence and selfishness. But I do not believe that those who undergo this very common change voluntarily choose the lower description of pleasures in preference to the higher. I believe that, before they devote themselves exclusively to the one, they have already become incapable of the other. Capacity for the nobler feelings is in most natures a very tender plant, easily killed, not only by hostile influences, but by mere want of sustenance; and in the majority of young persons it speedily dies away if the occupations to which their position in life has devoted them, and the society into which it has thrown them, are not favorable to keeping that higher capacity in exercise. Men lose their high aspirations as they lose their intellectual tastes, because they have not time or opportunity for indulging them; and they addict themselves to inferior pleasures, not because they deliberately prefer them, but because they are either the only ones to which they have access or the only ones which they are any longer capable of enjoying. It may be questioned whether anyone who has remained equally susceptible to both classes of pleasures ever knowingly and calmly preferred the lower, though many, in all ages, have broken down in an ineffectual attempt to combine both.

From this verdict of the only competent judges, I apprehend there can be no appeal. On a question which is the best worth having of two pleasures, or which of two modes of existence is the most grateful to the feelings, apart from its moral attributes and from its consequences, the judgment of these who are qualified by knowledge of both, or, if they differ, that of the majority among them, must be admitted as final. And there needs be the less hesitation to accept this judgment respecting the quality of pleasures, since there is no other tribunal to be referred to even on the question of quantity. What means are there of determining which is the acutest of two pains, or the intensest of two pleasurable sensations, except the general suffrage of those who are familiar with both? Neither pains nor pleasures are homogeneous, and pain is always heterogeneous with pleasure. What is there to decide whether a particular pleasure is worth purchasing at the cost of a particular pain, except the feelings and judgment of the experienced? When, therefore, those feelings and judgment declare the pleasures derived from the higher faculties to be preferable *in kind,* apart from the question of intensity, to those of which the animal nature, disjoined from the higher faculties, is susceptible, they are entitled on this subject to the same regard.

I have dwelt on this point as being part of a perfectly just conception of utility or happiness considered as the directive rule of human conduct. But it is by no means an indispensable condition to the acceptance of the utilitarian standard; for that standard is not the agent's own greatest happiness, but the greatest amount of happiness altogether; and if it may possibly be doubted whether a noble character is always the happier for its nobleness, there can be no doubt that it makes other people happier, and that the world in general is immensely a gainer by it. Utilitarianism, therefore, could only attain its end by the general cultivation of nobleness of character, even if each individual were only benefited by the nobleness of others, and his own, so far as happiness is concerned, were a sheer deduction from the benefit. But the bare enunciation of such an absurdity as this last renders refutation superfluous.

According to the greatest happiness principle, as above explained, the ultimate end, with reference to and for the sake of which all other things are desirable—whether we are considering our own good or that of other people—is an existence exempt as far as possible from pain, and as rich as possible in enjoyments, both in point of quantity and quality; the test of quality and the rule for measuring it against quality being the preference felt by those who, in their opportunities of experience, to which must be added their habits of self-consciousness and self-observation, are best furnished with the means of comparison. This, being according to the utilitarian opinion the end of human action, is necessarily also the standard of morality, which may accordingly be defined "the rules and precepts for human conduct," by the observance of which an existence such as has been described might be, to the greatest extent possible, secured to all mankind; and not to them only, but, so far as the nature of things admits, to the whole sentient creation.

Against this doctrine, however, arises another class of objectors who say that happiness, in any form, cannot be the rational purpose of human life and action; because, in the first place, it is unattainable; and they contemptuously ask, What right hast thou to be happy?—a question which Mr. Carlyle clinches by the addition, What right, a short time ago, hadst thou even *to be?* Next they say that men can do *without* happiness; that all noble human beings have felt this, and could not have become noble but by learning the lesson of *Entsagen*, or renunciation; which lesson, thoroughly learned and submitted to, they affirm to be the beginning and necessary condition of all virtue.

The first of these objectives would go to the root of the matter were it well founded; for if no happiness is to be had at all by human beings, the attainment of it cannot be the end of morality or of any rational conduct. Though, even in that case, something might still be said for the utilitarian theory, since utility includes not solely the pursuit of happiness, but the prevention or mitigation of unhappiness; and if the former aim be chimerical, there will be all the greater scope and more imperative need for the latter, so long at least as mankind think fit to live and do not take refuge in the simultaneous act of suicide recommended under certain conditions by Novalis. When, however, it is thus positively asserted to be impossible that human life should be happy, the assertion, if not something like a verbal quibble, is at least an exaggeration. If by happiness be meant a continuity of highly pleasurable excitement, it is evident enough that this is impossible. A state of exalted pleasure lasts only moments or in some cases, and with some intermissions, hours or days, and is the occasional brilliant flash of enjoyment, not its permanent and steady flame. Of this the philosophers who have taught that happiness is the end of life were as fully aware as those who taunt them. The happiness which they meant was not a life of rapture, but moments of such, in an existence made up of few and transitory pains, many and various pleasures, with a decided predominance of the active over the passive, and having as the foundation of the whole not to expect more from life than it is capable of bestowing. A life thus composed, to those who have been fortunate enough to obtain it, has always appeared worthy of the name of happiness. And such an existence is even now the lot of many during some considerable portion of their lives. The present wretched education and wretched social arrangements are the only real hindrance to its being attainable by almost all.

The objectors perhaps may doubt whether human beings, if taught to consider happiness as the end of life, would be satisfied with such a moderate share of it. But great numbers of mankind have been satisfied with much less. The main constituents of a satisfied life appear to be two, either of which by itself is often found sufficient for the purpose: tranquillity and excitement. With much tranquillity, many find that they can be content with very little pleasure; with much excitement, many can reconcile themselves to a considerable quantity of pain. There is assuredly no inherent impossibility of enabling even the mass of mankind to unite both, since the two are so far from being incompatible that they are in natural alliance, the prolongation of either being a preparation for, and exciting a wish for, the other. It is only those in whom indolence amounts to a vice that do not desire excitement after an interval of respose; it is only those in whom the need of excitement is a disease that feel the tranquillity which follows excitement dull and insipid, instead of pleasurable in direct proportion to the excitement which preceded it. When people who are tolerably fortunate in their outward lot do not find in life sufficient enjoyment to make it valuable to them, the cause generally is caring for nobody but themselves. To those who have neither public nor private affections, the excitements of life are much curtailed, and in any case dwindle in value as the time approaches when all selfish interests must be terminated by death; while those who leave after them objects of personal affection, and especially those who have also cultivated a fellow-feeling with the collective interests of mankind, retain as lively an interest in life on the eve of death as in the vigor of youth and health. Next to selfishness, the principle cause which makes life unsatisfactory is want of mental cultivation. A cultivated mind—I do not mean that a philosopher, but any mind to which the fountains of knowledge have been opened, and which has been taught, in any tolerable degree, to exercise its faculties—finds sources of inexhaustible interest in all that surrounds it: in the objects of nature, the achievements of art, the imaginations of poetry, the incidents of history, the ways of mankind, past and present, and their prospects in the future. It is possible, indeed, to become indifferent to all this, and that too without having exhausted a thousandth part of it, but only when one has had from the beginning no moral or human interest in these things and has sought in them only the gratification of curiosity.

Now there is absolutely no reason in the nature of things why an amount of mental culture sufficient to give an intelligent interest in these objects of contemplation should not be the inheritance of everyone born in a civilized country. As little is there an inherent necessity that any human being should be a selfish egotist, devoid of every feeling or care but those which center in his own miserable individuality. Something far superior to this is sufficiently common even now, to give ample earnest of what the human species may be made. Genuine private affections and a sincere interest in the public good are possible, though in unequal degrees, to every rightly brought up human being. In a world in which there is so much to interest, so much to enjoy, and so much also to correct and improve, everyone who has this moderate amount of moral and intellectual requisites is capable of an existence which may be called enviable; and unless such a person, through bad laws or subjection to the will of others, is denied the liberty to use the sources of happiness within his reach, he will not fail to find this enviable existence, if he escapes the positive evils of life, the great sources of physical and mental suffering—such as indigence, disease, and the unkindness, worthlessness, or premature loss of objects of affection. The main stress of the problem lies, therefore, in the contest with these calamities from which it is a rare good fortune entirely to escape; which, as things now are, cannot be obviated, and often cannot be in any material degree mitigated. Yet no one whose opinion deserves a moment's consideration can doubt that most of the great positive evils of the world are in themselves removable, and will, if human affairs continue to improve, be in the end reduced within narrow limits. Poverty, in any sense implying suffering, may be completely extinguished by the wisdom of society combined with the good sense and providence of individuals. Even that most intractable of enemies, disease, may be indefinitely reduced in dimensions by good physical and moral education and proper control of noxious influences, while the progress of science holds out a promise for the future of still more direct conquests over this detestable foe. And every advance in that direction relieves us from some, not only of the chances which cut short our own lives, but, what concerns us still more, which deprive us of those in whom our happiness is wrapt up. As for vicissitudes of fortune and other disappointments connected with worldly circumstances, these are principally the effect either of gross imprudence, of ill-regulated desires, or of bad or imperfect social institutions. All the grand sources, in short, of human suffering are in a great degree, many of them almost entirely, conquerable by human care and effort; and though their removal is grievously slow—though a long succession of generations will perish in the breach before the conquest is completed, and this world becomes all that, if will and knowledge were not wanting, it might easily be made—yet every mind sufficiently intelligent and generous to bear a part, however small and inconspicuous, in the endeavor will draw a noble enjoyment from the contest itself, which he would not for any bribe in the form of selfish indulgence consent to be without.

And this leads to the true estimation of what is said by the objectors concerning the possibility and the obligation of learning to do without happiness. Unquestionably it is possible to do without happiness; it is done involuntarily by nineteen-twentieths of mankind, even in those parts of our present world which are least deep in barbarism; and it often has to be done voluntarily by the hero or the martyr, for the sake of something which he prizes more than his individual happiness. But this something, what is it, unless the happiness of others or some of the requisites of happiness? It is noble to be capable of resigning entirely one's own portion of happiness, or chances of it; but, after all, this self-sacrifice must be for some end; it is not its own end; and if we are told that its end is not happiness but virtue, which is better than happiness, I ask, would the sacrifice be made if the hero or martyr did not believe that it would earn for others immunity from similar sacrifices? Would it be made if he thought that his renunciation of happiness for himself would produce no fruit for any of his fellow creatures, but to make their lot like his and place them also in the condition of persons who have renounced happiness? All honor to those who can abnegate for themselves the personal enjoyment of life when by such renunciation they contribute worthily to increase the amount of happiness in the world; but he who does it or professes to do it for any other purpose is no more deserving of admiration than the ascetic mounted on his pillar. He may be an inspiriting proof of what men *can* do, but assuredly not an example of what they *should*.

Though it is only in a very imperfect state of the world's arrangements that anyone can best serve the happiness of others by the absolute sacrifice of his own, yet, so long as the world is in that imperfect state, I fully acknowledge that the readiness to make such a sacrifice is the highest virtue which can be found in man. I will add that in this condition of the world, paradoxical as the assertion may be, the conscious ability to do without happiness gives the best prospect of realizing such happiness as is attainable. For nothing except that consciousness can raise a person above the chances of life by making him feel that, let fate and fortune do their worst, they have no power to subdue him; which, once felt, frees him from excess of anxiety concerning the evils of life and enables him, like many a Stoic in the worst times of the Roman Empire, to cultivate in tranquillity the sources of satisfacation accessible to him, without concerning himself about the uncertainty of their duration any more than about their inevitable end.

Meanwhile, let utilitarians never cease to claim the morality of self-devotion as a possession which belongs by as good a right to them as either to the Stoic or to the Transcendentalist. The utilitarian morality does recognize in human beings the power of sacrificing their own greatest good for the good of others. It only refuses to admit that the sacrifice is itself a good. A sacrifice which does not increase or tend to increase the sum total of happiness, it considers as wasted. The only self-renunciation which it applauds is devotion to the happiness, or to some of the means of happiness, of others, either of mankind collectively or of individuals within the limits imposed by the collective interests of mankind.

I must again repeat that the assailants of utilitarianism seldom have the justice to acknowledge, that the happiness which forms the utilitarian standard of what is right in conduct is not the agent's own happiness but that of all concerned. As between his own happiness and that of others, utilitarianism requires him to be as strictly impartial as a disinterested and benevolent spectator. In the golden rule of Jesus of Nazareth, we read the complete spirit of the ethics of utility. "To do as you would be done by," and "to love your neighbor as yourself," constitute the ideal perfection of utilitarian morality. As the means of making the nearest approach to this ideal, utility would enjoin, first, that laws and social arrangements should place the happiness or (as, speaking practically, it may be called) the interest of every individual as nearly as possible in harmony with the interest of the whole; and, secondly, that education and opinion, which have so vast a power over human character, should so use that power as to establish in the mind of every individual an indissoluble association between his own happiness and the good of the whole, especially between his own happiness and the practice of such modes of conduct, negative and positive, as regard for the universal happiness prescribes; so that not only he may be unable to conceive the possibility of happiness to himself, consistently with conduct opposed to the general good, but also that a direct impulse to promote the general good may be in every individual one of the habitual motives of action, and the sentiments connected therewith may fill a large and prominent place in every human being's sentient existence. If the impugners of the utilitarian morality represented it to their own minds in this its true character, I know not what recommendation possessed by any other morality they could possibly affirm to be wanting to it; what more beautiful or more exalted developments of human nature any other ethical system can be supposed to foster, or what springs of action, not accessible to the utilitarian, such systems rely on for giving effect to their mandates.

The objectors to utilitarianism cannot always be charged with representing it in a discreditable light. On the contrary, those among them who entertain anything like a just idea of its disinterested character sometimes find fault with its standard as being too high for humanity. They say it is exacting too much to require that people shall always act from the inducement of promoting the general interest of society. But this is to mistake the very meaning of a standard of morals and confound the rule of action with the motive of it. It is the business of ethics to tell us what are our duties, or by what test we may know them; but no system of ethics requires that the sole motive of all we do shall be a feeling of duty; on the contrary, ninety-nine hundredths of all our actions are done from other motives, and rightly so done if the rule of duty does not condemn them. It is the more unjust to utilitarianism that this particular misapprehension should be made a ground of objection to it, inasmuch as utilitarian moralists have gone beyond almost all others in affirming that the motive has nothing to do with the morality of the action, though much with the worth of the agent. He who saves a fellow creature from drowning does what is morally right, whether his motive be duty or the hope of being paid for his trouble; he who betrays the friend that trusts him is guilty of a crime, even if his object be to serve another friend to whom he is under greater obligations.[2] But to

[2] An opponent, whose intellectual and moral fairness it is a pleasure to acknowledge (the Rev. J. Llewellyn Davies), has objected to this passage, saying "Surely the rightness or wrongness of saving a man from drowning does depend very much upon the motive with which it is done. Suppose that a tyrant, when his enemy jumped into the sea to escape from him, saved him from drowning simply in order that he might inflict upon him more exquisite tortures, would it tend to clearness to speak of that rescue as 'a morally right action'? Or suppose again, according to one of the stock illustrations of ethical inquires, that a man betrayed a trust received from a friend, because the discharge of it would fatally injure that friend himself or someone belonging to him, would utilitarianism compel one to call the betrayal 'a crime' as much as if it had been done from the meanest motive?"

I submit that he who saves another from drowning in order to kill him by torture afterwards does not differ only in motive from him who does the same thing from duty or benevolence; the act itself is different. The rescue of the man is, in the case supposed, only the necessary first step of an act far more atrocious than leaving him to drown would have

speak only of actions done from the motive or duty, and in direct obedience to principle: it is a misapprehension of the utilitarian mode of thought to conceive it as implying that people should fix their minds upon so wide a generality as the world, or society at large. The great majority of good actions are intended not for the benefit of the world, but for that of individuals, of which the good of the world is made up; and the thoughts of the most virtuous man need not on these occasions travel beyond the particular persons concerned, except so far as is necessary to assure himself that in benefiting them he is not violating the rights, that is, the legitimate and authorized expectations, of anyone else. The multiplication of happiness is, according to the utilitarian ethics, the object of virtue: the occasions on which any person (except one in a thousand) has it in his power to do this on an extended scale—in other words, to be a public benefactor—are but exceptional; and on these occasions alone is he called on to consider public utility; in every other case, private utility, the interest or happiness of some few persons, is all he has to attend to. Those alone the influence of whose actions extends to society in general need concern themselves habitually about so large an object. In the case of abstinences indeed—of things which people forbear to do from moral considerations, though thecon-sequences in the particular case might be beneficial—it would be unworthy of an intelligent agent not to be consciously aware that the action is of a class which, if practiced generally, would be generally injurious, and that this is the ground of the obligation to abstain from it. The amount of regard for the public interest implied in this recognition is not greater than is demanded by every system of morals, for they all enjoin to abstain from whatever is manifestly pernicious to society.

The same considerations dispose of another reproach against the doctrine of utility, founded on a still grosser misconception of the purpose of a standard of morality and of the very meaning of the words "right" and "wrong." It is often affirmed that utilitarianism renders men cold and unsympathizing; that is chills their moral feelings toward

been. Had Mr. Davies said, "The rightness or wrongness of saving a man from drowning does depend very much"—not upon the motive, but—"upon the *intention*," no utilitarian would have differed from him. Mr. Davies, by an oversight too common not to be quite venial, has in this case confounded the very different ideas of Motive and Intention. There is no point which utilitarian thinkers (and Bentham pre-eminently) have taken more pains to illustrate than this. The morality of the action depends entirely upon the intention—that is, upon what the agent *wills to do*. But the motive, that is, the feeling which makes him will so to do, if it makes no difference in the act, makes none in the morality: though it makes a great difference in our moral estimation of the agent, especially if it indicates a good or a bad habitual *disposition*—a bent of character from which useful, or from which hurtful actions are likely to arise.

individuals; that it makes them regard only the dry and hard consideration of the consequences of actions, not taking into their moral estimate the qualities from which those actions emanate. If the assertion means that they do not allow their judgment respecting the rightness or wrongness of an action to be influenced by their opinion of the qualities of the person who does it, this is a complaint not against utilitarianism, but against any standard or morality at all; for certainly no known ethical standard decides an action to be good or bad because it is done by a good or bad man, still less because done by an amiable, or brave, or a benevolent man, or the contrary. These considerations are relevant, not to the estimation of actions, but of persons; and there is nothing in the utilitarian theory inconsistent with the fact that there are other things which interest us in persons besides the rightness and wrongness of their actions. The Stoics, indeed, with the paradoxical misuse of language which was part of their system, and by which they strove to raise themselves above all concern about anything but virtue, were fond of saying that he who has that has everything; that he, and only he, is rich, is beautiful, is a king. But no claim of this description is made for the virtuous man by the utilitarian doctrine. Utilitarians are quite aware that there are other desirable possessions and qualities besides virtue, and are perfectly willing to allow to all of them their full worth. They are also aware that right action does not necessarily indicate a virtuous character, and that actions which are blamable often proceed from qualities entitled to praise. When this is apparent in any particular case, it modifies their estimation, not certainly of the act, but of the agent. I grant that they are, notwithstanding, of opinion that in the long run the best proof of a good character is good actions; and resolutely refuse to consider any mental disposition as good of which the predominant tendency is to produce bad conduct. This makes them unpopular with many people, but it is an unpopularity which they must share with everyone who regards the distinction between right and wrong in a serious light; and the reproach is not one which a conscientious utilitarian need be anxious to repel.

If no more be meant by the ojection than that many utilitarians look on the morality of actions, as measured by the utilitarian standards, with too exclusive a regard, and do not lay sufficient stress upon the other beauties of character which go toward making a human being lovable or admirable, this may be admitted. Utilitarians who have cultivated their moral feelings, but not their sympathies, nor their artistic perceptions, do fall into this mistake; and so do all other moralists under the same conditions. What can be said in excuse for other moralists is equally available for them, namely, that, if there is to be any error, it is better that it should be on that side. As a matter of fact, we may affirm that among utilitarians, as among adherents of other systems, there is every imaginable degree of rigidity and of laxity in the application of their standard; some are even puritanically rigorous, while others are as indulgent as can possibly be desired by sinner or by sentimentalist. But on the whole, a doctrine which brings prominently forward the interest that mankind have in the repression and prevention of conduct which violates the moral law is likely to be inferior to no other in turning the sanctions of opinion against such violations. It is true, the question "What does violate the moral law?" is one on which those who recognize different standards of morality are likely now and then to differ. But difference of opinion on moral question was not first introduced into the world by utilitarianism, while that doctrine does supply, if not always an easy, at all events a tangible and intelligible, mode of deciding such differences.

It may not be superfluous to notice a few more of the common misapprehensions of utilitarian ethics, even those which are so obvious and gross that it might appear impossible for any person of candor and intelligence to fall into them; since persons, even of considerable mental endowment, often give themselves so little trouble to understand the bearings of any opinion against which they entertain a prejudice, and men are in general so little conscious of this voluntary ignorance as a defect that the vulgarest misunderstandings of ethical doctrines are continually met within the deliberate writings of persons of the greatest pretensions both to high principle and to philosophy. We not uncommonly hear the doctrine of utility inveighed against [as] a *godless* doctrine. If it be necessary to say anything at all against so mere an assumption, we may say that the question depends upon what idea we have formed of the moral character of the Deity. If it be a true belief that God desires, above all things, the happiness of his creatures, and that this was his purpose in their creation, utility is not only not a godless doctrine, but more profoundly religious than any other. If it be meant that utilitarianism does not recognize the revealed will of God as the supreme law of morals, I answer that a utilitarian who believes in the perfect goodness and wisdom of *God* necessarily believes that whatever God has thought fit to reveal on the subject of morals must fulfill the requirements of utility in a supreme degree. But others besides utilitarians have been of opinion that the Christian revelation was intended, and is fitted, to inform the hearts and minds of mankind with a spirit which should enable them to find for themselves what is right, and incline them to do it when found, rather than to tell them, except in a very general way, what it is; and that we need a doctrine of ethics, carefully followed out, to *interpret* to us the will of God. Whether this opinion is correct or not, it is superfluous here to discuss; since whatever aid religion, either natural or revealed, can afford to ethical investigation is as open to the utilitarian moralist as to any other. He can use it as the testimony of God to the usefulness or hurtfulness of any given course of action by as good a right as others can use it for the indication of a transcendental law having no connection with usefulness or with happiness.

Again, utility is often summarily stigmatized as an immoral doctrine by giving it the name of "expediency," and taking advantage of the popular use of that term to contrast it with principle. But the expedient, in the sense in which it is opposed to the right, generally means that which is expedient for the particular interest of the agent himself; as when a minister sacrifices the interests of his country to keep himself in place. When it means anything better than this, it means that which is expedient for some immediate object, some temporary purpose, but which violates a rule whose observance is expedient in a much higher degree. The expedient, in this sense, instead of being the same thing with the useful, is a branch of the hurtful. Thus it would often be expedient, for the purpose of getting over some momentary embarrassment, or attaining some object immediately useful to ourselves or others, to tell a lie. But inasmuch as the cultivation in ourselves of a sensitive feeling on the subject of veracity is one of the most useful, and the enfeeblement of that feeling one of the most hurtful, things to which our conduct can be instrumental; and inasmuch as any, even unintentional, deviation from truth does that much toward weakening the trustworthiness of human assertion, which is not only the principal support of all present social well-being, but the insufficiency of which does more than any one thing that can be named to keep back civilization, virtue, everything on which human happiness on the largest scale depends—we feel that the violation, for a present advantage, of a rule of such transcendent expediency is not expedient, and that he who, for the sake of convenience to himself or to some other individual, does what depends on him to deprive mankind of the good, and inflict upon them the evil, involved in the greater or less reliance which they can place in each other's words, acts the part of one of their worst enemies. Yet that even this rule, sacred as it is, admits of possible exceptions is acknowledged by all moralists; the chief of which is when the withholding of some fact (as of information from a malefactor, or of bad news from a person dangerously ill) would save an individual (especially an individual other than oneself) from great and unmerited evil, and when the withholding can only be effected by denial. But in order that the exception may not extend itself beyond the need, and may have the least possible effect in weakening reliance of veracity, it ought to be recognized and, if possible, its limits defined; and, if the principle of utility is good for anything, it must be good for weighing these conflicting utilities against one another and marking out the region within which one or the other preponderates.

Again, defenders of utility often find themselves called upon to reply to such objections as this—that there is not time, previous to action, for calculating and weighing the effects of any line of conduct on the general happiness. This is exactly as if anyone were to say that it is impossible to guide our conduct by Christianity because there is not time, on every occasion on which anything has to be done, to read through the Old and New Testaments. The answer to the objection is that there has been ample time, namely, the whole past duration of the human species. During all the time mankind have been learning by experience the tendencies of actions; on which experience all the prudence as well as all the morality of life are dependent. People talk as if the commencement of this course of experience had hitherto been put off, and as if, at the moment when some man feels tempted to meddle with the property or life of another, he had to begin considering for the first time whether murder and theft are injurious to human happiness. Even then I do not think that he would find the question very puzzling; but, at all events the matter is now done to his hand. It is truly a whimsical supposition that, if mankind were agreed in considering utility to be the test of morality, they would remain without any agreement as to what *is* useful, and would take no measures for having their notions on the subject taught to the young and enforced by law and opinion. There is no difficulty in proving any ethical standard whatever to work ill if we suppose universal idiocy to be conjoined with it; but on any hypothesis short of that, mankind must by this time have acquired positive beliefs as to the effects of some actions on their happiness; and the beliefs which have thus come down are the rules of morality for the multitude, and for the philosopher until he has succeeded in finding better. That philosophers might easily do this, even now, on many subjects; that the received code of ethics is by no means of divine right; and that mankind have still much to learn as to the effects of actions on the general happiness, I admit or rather earnestly maintain. The corollaries from the principle of utility, like the precepts of every practical art, admit the indefinite improvement, and, in a progressive state of the human mind, their improvement is perpetually going on. But to consider the rules of morality as improvable is one thing; to pass over the intermediate generalization entirely and endeavor to test each individual action directly by the first principle is another. It is a strange notion that the acknowledgment of a first principle is inconsistent with the admission of secondary ones. To inform a traveler respecting the place of his ultimate destination is not to forbid the use of landmarks and direction-posts on the way. The proposition that happiness is the end and aim of morality does not mean that no road ought to be laid down to that goal, or that persons going thither should not be advised to take one direction rather than another. Men really ought to leave off talking a kind of nonsense on this subject, which they would neither talk nor listen to on other matters of practical concernment. Nobody argues that the art of navigation is not founded on astronomy because sailors cannot wait to calculate the Nautical Almanac. Being rational creatures, they go to sea with it ready calculated; and all rational creatures go out upon the sea of life with their minds made up on the common question of right and wrong, as well as on many of the far more difficult questions of wise and foolish. And this, as long as foresight is a human quality, it is to be presumed they will continue to do. Whatever we adopt as the fundamental principle of morality, we require subordinate principles to apply it by; the impossibility of doing without them, being common to all systems, can afford no argument against any one in particular; but gravely to argue as if no such secondary principles could be had, and as if mankind had remained till now, and always must remain, without drawing any general conclusions from the experience of human life is as high a pitch, I think, as absurdity has ever reached in philosophical controversy.

The remainder of the stock arguments against utilitarianism mostly consist in laying to its charge the common infirmities of human nature, and the general difficulties which embarrass conscientious persons in shaping their course through life. We are told that a utilitarian will be apt to make his own particular case an exception to moral rules, and, when under temptation, will see a utility in the breach of a rule, greater than he will see in its observance. But is utility the only creed which is able to furnish us with excuses for evil-doing and means of cheating our own conscience? They are afforded in abundance by all doctrines which recognize as a fact in morals the existence of conflicting considerations, which all doctrines do that have been believed by sane persons. It is not the fault of any creed, but of the complicated nature of human affairs, that rules of conduct cannot be so framed as to require no exceptions, and that hardly any kind of action can safely be laid down as either always obligatory or always condemnable. There is no ethical creed which does not temper the rigidity of its laws by giving a certain latitude, under the moral responsibility of the agent, for accommodation to peculiarities of circumstances; and under every creed, at the opening thus made, self-deception and dishonest casuistry get in. There exists no moral system under which there do not arise unequivocal cases of conflicting obligation. These are the real difficulties, the knotty points both in the theory of ethics and in the conscientious guidance of personal conduct. They are overcome practically, with greater or with less success, according to the intellect and virtue of the individual; but it can hardly be pretended that anyone will be the less qualified for dealing with them, from possessing an ultimate standard to which conflicting rights and duties can be referred. If utility is the ultimate source of moral obligations, utility may be invoked to decide between them when their demands are incompatible. Though the application of the standard may be difficult, it is better than none at all; while in other systems, the moral laws all claiming independent authority, there is no common umpire entitled to interfere between them; their claims to precedence one over another rest on little better than sophistry, and, unless determined, as they generally are, by the unacknowledged influence of consideration of utility, afford a free scope of the action of personal desires and partialities. We must remember that only in these cases of conflict between secondary principles is it requisite that first principles should be appealed to. There is no case of moral obligation in which some secondary principle is not involved; and if only one, there can seldom be any real doubt which one it is, in the mind of any person by whom the principle itself is recognized. . . .

Of What Sort of Proof The Principle of Utility is Susceptible

It has already been remarked that questions of ultimate ends do not admit of proof, in the ordinary acception of the term. To be incapable of proof by reasoning is common to all first principles, to the first premises of our knowledge, as well as to those of our conduct. But the former, being matters of fact, may be the subject of a direct appeal to the faculties which judge of fact—namely, our senses and our internal consciousness. Can an appeal be made to the same faculties on questions of practical needs? Or by what other faculty is cognizance taken of them?

Questions about ends are, in other words, questions what things are desirable. The utilitarian doctrine is that happiness is desirable, and the only thing desirable, as an end; all other things being only desirable as means to that end. What ought to be required of this doctrine, what conditions is it requisite that the doctrine should fulfill—to make good its claim to be believed?

The only proof capable of being given that an object is visible is that people actually see it. The only proof that a sound is audible is that people hear it; and so of the other sources of our experience. In like manner, I apprehend, the sole evidence it is possible to produce that anything is desirable is that people do actually desire it. If the end which the utilitarian doctrine proposes to itself were not, in theory and in practice, acknowledged to be an end, nothing could ever convince any person that it was so. No reason can be given why the general happiness is desirable, except that each person, so far as he believes it to be attainable, desires his own happiness. This, however, being a fact, we have not only all the proof which the case admits of, but all which it is possible to require, that happiness is a good, that each person's happiness is a good to that person, and the general happiness, therefore, a good to the aggregate of all persons. Happiness has made out its title as *one* of the ends of conduct and, consequently, one of the criteria of morality.

But it has not, by this alone, proved itself to be the sole criterion. To do that, it would seem, by the same rule, necessary to show, not only that people desire happiness, but that they never desire anything else. Now it is palpable that they do desire things which, in common language, are decidedly distinguished from happiness. They desire, for example, virtue and the absence of vice no less really than pleasure and the absence of pain. The desire of virtue is not as universal, but it is as authentic a fact as the desire of happiness. And hence the opponents of the utilitarian standard deem that they have a right to infer that there are other ends of human action besides happiness, and that happiness is not the standard of approbation and disapprobation.

But does the utilitarian doctrine deny that people desire virtue, or maintain that virtue is not a thing to be desired? The very reverse. It maintains not only that virtue is to be desired, but that it is to be desired disinterestedly, for itself. Whatever may be the opinion of utilitarian moralists as to the original conditions by which virtue is made virtue, however they may believe (as they do) that actions and dispositions are only virtuous because they promote another end than virtue, yet this being granted, and it having been decided, from considerations of this description, what *is* virtuous, they not only place virtue at the very head of the things which are good as means to the ultimate end, but they also recognize as a psychological fact the possibility of its being, to the individual, a good in itself, without looking to any end beyond it; and hold that the mind is not in a right state, not in a state conformable to utility, not in the state most conducive to the general happiness, unless it does love virtue in this manner—as a thing desirable in itself, even although, in the individual instance, it should not produce those other desirable consequences which it tends to produce, and on account of which it is held to be virtue. This opinion is not, in the smallest degree, a departure from the happiness principle. The ingredients of happiness are very various, and each of them is desirable in itself, and not merely when considered as swelling an aggregate. The principle of utility does not mean that any given pleasure, as music, for instance, or any given exemption from pain, as for example health, is to be looked upon as means to a collective something termed happiness, and to be desired on that account. They are desired and desirable in and for themselves; besides being means, they are a part of the end. Virtue, according to the utilitarian doctrine, is not naturally and originally part of the end, but is capable of becoming so; and in those who live it disinterestedly it has become so, and is desired and cherished, not as a means to happiness, but as a part of their happiness.

To illustrate this further, we may remember that virtue is not the only thing originally a means, and which if it were not a means to anything else would be and remain indifferent, but which by association with what it is a means to comes to be desired for itself, and that too with the utmost intensity. What, for example, shall we say of the love of money? There is nothing originally more desirable about money than about any heap of glittering pebbles. Its worth is solely that of the things which it will buy; the desires for other things than itself, which it is a means of gratifying. Yet the love of money is not only one of the strongest moving forces of human life, but money is, in many cases, desired in and for itself; the desire to possess it is often stronger than the desire to use it, and goes on increasing when all the desires which point to ends beyond it, to be compassed by it, are falling off. It may, then, be said truly that money is desired not for the sake of an end, but as part of the end. From being a means to happiness, it has come to be itself a principal ingredient of the individual's conception of happiness. The same may be said of the majority of the great objects of human life: power, for example, or fame, except that to each of these there is a certain amount of immediate pleasure annexed, which has at least the semblance of being naturally inherent in them—a thing which cannot be said of money. Still, however, the strongest natural attraction, both of power and of fame, is the immense aid they give to the attainment of our other wishes; and it is the strong association thus generated between them and all our objects of desire which gives to the direct desire of them the intensity it often assumes, so as in some characters to surpass in strength all other desires. In these cases the means have become a part of the end, and a more important part of it than any of the things which they are means to. What was once desired as an instrument for the attainment of happiness has come to be desired for its own sake. In being desired for its own sake it is, however, desired as *part* of happiness. The person is made, or thinks he would be made, happy by its mere possession; and is made unhappy by failure to obtain it. The desire of it is not a different thing from the desire of happiness any more than the love of music or the desire of health. They are included in happiness. They are some of the elements of which the desire of happiness is made up. Happiness is not an abstract idea but a concrete whole; and these are some of its parts. And the utilitarian standard sanctions and approves their being so. Life would be a poor thing, very ill provided with sources of happiness, if there were not this provision of nature by which things originally indifferent, but conducive to, or otherwise associated with, the satisfaction of our primitive desires, become in themselves sources of pleasure more valuable than the primitive pleasures, both in permanency, in the space of human existence that they are capable of covering, and even in intensity.

Virtue, according to the utilitarian conception, is a good of this description. There was no original desire of it, or motive to it, save its conduciveness to pleasure, and especially to protection from pain. But through the association thus formed it may be felt a good in itself, and desired as such with as great intensity as any other good; and with this difference between it and the love of money, of power, or of fame—that all of these may, and often do, render the individual noxious to the other members of the society to which he belongs, whereas there is nothing which makes him so much a blessing to them as the cultivation of the disinterested love of virtue. And consequently, the utilitarian standard, while it tolerates and approves those other acquired desires, up to the point beyond which they would be more injurious to the general happiness than promotive of it, enjoins and requires the cultivation of the love of virtue up to the greatest strength possible, as being above all things important to the general happiness.

It results from the preceding considerations that there is in reality nothing desired except happiness. Whatever is desired otherwise than as a means to some end beyond itself, and ultimately to happiness, is desired as itself a part of happiness, and is not desired for itself until it has become so. Those who desire virtue for its own sake desire it either because the consciousness of it is a pleasure, or because the consciousness of being without it is a pain, or for both reasons united; as in truth the pleasure and pain seldom exist separately, but almost always together—the same person feeling pleasure in the degree of virtue attained, and pain in not having attained more. If one of these gave him no pleasure, and the other no pain, he would not love or desire virtue, or would desire it only for the other benefits which it might produce to himself or to persons whom he cared for.

We have now, then, an answer to the question, of what sort of proof the principle of utility is susceptible. If the opinion which I have now stated is psychologically true—if human nature is so constituted as to desire nothing which is not either a part of happiness or a means of happiness—we can have no other proof, and we require no other, that these are the only things desirable. If so, happiness is the sole end of human action, and the promotion of it the test by which to judge of all human conduct; from whence it necessarily follows that it must be the criterion of morality, since a part is included in the whole.

And now to decide whether this is really so, whether mankind do desire nothing for itself but that which is a pleasure to them, or of which the absence is a pain, we have evidently arrived at a question of fact and experience, dependent, like all similar questions, upon evidence. It can only be determined by practiced self-consciousness and self-observation, assisted by observation of others. I believe that these sources of evidence, impartially consulted, will declare that desiring a thing and finding it pleasant, aversion to it and thinking of it as painful, are phenomena entirely inseparable or, rather, two parts of the same phenomenon—in strictness of language, two different modes of naming the same psychological fact; that to think of an object as desirable (unless for the sake of its consequences) and to think of it as pleasant are one and the same thing; and that to desire anything except in proportion as the idea of it is pleasant is a physical and metaphysical impossibility.

So obvious does this appear to me that I expect it will hardly be disputed; and the objection made will be, not that desire can possibly be directed to anything ultimately except pleasure and exemption from pain, but that the will is a different thing from desire; that a person of confirmed virtue or any other person whose purposes are fixed carries out his purposes without any thought of the pleasure he has in contemplating them or expects to derive from their fulfillment, and persists in acting on them, even though these pleasures are much diminished by changes in his character or decay of his passive sensibilities, or are outweighed by the pains which the pursuit of the purposes may bring upon him. All this I fully admit and have stated it elsewhere as positively and emphatically as anyone. Will, the active phenomenon, is a different thing from desire, the state of passive sensibility, and, though originally an offshoot from it, may in time take root and detach itself from the parent stock, so much so that in the case of a habitual purpose, instead of willing the thing because we desire it, we often desire it only because we will it. This, however, is but an instance of that familiar fact, the power of habit, and is nowise confined to the case of virtuous actions. Many indifferent things which men originally did from a motive of some sort they continue to do from habit. Sometimes this is done unconsciously, the consciousness coming only after the action; at other times with conscious volition, but volition which has become habitual and is put in operation by the force of habit, in opposition perhaps to the deliberate preference, as often happens with those who have contracted habits of vicious or hurtful indulgence. Third and last comes the case in which the habitual act of will in the individual instance is not in contradiction to the general intention prevailing at other times, but in fulfillment of it, as in the case of the person of confirmed virtue and of all who pursue deliberately and consistently any determinate end. The distinction between will and desire thus understood is an authentic and highly important psychological fact; but the fact consists solely in this—that will, like all other parts of our constitution, is amenable to habit, and that we may will from habit what we no longer desire for itself, or desire only because we will it. It is not the less true that will, in the beginning, is entirely produced by desire, including in that term the repelling influence of pain as well as the attractive one of pleasure. Let us take into consideration no longer the person who has a confirmed will to do right but him in whom that virtuous will is still feeble, conquerable by temptation, and not to be fully relied on; by what means can it be strengthened? How can the will to be virtuous, where it does not exist in sufficient force, be implanted or awakened? Only by making the person *desire* virtue—by making him think of it in a pleasurable light, or of its absence in a painful one. It is by associating the doing right with pleasure, or the wrong with pain, or by eliciting and impressing and bringing home to the person's experience the pleasure naturally involved in the one or the pain in the other, that it is possible to call forth that will to be virtuous which, when confirmed, acts without any thought of either pleasure or pain. Will is the child of desire, and passes out of the dominion of its parent only to come under that of habit. That which is the result of habit affords no presumption of being intrinsically good; and there would be no reason for wishing that the purpose of virtue should become independent of pleasure and pain were it not that the influence of the pleasurable and painful associations which prompt to virtue is not sufficiently to be depended on for unerring constancy of action until it has acquired the support of habit. Both in feeling and in conduct, habit is the only thing which imparts certainty, and it is because of the importance to others of being able to rely absolutely on one's feelings and conduct, and to oneself of being able to rely on one's own, that the will to do right ought to be cultivated into this habitual independence. In other words, this state of will is a means to good, not intrinsically a good; and does not contradict the doctrine that nothing is a good to human beings but in so far as it is either itself pleasurable or a means of attaining pleasure or averting pain.

But if this doctrine be true, the principle of utility is proved. Whether it is so or not must now be left to the consideration of the thoughtful reader. . . .

Richard B. Brandt

Some Merits of One Form of Rule-Utilitarianism

1. Utilitarianism is the thesis that the moral predicates of an act—at least its objective rightness or wrongness, and sometimes also its moral praiseworthiness or blameworthiness—are functions in some way, direct or indirect, of consequences for the welfare of sentient creatures, and of nothing else. Utilitarians differ about what precise function they are; and they differ about what constitutes welfare and how it is to be measured. But they agree that all one needs to know, in order to make moral appraisals correctly, is the consequences of certain things for welfare. . . .

2. If an analysis of concepts like "morally wrong" and "morality" and "moral code" does not enable us to establish the truth of the utilitarian thesis, the question arises what standard a normative theory like utilitarianism has to meet in order for a reasonable presumption to be established in its favor. It is well known that the identity and justification of any such standard can be debated at length. In order to set bounds to the present discussion, I shall state briefly the standard I shall take for granted for purposes of the present discussion. Approximately this standard would be acceptable to a good many writers on normative ethics. However this may be, it would be agreed that it is worth knowing whether some form of utilitarianism meets this standard better than any other form of utilitarian theory, and it is this question which I shall discuss.

The standard which I suggest an acceptable normative moral theory has to meet is this: The theory must contain no unintelligible concepts or internal inconsistencies; it must not be inconsistent with known facts; it must be capable of precise formulation so that its implications for action can be determined; and—most important—its implications must be acceptable to thoughtful persons who have had reasonably wide experience, when taken in the light of supporting remarks that can be made, and when compared with the implications of other clearly statable normative theories. It is not required that the implications of a satisfactory theory be consonant with the uncriticized moral intuitions of intelligent and experienced people, but only with those intuitions which stand in the light of supporting remarks, etc. Furthermore, it is not required of an acceptable theory that the best consequences would be produced by people adopting that theory, in contrast to other theories by which they might be convinced. (The theory might be so complex that it would be a good thing if most people did not try their hand at applying it to concrete situations!) It may be a moving *ad hominem* argument, if one can persuade an act-utilitarian that it would have bad consequences for people to try to determine the right act according to that theory, and to live by their conclusions; but such a showing would not be a reasonable ground for rejecting that normative theory.

3. Before turning to the details of various types of utilitarian theory, it may be helpful to offer some "supporting remarks" which will explain some reasons why some philosophers are favorably disposed toward a utilitarian type of normative theory.

(a) The utilitarian principle provides a clear and definite procedure for determining which acts are right or wrong (praiseworthy or blameworthy), by observation and the methods of science alone and without the use of any supplementary intuitions (assuming that empirical procedures can determine when something maximizes utility), for all cases, including the complex ones about which intuitions are apt to be mute, such as whether kleptomanic behavior is blameworthy or whether it is right to break a confidence in certain circumstances. The utilitarian presumably frames his thesis so as to conform with enlightened intuitions which are clear, but his thesis, being general, has implications for all cases, including those about which his intuitions are not clear. The utilitarian principle is like a general scientific theory, which checks with observations at many points, but can also be used as a guide to beliefs on matters inaccessible to observation (like the behavior of matter at absolute zero temperature).

Utilitarianism is not the only normative theory with the desirable property; egoism is another, and, with some qualifications, so is Kant's theory.

(b) Any reasonably plausible normative theory will give a large place to consequences for welfare in the moral assessment of actions, for this consideration enters continuously and substantially into ordinary moral thinking. Theories which ostensibly make no appeal of this sort admit utilitarian considerations by the back door, or have counter-intuitive consequences. Therefore the ideal of simplicity leads us to hope for the possibility of a pure utilitarian theory. Moreover, utilitarianism avoids the necessity of weighing disparate things such as justice and utility.

(c) If a proposed course of action does not raise moral questions, it is generally regarded as rational, and its agent well advised to perform it, if and only if it will maximize expectable utility for the agent. In a similar vein, it can be argued that society's "choice" of an institution of morality is rational and well advised, if and only if having it will maximize expectable social utility—raise the expectable level of the average "utility curve" of the population. If morality is a system of traditional and arbitrary constraints on behavior, it cannot be viewed as a rational institution. But it can be, if the system of morality is utilitarian. In that case the institution of morality can be recommended to a person of broad human sympathies, as an institution which maximizes the expectation of general welfare; and to a selfish person, as an institution which, in the absence of particular evidence about his own case, may be expected to maximize his own expectation of welfare (his own welfare being viewed as a random sample from the population). To put it in other words, a utilitarian morality can be "vindicated" by appeal either to the humanity or to the selfishness of human beings.

To say this is not to deny that nonutilitarian moral principles may be capable of vindication in a rather similar way. For instance, to depict morality as an institution which fosters human equality is to recommend it by appeal to something which is perhaps as deep in man as his sympathy or humanity.[1]

4. The type of utilitarianism on which I wish to focus is a form of rule-utilitarianism, as contrasted with act-utilitarianism. According to the latter type of theory (espoused by Sidgwick and Moore), an act is objectively right if no other act the agent could perform would produce better consequences. (On this view, an act is blameworthy if and only if it is right to perform the act of blaming or condemning it; the principles of blameworthiness are a special case of the principle of objectively right actions.) Act-utilitarianism is hence a rather atomistic theory: the rightness of a single act is fixed by its effects on the world. Rule-utilitarianism, in contrast, is the view that the rightness of an act is fixed, not by its relative utility, but by the utility of having a relevant moral rule, or of most or all members of a certain class of acts being performed.

The implications of act-utilitarianism are seriously counter-intuitive, and I shall ignore it except to consider whether some ostensibly different theories really are different.

5. Rule-utilitarianisms may be divided into two main groups, according as the rightness of a particular act is made a function of ideal rules

[1]It would not be impossible to combine a restricted principle of utility with a morality of justice or equality. For instance, it might be said that an act is right only if it meets a certain condition of justice, and also if it is one which, among all the just actions open to the agent, meets a requirement of utility as well as any other.

in some sense, or of the actual and recognized rules of a society. The variety of theory I shall explain more fully is of the former type.

According to the latter type of theory, a person's moral duties or obligations in a particular situation are determined, with some exceptions, solely by the moral rules, or institutions, or practices prevalent in the society, and not by what rules (etc.) it would ideally be best to have in the society. (It is sometimes held that actual moral rules, practices, etc., are only a necessary condition of an act's being morally obligatory or wrong.) Views roughly of this sort have been held in recent years by A. MacBeath, Stephen Toulmin, John Rawls, P. F. Strawson, J. O. Urmson,and B. J. Diggs. Indeed, Strawson says in effect that for there to be a moral obligation on one is just for there to be a socially sanctioned demand on him, in a situation where he has an interest in the system of demands which his society is wont to impose on its members, and where such demands are generally acknowledged and respected by members of his society.[2] And Toulmin asserts that when a person asks, "Is this the right thing to do?" what he is normally asking is whether a proposed action "conforms to the moral code" of his group, "whether the action in question belongs to a class of actions generally approved of in the agent's community." In deliberating about the question what is right to do, he says, "there is no more general 'reason' to be given beyond one which related the action . . . to an accepted social practice."[3]

So far the proposal does not appear to be a form of utilitarianism at all. The theory is utilitarian, however, in the following way: it is thought that what is relevant for a decision whether to try to change moral codes, institutions, etc., or for a justification of them, is the relative utility of the code, practice, etc. The recognized code or practice determined the individual's moral obligations in a particular case; utility of the code or practice determines whether it is justified or ought to be changed. Furthermore, it is sometimes held that utilitarian considerations have some relevance to the rightness of a particular action. For instance, Toulmin thinks that in case the requirements of the recognized code or practice conflict in a particular case, the individual ought (although strictly, he is not morally obligated) to do what will maximize utility in the situation, and that in case an individual can relieve the distress of

[2]P.F. Strawson, "Social Morality and Individual Ideal," *Philosophy*, XXXVI (1961), 1–17.

[3] Stephen Toulmin, *An Examination of the Place of Reason in Ethics* (Cambridge University Press, 1950), pp. 144–45. See various acute criticisms, with which I mostly agree, in Rawls's review, *Philosophical Review*, LX (1951), 572–80.

another, he ought (strictly, is not morally obligated) to do so, even if the recognized code does not require him to.[4]

This theory, at least in some of its forms or parts, has such conspicuously counter-intuitive implications that it fails to meet the standard for a satisfactory normative theory. In general, we do not believe that an act's being prohibited by the moral code of one's society is sufficient to make it morally wrong. Moral codes have prohibited such things as work on the Sabbath, marriage to a divorced person, medically necessary abortion, and suicide; but we do not believe it was really wrong for persons living in a society with such prohibitions, to do these things.[5]

Neither do we think it a necessary condition of an act's being wrong that it be prohibited by the code of the agent's society, or of an act's being obligatory that it be required by the code of his society. A society may permit a man to have his wife put to death for infidelity, or to have a child put to death for almost any reason; but we still think such actions wrong. Moreover, a society may permit a man absolute freedom in divorcing his wife, and recognize no obligations on his part toward her; but we think, I believe, that a man has some obligations for the welfare of a wife of thirty year's standing (with some qualifications), whatever his society may think.[6]

Some parts of the theory in some of its forms, however, appear to be correct. In particular, the theory in some forms implies that, if a person has a certain recognized obligation in an institution or practice (e.g., a child to support his aged parent, a citizen to pay his taxes), then he morally does have this obligation, with some exceptions, irrespective of whether in an ideal institution he would or would not have. This we do

[4] Toulmin and Rawls sometimes go further, and suggest that a person is morally free to do something which the actual code or practice of his society prohibits, if he is convinced that the society would be better off if the code or practice were rewritten so as to permit that sort of thing, and he is prepared to live according to the ideally revised code. If their theory were developed in this direction, it need not be different from some "ideal" forms of rule-utilitarianism, although, as stated, the theory makes the recognized code the standard for moral obligations, with exceptions granted to individuals who hold certain moral opinions. See Toulmin, op. cit., pp. 151–52, and Rawls, "Two Concepts of Rules," *Philosophical Review*, LXIV (1955), 28–29, especially ftnt. 25. It should be noticed that Rawls's proposal is different from Toulmin's in an important way. He is concerned with only a segment of the moral code, the part which can be viewed as the rules of practices. As he observes, this may be only a small part of the moral code.

[5] Does a stranger living in a society have a moral obligation to conform to its moral code? I suggest we think that he does not, unless it is the right moral code or perhaps at least he thinks it is, although we think that offense he might give to the feelings of others should be taken into account, as well as the result his nonconformity might have in weakening regard for moral rules in general.

[6] It is a different question whether we should hold offenders in such societies seriously morally blameworthy. People cannot be expected to rise much above the level of recognized morality, and we condemn them little when they do.

roughly believe, although we need not at the same time accept the reasoning which has been offered to explain how the fact of a practice or institution leads to the moral obligation. The fact that the theory seems right in this would be a strong point in its favor if charges were correct that "ideal" forms of rule-utilitarianism necessarily differ at this point. B. J. Diggs, for instance, has charged that the "ideal" theories imply that:

> one may freely disregard a rule if ever he discovers that action on the rule is not maximally felicific, and in this respect makes moral rules like 'practical maxims.' . . . It deprives social and moral rules of their authority and naturally is in sharp conflict with practice. On this alternative rule-utilitarianism collapses into act-utilitarianism. Surely it is a mistake to maintain that a set of rules, thought to be ideally utilitarian or felicific, is the criterion of right action. . . . If we are presented with a list [of rules], but these are not rules in practice, the most one could reasonably do is to try to get them adopted.[7]

I believe, however, and shall explain in detail later that this charge is without foundation.

6. Let us turn now to "ideal" forms of rule-utilitarianism, which affirm that whether it is morally obligatory or morally right to do a certain thing in a particular situation is fixed, not by the actual code or practice of the society (these may be indirectly relevant, as forming part of the situation), but some "ideal" rule—that is, by the utility of having a certain general moral rule, or by the utility of all or most actions being performed which are members of a relevant class of actions.

If the rightness of an act is fixed by the utility of a relevant rule (class), are we to say that the rule (class) which qualifies must be the optimific rule (class), the one which maximizes utility, or must the rule (class) meet only some less stringent requirement (e.g., be better than the absence of any rule regulating the type of conduct in question)? And, if it is to be of the optimific type, are all utilities to be counted, or perhaps only "negative" utilities, as is done when it is suggested that the rule (class) must be the one which minimizes suffering?[8]

The simplest proposal—that the rule (class) which qualifies is the one that maximizes utility, with all utilities, whether "positive" or "negative," being counted—also seems to me to be the best, and it is the one I shall shortly explain more fully. Among the several possible theories

[7] "Rules and Utilitarianism," *American Philosophical Quarterly*, I (1964), 32–44.

[8] In a footnote to Chapter 9 of *The Open Society*, Professor Popper suggested that utilitarianism would be more acceptable if its test were minimized suffering rather than maximizing welfare, to which J. J. C. Smart replied (*Mind*, 1958, pp. 542–43) that the proposal implies that we ought to destroy all living beings, as the surest way to eliminate suffering. It appears, however, that Professor Popper does not seriously advocate what seemed to be the position of the earlier footnote (Addendum to fourth edition, p. 386).

different from this one I shall discuss briefly only one, which seems the most plausible of its kind, and is at least closely similar to the view defended by Professor Marcus Singer.

According to this theory, an action (or inaction) at time *t* in circumstances C is wrong if and only if, were everyone in circumstances C to perform a relevantly similar action, harm would be done—meaning by "doing harm" that affected persons would be made worse off by the action (or inaction) than they already were at time *t*. (I think it is not meant that the persons must be put in a state of "negative welfare" in some sense, but simply made worse off than they otherwise would have been.) Let us suppose a person is deciding whether to do A in circumstances C at *t*. The theory, then, implies the following: (1) If everyone doing A in circumstances C would make people worse off than they already were at *t* (A can be inaction, such as failing to pull a drowning man from the water) whereas some other act would not make them so, then it is wrong for anyone to do A. (2) If everyone doing A would not make people worse off, then even if everyone doing something else would make them better off, it is not wrong to do A. (3) If everyone doing A would make people worse off, but if there is no alternative act, the performance of which by everyone would avoid making people worse off, then it is right to do A, even though doing A would make people relatively much worse off than they would have been made by the performance of some other action instead. The "optimific rule" theory, roughly, would accept (1), but reject (2) and (3).

Implication (3) of the theory strikes me as clearly objectionable; I am unable to imagine circumstances in which we should think it not morally incumbent on one to avoid very bad avoidable consequences for others, even though a situation somewhat worse than the status quo could not be avoided. Implication (2) is less obviously dubious. But I should think we do have obligations to do things for others, when we are not merely avoiding being in the position of making them worse off. For instance, if one sees another person at a cocktail party, standing by himself and looking unhappy, I should suppose one has some obligation to make an effort to put him at his ease, even though doing nothing would hardly make him worse off than he already is.

Why do proponents of this view, like Professor Singer, prefer his view to the simpler, "maximize utility" form of rule-utilitarianism? This is not clear. One objection sometimes raised is that an optimific theory implies that every act is morally weighty and none morally indifferent. And one may concede that this is a consequence of some forms of utilitarianism, even rule-utilitarianism of the optimific variety; but we shall see that it is by no means a consequence of the type of proposal described below. For the theory below will urge that an action is not morally indifferent only if it falls under some prescription of an optimific moral code, and, since there are disadvantages in a moral code regulating actions, optimific moral codes will prohibit or require actions of a certain type only when there are significant utilitarian reasons for it. As a consequence, a great many types of action are morally indifferent, according to the theory. Professor Singer also suggests that optimific-type theories have objectionable consequences for state-of-nature situtations;[9] we may postpone judgment on this until we have examined these consequences of the theory here proposed, at a later stage. Other objections to the optimizing type of rule-utilitarianism with which I am familiar either confuse rule-utilitarianism with act-utilitarianism, or do not distinguish among the several possible forms of optimizing rule-utilitarianisms.

7. I propose, then, that we tentatively opt for an "ideal" rule-utilitarianism, of the "maximizing utility" variety. This decision, however, leaves various choices still to be made, between theories better or worse fitted to meet various problems. Rather than attempt to list alternatives, and explain why one choice rather than another between them would work out better, I propose to describe in some detail the type of theory which seems most plausible. I shall later show how this theory meets the one problem to which the "actual rule" type theories seemed to have a nice solution; and I shall discuss its merits, as compared with another quite similar type of theory which has been suggested by Jonathan Harrison and others.

The theory I wish to describe is rather similar to one proposed by J. D. Mabbott in his 1953 British Academy lecture, "Moral Rules." It is also very similar to the view defended by J. S. Mill in *Utilitarianism*, although Mill's formulation is ambiguous at some points, and he apparently did not draw some distinctions he should have drawn. (I shall revert to this historical point.)

For convenience I shall refer to the theory as the "ideal moral code" theory. The essence of it is as follows: Let us first say that a moral code is "ideal" if its currency in a particular society would produce at least as much good per person (the total divided by the number of persons) as the currency of any other moral code. (Two different codes might meet this condition, but, in order to avoid complicated formulations, the following discussion will ignore this possibility.) Given this stipulation

[9] M. G. Singer, *Generalization in Ethics* (New York: Alfred A. Knopf, Inc., 1961), p. 192.

for the meaning of "ideal," the Ideal Moral Code theory consists in the assertion of the following thesis: *An act is right if and only if it would not be prohibited by the moral code ideal for the society; and an agent is morally blameworthy (praiseworthy) for an act if, and to the degree that, the moral code ideal in that society would condemn (praise) him for it.* It is a virtue of this theory that it is a theory about objective rightness and about moral blameworthiness (praiseworthiness) of actions, but the assertion about blameworthiness will be virtually ignored in what follows.

8. In order to have a clear proposal before us, however, the foregoing summary statement must be filled out in three ways: (1) by explaining what it is for a moral code to have currency; (2) by making clear what is the difference between the rules of a society's moral code and the rules of its institutions; and (3) by describing how the relative utility of a moral code is to be estimated.

First, then, the notion of a moral code having currency in a society.

For a moral code to have currency in a society; two things must be true. First, a high proportion of the adults in the society must subscribe to the moral principles, or have the moral opinions, constitutive of the code. Exactly how high the proportion should be, we can hardly decide on the basis of the ordinary meaning of "the moral code"; but probably it would not be wrong to require at least ninety per cent agreement. Thus, if at least ninety per cent of the adults subscribe to principle A, and ninety per cent to principle B, etc., we may say that a code consisting of A and B (etc.) has a currency in the society, provided the second condition is met. Second, we want to say that certain principles A, B, etc. belong to the moral code of a society only if they are recognized as such. That is, it must be that a large proportion of the adults of the society would respond correctly if asked, with respect to A and B, whether most members of the society subscribed to them. (It need not be required that adults base their judgments on such good evidence as recollection of moral discussions; it is enough if for some reason the correct opinion about what is accepted is widespread). It is of course possible for certain principles to constitute a moral code with currency in a society even if some persons in the society have no moral opinions at all, or if there is disagreement, e.g., if everyone in the society disagrees with every other person with respect to at least one principle.

The more difficult question is what it is for an individual to subscribe to a moral principle or to have a moral opinion. What is it, then, for someone to think sincerely that any action of the kind F is wrong? (1) He is to some extent motivated to avoid actions which he thinks are F, and often, if asked why he does not perform such an action when it appears to be to his advantage, offers, as one of his reasons, that it is F. In addition, the person's motivation to avoid F-actions does not derive entirely from his belief that F-actions on his part are likely to be harmful to him or to persons to whom he is somehow attached. (2) If he thinks he has just performed an F-action, he feels quilty or remorseful or uncomfortable about it, unless he thinks he has some excuse—unless, for instance, he knows that at the time of action he did not think his action would be an F-action. "Guilt" (etc.) is not to be understood as implying some special origin such as interiorization of parental prohibitions, or as being a vestige of anxiety about punishment. It is left open that it might be an unlearned emotional response to the thought of being the cause of the suffering of another person. Any feeling which must be viewed simply as anxiety about anticipated consequences, for one's self or person to whom one is attached, is not, however, to count as a "guilt" feeling. (3) If he believes that someone has performed an F-action, he will tend to admire him less as a person, unless he thinks that the individual has a good excuse. He thinks that action of this sort, without excuse, reflects on character—this being spelled out, in part, by reference to traits like honesty, respect for the rights of others, and so on. (4) He thinks that these attitudes of his are correct or well justified, in some sense, but with one restriction: it is not enough if he thinks that what justifies them is simply the fact that they are shared by all or most members of his society. This restriction corresponds with our distinction between a moral conviction and something else. For instance, we are inclined to think no moral attitude is involved if an Englishman disapproves of something but says that his disapproval is justified by the fact that it is shared by "well-bred Englishmen." In such cases we are inclined to say that the individual subscribes only to a custom, or to a rule of etiquette or manners. On the other hand, if the individual thinks that what justifies his attitude unfavorable to F-actions is that F-actions are contrary to the will of God (and the individual's attitude is not merely a prudential one), or inconsistent with the welfare of mankind, or contrary to human nature, we are disposed to say the attitude is a moral attitude and the opinion expressed a moral one. And the same if he thinks his attitude justified, but can give no reason. There are perhaps other restrictions we should make on acceptable justifications (perhaps to distinguish a moral code from a code of honor), and other types of justification we should wish to list as clearly acceptable (perhaps an appeal to human equality).

9. It is important to distinguish between the moral code of a society and its institutions, or the rules of its institutions. It is especially

important for the Ideal Moral Code theory, for this theory involves the conception of a moral code ideal for a society in the context of its institutions, so that it is necessary to distinguish the moral code which a society does or might have from its institutions and their rules. The distinction is also one we actually do make in our thinking, although it is blurred in some cases. (For instance, is "Honor thy father and thy mother" a moral rule, or a rule of the family institution, in our society?)[10]

An institution is a set of positions or statuses, with which certain privileges and jobs are associated. (We can speak of these as "rights" and "duties" if we are careful to explain that we do not mean moral rights and duties.) That is, there are certain, usually nameable, positions which consist in the fact that anyone who is assigned to the position is expected to do certain things, and at the same time is expected to have certain things done for him. The individuals occupying these positions are a group of cooperating agents in a system which as a whole is thought to have the aim of serving certain ends. (E.g., a university is thought to serve the ends of education, research, etc.) The rules of the system concern jobs that must be done in order that the goals of the institution be achieved; they allocate the necessary jobs to different positions. Take, for instance, a university. There are various positions in it: the presidency, the professorial ranks, the registrars, librarians, etc. It is understood that one who occupies a certain post has certain duties, say teaching a specified number of classes or spending time working on research in the case of the instructing staff. Obviously the university cannot achieve its ends unless certain persons do the teaching, some tend to the administration, some do certain jobs in the library, and so on. Another such system is the family. We need not speculate on the "purpose" of the family, whether it is primarily a device for producing a new generation, etc. But it is clear that when a man enters marriage, he takes a position to which certain jobs are attached, such as providing support for the family to the best of his ability, and to which also certain rights are attached, such as exclusive sexual rights with his wife, and the right to be cared for should he become incapacitated.

If an "institution" is defined in this way, it is clear that the moral code

[10] The confusion is compounded by the fact that terms like "obligation" and "duty" are used sometimes to speak about moral obligations and duties, and sometimes not. The fact that persons have a certain legal duty in certain situations is a rule of legal institutions of the society; a person may not have a moral duty to do what is his legal duty. The fact that a person has an obligation to invite a certain individual to dinner is a matter of manners or etiquette, and at least may not be a matter of moral obligation. See R. B. Brandt, "The Concepts of Duty and Obligation," *Mind*, LXXIII (1964), especially 380–84.

of a society cannot itself be construed as an institution, nor its rules as rules of an institution. The moral code is society-wide, so if we were to identify its rules as institutional rules, we should presumably have to say that everyone belongs to this institution. But what is the "purpose" of society as a whole? Are there any distinctions of status, with rights and duties attached, which we could identify as the "positions" in the moral system? Can we say that moral rules consist in the assignment of jobs in such a way that the aims of the institution may be achieved? It is true that there is a certain analogy: society as a whole might be said to be aiming at the good life for all, and the moral rules of the society be viewed as the rules with which all must conform in order to achieve this end. But the analogy is feeble. Society as a whole is obviously not an organization like a university, an educational system, the church, General Motors, etc.; there is no specific goal in the achievement of which each position has a designated role to play. Our answer to the above questions must be in the negative: morality is not an institution in the explained sense; nor are moral rules institutional expectations or rules.

The moral code of a society may, of course, have implications that bear on institutional rules. For one thing, the moral code may imply that an institutional system is morally wrong and ought to be changed. Moreover, the moral code may imply that a person has also a moral duty to do something which is his institutional job. For instance, it may be a moral rule that a person ought to do whatever he has undertaken to do, or that he ought not to accept the benefits of a position without performing its duties. Take for instance the rules, "A professor should meet his classes" or "Wives ought to make the beds." Since the professor has undertaken to do what pertains to his office, and the same for a wife, and since these tasks are known to pertain to the respective offices, the moral rule that a person is morally bound (with certain qualifications) to do what he has undertaken to do implies, in context, that the professor is morally bound to meet his classes and the wife to make the beds, other things being equal (viz., there being no contrary moral obligations in the situation). But these implications are not themselves part of the moral code. No one would say that a parent had neglected to teach his child the moral code of the society if he had neglected to teach him that professors must meet classes, and that wives must make the beds. A person becomes obligated to do these things only by participating in an institution, by taking on the status of professor or wife. Parents do not teach children to have guilt feelings about missing classes, or making beds. The moral code consists only of more general rules, defining what is to be done in certain types of situations in which practically everyone will find himself. ("Do what you have promised!")

Admittedly some rules can be both moral and institutional: "Take care of your father in his old age" might be both an institutional rule of the family organization and also a part of the moral code of a society. (In this situation, one can still raise the question whether this moral rule is optimific in a society with that institutional rule; the answer could be negative.)

It is an interesting question whether "Keep your promises" is a moral rule, an institutional rule (a rule of an "institution" of promises), or both. Obviously it is a part of the moral code of western societies. But is it also a rule of an institution? There are difficulties in the way of affirming that it is. There is no structure of cooperating individuals with special functions, which serves to promote certain aims. Nor, when one steps into the "role" of a promisor, does one commit one's self to any specific duties; one fixes one's own duties by what one promises. Nor, in order to understand what one is committing one's self to be promising, need one have any knowledge of any system of expectations prevalent in the society. A three-year-old, who has never heard of any duties incumbent on promisors, can tell his friends, who wish to play baseball that afternoon, that he will bring the ball and bat, and that they need give no thought to the availability of these items. His invitation to rely on him for something needed for their common enjoyment, and his assurance that he will do something and his encouraging them thereby to set their minds at rest, *is* to make a promise. No one need suppose that the promisor is stepping into a socially recognized position, with all the rights and duties attendant on the same, although it is true he has placed himself in a position where he will properly be held responsible for the disappointment if he fails, and where inferences about his reliability as a person will properly be drawn if he forgets, or worse, if it turns out he was never in a position to perform. The bindingness of a promise is no more dependent on a set of expectations connected with an institution, than is the wrongness of striking another person without justifying reason.

Nevertheless, if one thinks it helpful to speak of a promise as an institution or a practice, in view of certain analogies (promisor and promisee may be said to have rights and duties like the occupants of roles in an institution, and there is the ritual word "promise" the utterance of which commits the speaker to certain performances), there is no harm in this. The similarities and dissimilarities are what they are, and as long as these are understood it seems to make little difference what we say. Nevertheless, even if making a promise is participating in a practice or institution, there is still the *moral* question whether one is morally bound to perform, and in what conditions, and for what reasons. This question is left open, given the institution is whatever it is—as is the case with all rules of institutions.

10. It has been proposed above that an action is right if and only if it would not be prohibited by the moral code ideal for the society in which it occurs, where a moral code is taken to be "ideal" if and only if its currency would produce at least as much good per person as the currency of any other moral code.[11] We must now give more attention to the conception of an ideal moral code, and how it may be decided when a given moral code will produce as much good per person as any other. We may, however, reasonably bypass the familiar problems of judgments of comparative utilities, especially when different persons are involved, since these problems are faced by all moral theories that have any plausibility. We shall simply assume that rough judgments of this sort are made and can be justified.

(a) We should first notice that, as "currency" has been explained above, a moral code could not be current in a society if it were too complex to be learned or applied. We may therefore confine our consideration to codes simple enough to be absorbed by human beings, roughly in the way in which people learn actual moral codes.

(b) We have already distinguished the concept of an institution and its rules from the concept of a moral rule, or rule of the moral code. (We have, however, pointed out that in some cases a moral rule may prescribe the same thing that is also an institutional expectation. But this is not a necessary situation, and a moral code could condemn an institutional expectation.) Therefore, in deciding how much good the currency of a specific moral system would do, we consider the institutional setting as it is, as part of the situation. We are asking which moral code would produce the most good in the long run in this setting. One good to be reckoned, of course, might be that the currency of a given moral code would tend to change the institutional system.

(c) In deciding which moral code will produce the most per person good, we must take into account the probability that certain types of situation will arise in the society. For instance, we must take for granted

[11] Some utilitarians have suggested that the right act is determined by the total net intrinsic good produced. This view can have embarrassing consequences for problems of population control. The view here advocated is that the right act is determined by the per person, average, net intrinsic good produced.

that people will make promises and subsequently want to break them, that people will sometimes assault other persons in order to achieve their own ends, that people will be in distress and need the assistance of others, and so on. We may not suppose that, because an ideal moral code might have certain features, it need not have other features because they will not be required; for instance, we may not suppose, on the ground that an ideal moral system would forbid everyone to purchase a gun, that such a moral system needs no provisions about the possession and use of guns—just as our present moral and legal codes have provisions about self-defense, which would be unnecessary if everyone obeyed the provision never to assault anyone.

It is true that the currency of a moral code with certain provisions might bring about a reduction in certain types of situation, e.g., the number of assaults or cases of dishonesty. And the reduction might be substantial, if the moral code were current which prohibited these offenses very strongly. (We must remember that an ideal moral code might differ from the actual one not in what it prohibits or enjoins, but also in how strongly it prohibits or enjoins.) But it is consistent to suppose that a moral code prohibits a certain form of behavior very severely, and yet that the behavior will occur, since the "currency" of a moral code requires only ninety per cent subscription to it, and a "strong" subscription, on the average, permits a great range from person to person. In any case there must be doubt whether the best moral code will prohibit many things very severely, since there are serious human costs in severe prohibitions: the burden of guilt feelings, the traumas caused by the severe criticism by others which is a part of having a strong injunction in a code, the risks of any training process which would succeed in interiorizing a severe prohibition, and so on.

(d) It would be a great oversimplification if, in assessing the comparative utility of various codes, we confined ourselves merely to counting the benefits of people doing (refraining from doing) certain things, as a result of subscribing to a certain code. To consider only this would be as absurd as estimating the utility of some feature of a legal system by attending only to the utility of people behaving in the way the law aims to make them behave—and overlooking the fact that the law only reduces and does not eliminate misbehavior, as well as the disutility of punishment to the convicted, and the cost of the administration of criminal law. In the case of morals, we must weigh the benefit of the improvement in behavior as a result of the restriction built into conscience, against the cost of the restriction—the burden of guilt feelings, the effects of the training process, etc. There is a further necessary refinement. In both law and morals we must adjust our estimates of utility by taking into account the envisaged system of excuses. That *mens rea* is required as a condition of guilt in the case of most legal offenses is most important; and it is highly important for the utility of a moral system whether accident, intent, and motives are taken into account in deciding a person's liability to moral criticism. A description of a moral code is incomplete until we have specified the severity of condemnation (by conscience or the criticism of others) to be attached to various actions, along with the excuses to be allowed as exculpating or mitigating.

11. Philosophers have taken considerable interest in the question what implications forms of rule-utilitarianism have for the moral relevance of the behavior of persons other than the agent. Such implications, it is thought, bring into focus the effective difference between any form of rule-utilitarianism, and act-utilitarianism. In particular, it has been thought that the implications of rule-utilitarianisms for two types of situation are especially significant: (a) for situtations in which persons are generally violating the recognized moral code, or some feature of it; and (b) for situations in which, because the moral code is generally respected, maximum utility would be produced by violation of the code by the agent. An example of the former situation (sometimes called a "state of nature" situation) would be widespread perjury in making out income tax declarations. An example of the latter situation would be widespread conformity to the rule forbidding walking on the grass in a park.

What are the implications of the suggested form of rule-utilitarianism for these types of situation? Will it prescribe conduct which is not utility maximizing in these situations? If it does, it will clearly have implications discrepant with those of act-utilitarianism—but perhaps unpalatable to some people.

It is easy to see how to go about determining what is right or wrong in such situations, on the above described form of rule-utilitarianism—it is a question of what an "ideal" moral code would prescribe. But it is by no means easy to see where a reasonable person would come out, after going through such an investigation. Our form of rule-utilitarianism does not rule out, as morally irrelevant, reference to the behavior of other persons; it implies that the behavior of others is morally relevant precisely to the extent to which an optimific moral code (the one the currency of which is optimific) would take it into account. How far, then, we might ask, would an optimific moral code take into account the behavior of other persons, and what would its specific prescriptions be for the two types of situations outlined?

It might be thought, and it has been suggested, that an ideal moral code could take no cognizance of the behavior of other persons, and in particular of the possibility that many persons are ignoring some prohibitions of the code, sometimes for the reason, apparently, that it is supposed that a code of behavior would be self-defeating if it prescribed for situations of its own breach, on a wide scale. It is a sufficient answer to this suggestion, to point out that our actual moral code appears to contain some such prescriptions. For instance, our present code seems to permit, for the case in which almost everyone is understating his income, that others do the same, on the ground that otherwise they will be paying more than their fair share. It is, of course, true that a code simple enough to be learned and applied cannot include prescriptions for all possible types of situation involving the behavior of other persons; but it can contain some prescriptions pertinent to some general features of the behavior of others.

Granted, then, that an ideal moral code may contain some special prescriptions which pay attention to the behavior of other persons, how in particular will it legislate for special situations such as the examples cited above? The proper answer to this question is that there would apparently be no blanket provision for all cases of these general types, and that a moral agent faced with such a concrete situation would have to think out what an ideal moral code would imply for his type of concrete situation. Some things do seem clear. An ideal moral code would not provide that a person is permitted to be cruel in a society where most other persons are cruel; there could only be loss of utility in any special provision permitting that. On the other hand, if there is some form of cooperative activity which enhances utility only if most persons cooperate, and nonparticipation in which does not reduce utility when most persons are not cooperating, utility would seem to be maximized if the moral code somehow permitted all to abstain—perhaps by an abstract formula stating this very condition. (This is on the assumption that the participation by some would not, by example, eventually bring about the participation of most or all.) Will there be any types of situation for which an ideal moral code would prescribe infringement of a generally respected moral code, by a few, when a few infringements (provided there are not many) would maximize utility? The possibility of this is not ruled out. Obviously there will be some regulations for emergencies; one may cut across park grass in order to rush a heartattack victim to a hospital. And there will be rules making special exceptions when considerable utility is involved; the boy with no other place to play may use the grass in the park. But, when an agent has no special claim which others could not make, it is certainly not clear that ideal moral rules will make him an exception on the ground that some benefit will come to him, and that restraint by him is unnecessary in view of the cooperation of others.

The implications of the above form of rule-utilitarianism, for these situations, are evidently different from those of act-utilitarianism.[12]

12. The Ideal Moral Code theory is very similar to the view put forward by J. S. Mill in *Utilitarianism*.

Mill wrote that his creed held that "actions are right in proportion as they tend to promote happiness; wrong as they tend to produce the reverse of happiness." Mill apparently did not intend by this any form of act-utilitarianism. He was—doubtless with much less than full awareness—writing of act-*types*, and what he meant was that an act of a certain type is morally obligatory (wrong) if and only if acts of that type tend to promote happiness (the reverse). Mill supposed that it is unknown that certain kinds of acts, e.g., murder and theft, promote unhappiness, and that therefore we can say, with exceptions only for very special circumstances, that murder and theft are wrong. Mill recognized that there can be a discrepancy between the tendency of an act-type, and the probable effects, in context, of an individual act. He wrote: "In the case of abstinences, indeed—of things which people forbear to do from moral considerations, though the consequences in the particular case might be beneficial—, it would be unworthy of an intelligent agent not to be consciously aware that the action is of a class which, if practiced generally, would be generally injurious, and that this is the ground of the obligation to abstain from it."[13] Moreover, he specifically denied that one is morally obligated to perform (avoid) an act just on the ground that it can be expected to produce good consequences; he says that "there is no case of moral obligation in which some secondary principle is not involved" (op. cit., p. 33).

It appears, however, that Mill did not quite think that it is morally obligatory to perform (avoid) an act according as its general performance

[12] The above proposal is different in various respects from that set forth in the writer's "Toward a Credible Form of Utilitarianism," in Castaneda and Nakhnikian, *Morality and the Language of Conduct*, 1963. The former paper did not make a distinction between institutional rules and moral rules. (The present paper, of course, allows that both may contain a common prescription.) A result of these differences is that the present theory is very much simpler, and avoids some counter-intuitive consequences which some writers have pointed out in criticism of the earlier proposal.

[13] *Utilitarianism* (New York: Library of Liberal Arts, 1957), p. 25.

would promote (reduce) happiness in the world. For he said (p. 60) that "We do not call anything wrong unless we mean to imply that a person ought to be punished in some way or other for doing it—if not by law, by the opinion of his fellow creatures; if not by opinion, by the reproaches of his own conscience. This seems the real turning point of the distinction between morality and simple expediency." The suggestion here is that it is morally obligatory to perform (avoid) an act according as it is beneficial to have a system of sanctions (with what this promises in way of performance), whether formal, informal (criticism by others), or internal (one's own conscience), for enforcing the performance (avoidance) of the type of act in question. This is very substantially the Ideal Moral Code theory.

Not that there are no differences. Mill is not explicit about details, and the theory outlined above fills out what he actually said. Moreover, Mill noticed that an act can fall under more than one secondary principle and that the relevant principles may give conflicting rulings about what is morally obligatory. In such a case, Mill thought, what one ought to do (but it is doubtful whether he believed there is a strict moral obligation in this situation) is what will maximize utility in the concrete situation. This proposal for conflicts of "ideal moral rules" is not a necessary part of the Ideal Code theory as outlined above.

13. It is sometimes thought that a rule-utilitarianism rather like Mill's cannot differ in its implication about what is right or wrong from the act-utilitarian theory. This is a mistake.

The contention would be correct if two dubious assumptions happened to be true. The first is that one of the rules of an optimific moral code will be that a person ought always to do whatever will maximize utility. The second is that, when there is a conflict between the rules of an optimific code, what a person ought to do is to maximize utility. For then either the utilitarian rule is the only one that applies (and it always will be relevant), in which case the person ought to do what the act-utilitarian directs; or if there is a conflict among the relevant rules, the conflict resolving principle takes over, and this, of course, prescribes exactly what act-utilitarianism prescribes. Either way, we come out where the act-utilitarian comes out.

But there is no reason at all to suppose that there will be a utilitarian rule in an optimific moral code. In fact, obviously there will not be. It is true that there should be a directive to relieve the distress of others, when this can be done, say at relatively low personal cost; and there should be a directive not to injure other persons, except in special situations. And so on. But none of this amounts to a straight directive to do the most good possible. Life would be chaotic if people tried to observe any such moral requirement.

The second assumption was apparently acceptable to Mill. But a utilitarian principle is by no means the only possible conflict resolving principle. For if we say, with the Ideal Moral Code theory, that what is right is fixed by the content of the moral system with maximum utility, the possibility is open that the utility maximizing moral system will contain some rather different device for resolving conflicts between lowest-level moral rules. The ideal system might contain several higher-level conflict resolving principles, all different from Mill's. Or, if there is a single one, it could be a directive to maximize utility; it could be a directive to do what an intelligent person who had fully interiorized the rest of the ideal moral system would feel best satisfied with doing; and so on. But the final court of appeal need not be an appeal to direct utilities. Hence the argument that Mill-like rule-utilitarianism must collapse into direct utilitarianism is doubly at fault.[14]

In fact far from "collapsing" into act-utilitarianism, the Ideal Moral Code theory appears to avoid the serious objections which have been leveled at direct utilitarianism. One objection to the latter view is that it implies that various immoral actions (murdering one's elderly father, breaking solemn promises) are right or even obligatory if only they can be kept secret. The Ideal Moral Code theory has no such implication. For it obviously would not maximize utility to have a moral code which condoned secret murders or breaches of promise. W. D. Ross criticized act-utilitarianism on the ground that it ignored the personal relations important in ordinary morality, and he listed a half-dozen types of moral rule which he thought captured the main themes of thoughtful morality: obligations of fidelity, obligations of gratitude, obligations to make restitution for injuries, obligations to help other persons, to avoid injuring them, to improve one's self, and to bring about a just distribution of good things in life. An ideal moral code, however, would presumably contain substantially such rules in any society, doubtless not precisely as Ross stated them. So the rule-utilitarian need not fail to recognize the personal character of morality.

14. In contrast to the type of theory put forward by Toulmin and

[14] Could some moral problems be so unique that they would not be provided for by the set rules it is best for the society to have? If so, how should they be appraised morally? Must there be some appeal to rules covering cases most closely analogous, as seems to be the procedure in law? If so, should we say that an act is right if it is not prohibited, either explicitly or by close analogy, by an ideal moral code? I shall not attempt to answer these questions.

others, the Ideal Moral Code theory has the advantage of implying that the moral rules recognized in a given society are not necessarily morally binding. They are binding only in so far as they maximize welfare, as contrasted with other possible moral rules. Thus if, in a given society, it is thought wrong to work on the Sabbath, to perform socially desirable abortions, or to commit suicide, it does not follow, on the Ideal Moral Code theory, that these things are necessarily wrong. The question is whether a code containing such prohibitions would maximize welfare. Similarly, according to this theory, a person may act wrongly in doing certain things which are condoned by his sociey.

A serious appeal of theories like Toulmin's is, however, their implications for institutional obligations. For instance, if in society A it is a recognized obligation to care for one's aged father, Toulmin's theory implies that it really is a moral obligation for a child in that society to care for his aged parent (with some qualifications); whereas if in society B it is one's recognized obligation not to care for one's aged father, but instead for one's aged maternal uncle, his theory implies that it really is the moral obligation of a person in that society to care for his aged maternal uncle—even if a better institutional system would put the responsibilities in different places. This seems approximately what we do believe.

The Ideal Moral Code theory, however, has much the same implications. According to it, an institutional system forms the setting within which the best (utility maximizing) moral code is to be applied, and one's obligation is to follow the best moral rules in that institutional setting—not to do what the best moral rules would require for some other, more ideal, setting.

Let us examine the implications of the Ideal Moral Code theory by considering a typical example. Among the Hopi Indians, a child is not expected to care for his father (he is always in a different clan), whereas he is expected to care for his mother, maternal aunt, and maternal uncle, and so on up the female line (all in the same clan). It would be agreed by observers that this system does not work very well. The trouble with it is that the lines of institutional obligation and the lines of natural affection do not coincide, and, as a result, an elderly male is apt not to be cared for by anyone.

Can we show that an "ideal moral code" would call on a young person to take care of his maternal uncle, in a system of this sort? (It might also imply he should try to change the system, but that is another point.) One important feature of the situation of the young man considering whether he should care for his maternal uncle is that, the situation including the expectations of others being what it is, if he does nothing to relieve the distress of his maternal uncle, it is probable that it will not be relieved. His situation is very like that of the sole observer of an automobile accident; he is a mere innocent bystander, but the fact is that if he does nothing, the injured persons will die. So the question for us is whether an ideal moral code will contain a rule that, if someone is in a position where he can relieve serious distress, and where it is known that in all probability it will not be relieved if he does not do so, he should relieve the distress. The answer seems to be that it will contain such a rule: we might call it an "obligation of humanity." But there is a second, and more important point. Failure of the young person to provide for his maternal uncle would be a case of unfairness or free riding. For the family system operates like a system of insurance; it provides one with various sorts of privileges or protections, in return for which one is expected to make certain payments, or accept the risk of making certain payments. Our young man has already benefited by the system, and stands to benefit further, he has received care and education as a child, and later on his own problems of illness and old age will be provided for. On the other hand, the old man, who as (we assume) paid such premiums as the system calls on him to pay in life, is now properly expecting, in accordance with the system, certain services from a particular person whom the system designates as the one to take care of him. Will the ideal moral code require such a person to pay the premium in such a system? I suggest that it will, and we can call the rule in question an "obligation of fairness."[15] So, we may infer that our

[15] See John Rawls, in "Justice as Fairness," *Philosophical Reviews*, LXVII (1958), 164–94, especially 179–84.

It seems to be held by some philosophers that an ideal moral code would contain no rule of fairness. The line of argument seems to be as follows: Assume we have an institution involving cooperative behavior for an end which will necessarily be of benefit to all in the institution. Assume further that the cooperative behavior required is burdensome. Assume finally that the good results will be produced even if fewer than all cooperate—perhaps ninety per cent is sufficient. It will then be to an individual's advantage to shirk making his contribution, since he will continue to enjoy the benefits. Shirking on the part of some actually maximizes utility, since the work is burdensome, and the burdensome effort of those who shirk (provided there are not too many) is useless.

I imagine that it would be agreed that, in this sort of system, there should be an agreed and known rule for exempting individual's from useless work. (E.g., someone who is ill would be excused.) In the absence of this, a person should feel free to excuse himself for good and special reason. Otherwise, I think we suppose everyone should do his share, and that it is not a sufficient reason for shirking, to know that enough are cooperating to produce the desired benefits. Let us call this requirement, of working except for special reason (etc.) a "rule of fairness."

Would an ideal moral code contain a rule of fairness? At least, there could hardly be a public rule permitting people to shirk while a sufficient number of others work. For what

young man will have a moral obligation to care for his maternal uncle, on grounds both of humanity and fairness.

We need not go so far as to say that such considerations mean that an ideal moral code will underwrite morally every institutional obligation. An institution may be grossly inequitable; or some part of it may serve no purpose at all but rather be injurious (as some legal prohibitions may be). But I believe we can be fairly sure that Professor Diggs went too far in saying that a system of this sort "deprives social and moral rules of their authority and naturally is in sharp conflict with practice" and that it "collapses into act-utilitarianism."

15. It may be helpful to contrast the Ideal Moral Code theory with a rather similar type of rule-utilitarianism, which in some ways is simpler than the Ideal Moral Code theory, and which seems to be the only form of rule-utilitarianism recognized by some philosophers. This other type of theory is suggested in the writings of R. F. Harrod, Jonathan Harrison, perhaps John Hospers and Marcus Singer, although, as I shall describe it, it differs from the exact theory proposed by any of these individuals, in more or less important ways.

The theory is a combination of act utilitarianism with a Kantian universalizability requirement for moral action. It denies that an act is necessarily right if it will produce consequences no worse than would any other action the agent might perform; rather, it affirms that an act is right if and only if universal action on the "maxim" of the act would not produce worse consequences than universal action on some other maxim on which the agent could act. Or, instead of talking of universal action on the "maxim" of the act in question, we can speak of all members of the class of relevantly similar actions being performed; then the proposal is that an action is right if and only if universal performance of the class of relevantly similar acts would not have worse consequences than universal performance of the class of acts relevantly similar to some alternative action the agent might perform. Evidently it

---

would the rule be? It would be all too easy for most people to believe that a sufficient number of others were working (like the well-known difficulty in farm planning, that if one plants what sold at a good price the preceding year, one is apt to find that prices for that produce will drop, since most other farmers have the same idea). Would it even be a good idea to have a rule to the effect that if one absolutely knows that enough others are working, one may shirk? This seems highly doubtful.

Critics of rule-utilitarianism seem to have passed from the fact that the best system would combine the largest product with the least effort, to the conclusion that the best moral code would contain a rule advising not to work when there are enough workers already. This is a non sequitur.

is important how we identify the "maxim" of an act or the class of "relevantly similar" acts.

One proceeds as follows. One may begin with the class specified by the properties one thinks are the morally significant ones of the act in question. (One could as well start with the class defined by all properties of the act, if one practically could do this!) One then enlarges the class by omitting from its definition those properties which would not affect the average utility which would result from all the acts in the class being performed. (The total utility might be affected simply by enlarging the size of the class; merely enlarging the class does not affect the average utility.) Conversely, one must also narrow any proposed class of "relevantly similar" acts if it is found that properties have been omitted from the specification of it, the presence of which would affect the average utility which would result if all the acts in the class were performed. The relevant class must not be too large, because of omission of features which define subclasses with different utilities; or too small, because of the presence of features which make no difference to the utilities.

An obvious example of an irrelevant property is that of the agent having a certain name (in most situations), or being a certain person. On the other hand, the fact that the agent wants (does not want) to perform a certain act normally is relevant to the utility of the performance of that act.

So much by way of exposition of the theory.

For many cases this theory and the Ideal Moral Code theory have identical implications. For, when it is better for actions of type A to be performed in a certain situation than for actions of any type to be performed, it will often be a good thing to have type A actions prescribed by the moral code, directly or indirectly.

The theory also appears more simple than the Ideal Moral Code theory. In order to decide whether a given act is right or wrong we are not asked to do anything as grand as decide what some part of an ideal moral code would be like, but merely whether it would be better, or worse, for all in a relevant class of acts to be performed, as compared with some other relevant class. Thus it offers simple answers to questions such as whether one should vote ("What if nobody did?"), pick wildflowers along the road ("What if everyone did?"), join the army in wartime, or walk on the grass in a park.[16]

[16] One should not, however, overemphasize the simplicity. Whether one should vote in these circumstances is not decided by determining that it would have bad consequences if no one voted at all. It is a question whether it would be the best thing for all those people

Furthermore, the theory has a simple way of dealing with conflicts of rules: one determines whether it would be better, or worse, for all members of the more complex class (about which the rules conflict) of actions to be performed (e.g., promises broken in the situation where the breach would save a life).

In one crucial respect, however, the two theories are totally different. For, in contrast with the Ideal Moral Code theory, this theory implies that exactly those acts are objectively right which are objectively right on the act-utilitarian theory. Hence the implications of this theory for action include the very counter-intuitive ones which led its proponents to seek an improvement over act-utilitarianism.

It must be conceded that this assessment of the implications of the theory is not yet a matter of general agreement,[17] and depends on a rather complex argument. In an earlier paper (loc. cit.) I argued that the theory does have these consequences, although my statement of the theory was rather misleading. More recently Professor David Lyons has come to the same conclusion, after an extensive discussion in which he urges that the illusion of a difference between the consequences of this theory and those of act-utilitarianism arises because of failure to notice certain important features of the context of actions, primarily the relative frequency of similar actions at about the same time, and "threshold effects" which an action may have on account of these features.[18]

It may be worthwhile to draw attention to the features of the Ideal Moral Code theory which avoid this particular result. In the first place, the Ideal Moral Code theory sets a limit to the number and complexity of the properties which define a class of morally similar actions. For, on this theory, properties of an act make a difference to its rightness, only if a moral principle referring to them (directly or indirectly) can be learned as part of the optimific moral code. Actual persons, with their emotional and intellectual limitations, are unable to learn a moral code

---

to vote (or not vote) in the class of situations relevantly similar to this one. It should be added, however, that if I am correct in my (below) assessment of the identity of this theory with act-utilitarianism, in the end it is simple, on the theory, to answer these questions.

It hardly seems that an ideal moral code would contain prescriptions as specific as rules about these matters. But the implications for such matters would be fairly direct if, as suggested above, an ideal moral code would contain a principle enjoining fairness, i.e., commanding persons to do their share in common enterprises (or restraints), when everyone benefits if most persons do their share, when persons find doing their share a burden, and when it is not essential that everyone do his share although it is essential that most do so, for the common benefit to be realized.

[17] See, for instance, the interesting paper by Michael A. G. Stocker, "Consistency in Ethics," *Analysis* Supplement, XXV (January 1965), 116–22.

[18] David Lyond, *Forms and Limits of Utilitarianism* (Oxford: Clarendon Press, 1965).

which incorporates all the distinctions the other theory can recognize as morally relevant; and even if they could learn it, it would not be utility maximizing for them to try to apply it. In the second place, we noted that to be part of a moral code a proscription must be public, believed to be part of what is morally disapproved of by most adults. Thus whereas some actions (e.g., some performed in secret) would be utility maximizing, the Ideal Moral Code theory may imply that they are wrong, because it would be a bad thing for it to be generally recognized that a person is free to do that sort of thing.

16. I do not know of any reason to think that the Ideal Moral Code theory is a less plausible normative moral theory than any other form of utilitarianism. Other types of rule-utilitarianism are sufficiently like it, however, that it might be that relatively minor changes in formulation would make their implications for conduct indistinguishable from those of the Ideal Moral Code theory.

Two questions have not here been discussed. One is whether the Ideal Moral Code theory is open to the charge that it implies that some actions are right which are unjust in such an important way that they cannot be right. The second question is one a person would naturally wish to explore if he concluded that the right answer to the first question is affirmative: it is whether a rule-utilitarian view could be combined with some other principles like a principle of justice in a plausible way, without loss of all the features which make utilitarianism attractive. The foregoing discussion has not been intended to provide an answer to these questions.

Part II

Duties

Introduction

Egoism and utilitarianism are *consequentialist* theories. According to them, the fundamental criterion for determining the moral rightness of actions is the nature of their consequences. One should perform the action which, of all the available ones, produces the best results.

One of the difficulties with utilitarian theories is that the best consequences may require actions we normally consider immoral. The first reading in this section, a hypothetical case study, illlustrates how an action prescribed by utilitarian theories conflicts with an action justice requires. Police authorities must decide whether to choose to act so as to benefit the community or to respect the rights of an individual. Unfortunately, the action which has the best consequences for the community will also seriously injure an innocent person. It follows from utilitarian theories that in such conflicts beneficial consequences for the majority should override the welfare of the individual.

Nonconsequentialist theories hold that actions are to be judged on the basis of their conformity to moral rules, not in terms of their consequences. The second reading in this section is an excerpt from Immanuel Kant's (1724–1804) *Groundwork of the Metaphysics of Morals*. This work is the best known nonconsequentialist theory; it is based on the concept of absolute duty. Kant identifies the fundamental moral law, what he calls the Categorical Imperative. Actions are morally right only if they conform to the rules or maxims derived from this moral law. Thus, according to Kant, it is only the moral law, and not consequences, which determines whether an action is right. If it is right, it is our absolute duty to perform it.

In the third reading in this section, W. D. Ross presents a contemporary form of nonconsequentialism. He tries to avoid the problem with Kant's theory that absolute duties may conflict with each other. Ross proposes the concept of *prima facie* duties, in place of absolute ones, as the basic criterion for identifying right actions. *Prima facie* duties are known through intuition, the direct, immediate apprehension of self-evident truths. Ross recognizes that *prima facie* duties may conflict with each other. If this occurs, we have to rely on our intuitions as guided by reasoning. We may still make a mistake and act immorally, but, according to Ross, morality is difficult, there often are no easy answers.

By emphasizing the fundamental importance of moral rules, nonconsequentialism avoids problems that raise serious difficulties for utilitarianism. Moral rules protect the welfare of individuals from being overridden in the name of the common good. It is morally right to act so as to promote the common good, but respect for the welfare of individuals places a morally necessary constraint on how far it is permissible to go in pursuit of the common good. The specific ways in which individuals ought to be respected are referred as their *rights*. Part III builds on the previous two as we examine how morally justified social and political institutions protect the rights of individuals.

Problem Case: Justice and the Common Good

The civil war in Dystopia has been raging for more than a generation. Tens of thousands of citizens have been killed; politics, education, commerce and social life have all come to a standstill. Amidst chaos, brutality, and deep resentment, an apparently unbridgeable gulf separates two warring factions. All families have suffered losses and inflicted them in return.

For the first time, however, there is hope that the hostilities may come to an end. Some Dystopians, belonging to the opposing factions, but raised and educated elsewhere, have come together, worked out a compromise, and returned to their country to persuade the population to forget their resentments, put an end to the vicious cycle of hostilities, and try to live in peace. People appear to be listening. The intensity of the fighting has decreased, and both sides seem willing to accept the compromise proposed by the returned expatriates.

Against this background, there occurs a series of exceptionally brutal crimes. The victims are always women of one of the factions; they are sexually abused and tortured to death. There have already been more than a dozen victims, and each week brings another. The police are investigating, but the crimes are so cleverly committed that no clues are left. Indignation mounts. The faction whose women are being murdered suspects the extremists of the other side, while that side resents the accusation that they would do such a thing. Matters grow worse and it is feared that the fighting will flare up again, destroying the fragile compromise. Responding to great pressure, the police concentrate all their resources on finding the murderer.

At this time, a drifter is arrested. He is a foreigner, he has no family or friends, and circumstantial evidence ties him to the crimes. Though the case against him is quite weak, he is the only one against whom there is any case at all. His arrest is publicized, and everybody in Dystopia is relieved. The compromise may prevail after all, one faction does not have to seek revenge and the other faction does not have to bear the burden of these horrible crimes. And, most importantly, the crimes come to an end.

The police, however, discover that the drifter is innocent. He has claimed all along not to have been where the crimes were committed, but could not prove it. The police find conclusive corroborating evidence. But only a very few people know of this evidence.

If the drifter is released, the crimes will be unsolved, and the factions will once again be pitted against each other. The civil war will be likely to start again, and the usual hundreds, and then thousands, will be murdered. The fate of the country hangs in the balance. Yet, the drifter is innocent.

Does morality require that the drifter should be freed, since he is innocent, or does it require that he should be sacrificed for the common good?

Immanuel Kant

Groundwork for the Metaphysics of Morals

First Section

TRANSITION FROM THE COMMON RATIONAL KNOWLEDGE OF MORALITY TO THE PHILOSOPHICAL.

[The Good Will]*

NOTHING can possibly be conceived in the world, or even out of it, which can be called good without qualification, except a Good Will. Intelligence, wit, judgment, and the other *talents* of the mind, however they may be named, or courage, resolution, perseverance, as qualities of temperament, are undoubtedly good and desirable in many respects; but these gifts of nature may also become extremely bad and mischievous if the will which is to make use of them, and which, therefore, constitutes what is called *character*, is not good. It is the same with the *gifts of fortune*. Power, riches, honour, even health and the general well-being and contentment with one's condition which is called *happiness*, inspire pride, and often presumption, if there is not a good will to correct the influence of these on the mind, and with this also to rectify the whole principle of acting, and adapt it to its end. The sight of a being who is not adorned with a single feature of a pure and good will, enjoying unbroken prosperity, can never give pleasure to an impartial rational spectator. Thus a good will appears to constitute the indispensable condition even of being worthy of happiness.

There are even some qualities which are of service to this good will itself, and may facilitate its action, yet which have no intrinsic unconditional value, but always presuppose a good will, and this qualifies the esteem that we justly have for them, and does not permit us to regard them as absolutely good. Moderation in the affections and passions, self-control and calm deliberation are not only good in many respects, but even seem to constitute part of the intrinsic worth of the person; but they are far from deserving to be called good without qualification, although they have been so unconditionally praised by the ancients. For without the principles of a good will, they may become extremely bad, and the coolness of a villain not only makes him far more dangerous, but

* Headings enclosed in square brackets have been added to the text by the Editors.

also directly makes him more abominable in our eyes than he would have been without it.

A good will is good not because of what it performs or effects, not by its aptness for the attainment of some proposed end, but simply by virtue of the volition, that is, it is good in itself, and considered by itself is to be esteemed much higher than all that can be brought about by it in favour of any inclination, nay, even of the sum total of all inclinations. Even if it should happen that, owing to special disfavour of fortune, or the niggardly provision of a step-motherly nature, this will should wholly lack power to accomplish its purpose, if with its greatest efforts it should yet achieve nothing, and there should remain only the good will (not, to be sure, a mere wish, but the summoning of all means in our power), then, like a jewel, it would still shine by its own light, as a thing which has its whole value in itself. Its usefulness or fruitlessness can neither add to nor take away anything from this value. It would be, as it were, only the setting to enable us to handle it the more conveniently in common commerce or to attract to it the attention of those who are not yet connoisseurs, but not to recommend it to true connoisseurs, or to determine its value. . . .

[Duty]

We have then to develop the notion of a will which deserves to be highly esteemed for itself, and is good without a view of anything further, a notion which exists already in the sound natural understanding, requiring rather to be cleared than to be taught, and which in estimating the value of our actions always takes the first place, and constitutes the condition of all the rest. In order to do this we will take the notion of duty, which includes that of a good will, although implying certain subjective restrictions and hindrances. These, however, far from concealing it, or rendering it unrecognisable, rather bring it out by contrast, and make it shine forth so much the brighter.

I omit here all actions which are already recognised as inconsistent with duty, although they may be useful for this or that purpose, for with these the question whether they are done *from duty* cannot arise at all, since they even conflict with it. I also set aside those actions which really conform to duty, but to which men have *no* direct *inclination*, performing them because they are impelled thereto by some other inclination. For in this case we can readily distinguish whether the action which agrees with duty is done *from duty*, or from a selfish view. It is much harder to make this distinction when the action accords with duty, and the subject has besides a *direct* inclination to it. For example, it is always a matter of duty that a dealer should not overcharge an inexperienced purchaser, and wherever there is much commerce the prudent tradesman does not overcharge, but keeps a fixed price for everyone, so that a child buys of him as well as any other. Men are thus *honestly* served; but this is not enough to make us believe that the tradesman has so acted from duty and from principles of honesty: his own advantage required it; it is out of the question in this case to suppose that he might besides have a direct inclination in favour of the buyers, so that, as it were, from love he should give no advantage to one over another. Accordingly the action was done neither from duty nor from direct inclination, but merely with a selfish view.

On the other hand, it is a duty to maintain one's life; and, in addition, every one has also a direct inclination to do so. But on this account the often anxious care which most men take for it has no intrinsic worth, and their maxim has no moral import. They preserve their life *as duty requires,* no doubt, but not *because duty requires.* On the other hand, if adversity and hopeless sorrow have completely taken away the relish for life, if the unfortunate one, strong in mind, indignant at his fate rather than desponding or dejected, wishes for death, and yet preserves his life without loving it—not from inclination or fear, but from duty—then his maxim has a moral worth.

To be beneficent when we can is a duty; and besides this, there are many minds so sympathetically constituted that, without any other motive of vanity or self-interest, they find a pleasure in spreading joy around them, and can take delight in the satisfaction of others so far as it is their own work. But I maintain that in such a case an action of this kind, however proper, however amiable it may be, has nevertheless no true moral worth, but is on a level with other inclinations, *e.g.* the inclination to honour, which, if it is happily directed to that which is in fact of public utility and accordant with duty, and consequently honourable, deserves praise and encouragement, but not esteem. For the maxim lacks the moral import, namely, that such actions be done *from duty,* not from inclination. Put the case that the mind of that philanthropist were clouded by sorrow of his own extinguishing all sympathy with the lot of others, and that while he still has the power to benefit others in distress, he is not touched by their trouble because he is absorbed with his own; and now suppose that he tears himself out of his dead insensibility, and performs the action without any inclination to it, but simply from duty, then first has his action its genuine moral worth. Further still; if nature has put little sympathy in the heart of this or that man; if he, supposed to be an upright man, is by temperament cold and indifferent to the sufferings of others, perhaps because in respect of his own he is provided with the special gift of patience and fortitude, and supposes, or even requires, that others should have the same—and such a man would certainly not be the meanest product of nature—but if nature had not specially framed him for a philanthropist, would he not still find in himself a source from whence to give himself a far higher worth than that of a good-natured temperament could be? Unquestionably. It is just in this that the moral worth of the character is brought out which is incomparably the highest of all, namely, that he is beneficent, not from inclination, but from duty.

To secure one's own happiness is a duty, at least indirectly; for discontent with one's condition, under a pressure of many anxieties and amidst unsatisfied wants, might easily become a great *temptation to transgression of duty.* But here again, without looking to duty, all men have already the strongest and most intimate inclination to happiness, because it is just in this idea that all inclinations are combined in one total. But the precept of happiness is often of such a sort that it greatly interferes with some inclinations, and yet a man cannot form any definite and certain conception of the sum of satisfaction of all of them which is called happiness. It is not then to be wondered at that a single inclination, definite both as to what it promises and as to the time within which it can be gratified, is often able to overcome such a fluctuating idea, and that a gouty patient, for instance, can choose to enjoy what he likes, and to suffer what he may, since, according to his calculation, on this occasion at least, he has [only] not sacrificed the enjoyment of the present moment to a possibly mistaken expectation of a happiness which is supposed to be found in health. But even in this case, if the general desire for happiness did not influence his will, and supposing that in his particular case health was not a necessary element in this calculation, there yet remains in this, as in all other cases, this law, namely, that he should promote his happiness not from inclination but from duty, and by this would his conduct first acquire true moral worth. . . .

The second[1] proposition is: That an action done from duty derives its moral worth, *not from the purpose* which is to be attained by it, but from the maxim by which it is determined, and therefore does not depend on the realization of the object of the action, but merely on the *principle of volition* by which the action has taken place, without regard to any object

[1] [The first proposition was that, to have moral worth, an action must be done from duty.]

of desire. It is clear from what precedes that the purposes which we may have in view in our actions, or their effects regarded as ends and springs of the will, cannot give to actions any unconditional or moral worth. In what, then, can their worth lie, if it is not to consist in the will and in reference to its expected effect? It cannot lie anywhere but in the *principle of the will* without regard to the ends which can be attained by the action. For the will stands between its *à priori* principle, which is formal, and its *à posteriori* spring, which is material, as between two roads, and as it must be determined by something, it follows that it must be determined by the formal principle of volition when an action is done from duty, in which case every material principle has been withdrawn from it.

The third proposition, which is a consequence of the two preceding, I would express thus: *Duty is the necessity of acting from respect for the law.* I may have *inclination* for an object as the effect of my proposed action, but I cannot have *respect* for it, just for this reason, that it is an effect and not an energy of will. Similarly, I cannot have respect for inclination, whether my own or another's; I can at most, if my own, approve it; if another's, sometimes even love it; *i.e.* look on it as favourable to my own interest. It is only what is connected with my will as a principle, by no means as an effect—what does not subserve my inclination, but overpowers it, or at least in case of choice excludes it from its calculation—in other words, simply the law of itself which can be an object of respect, and hence a command. Now an action done from duty must wholly exclude the influence of inclination, and with it every object of the will, so that nothing remains which can determine the will except objectively the *law*, and subjectively *pure respect* for this practical law, and consequently the maxim[2] that I should follow this law even to the thwarting of all my inclinations.

Thus the moral worth of an action does not lie in the effect expected from it, nor in any principle of action which requires to borrow its motive from this expected effect. For all these affects—agreeableness of one's condition, and even the promotion of the happiness of others—could have been also brought about by other causes, so that for this there would have been no need of the will of a rational being; whereas it is in this alone that the supreme and unconditional good can be found. The pre-eminent good which we call moral can therefore consist in nothing else than *the conception of law* in itself, *which certainly is only possible in a rational being*, in so far as this conception, and not the

[2] A *maxim* is the subjective principle of volition. The objective principle (*i.e.* that which would also serve subjectively as a practical principle to all rational beings if reason had full power over the faculty of desire) is the practical *law*.

expected effect, determines the will. This is a good which is already present in the person who acts accordingly, and we have not to wait for it to appear first in the result.[3]

But what sort of law can that be, the conception of which must determine the will, even without paying any regard to the effect expected from it, in order that this will may be called good absolutely and without qualification? As I have deprived the will of every impulse which could arise to it from obedience to any law, there remains nothing but the universal conformity of its actions to law in general, which alone is to serve the will as a principle, *i.e.* I am never to act otherwise than so *that I could also will that my maxim should become a universal law.* Here now, it is the simple conformity to law in general, without assuming any particular law applicable to certain actions, that serves the will as its principle, and must so serve it, if duty is not to be a vain delusion and a chimerical notion. The common reason of men in its practical judgments perfectly coincides with this, and always has in view the principle here suggested. Let the question be, for example: May I when in distress make a promise with the intention not to keep it? I readily distinguish here between the two significations which the question may have: Whether it is prudent, or whether it is right, to make a false promise. The former may undoubtedly often be the case. I see clearly indeed that it is not enough to extricate myself from a present difficulty by means of this subterfuge, but it must be well considered whether there may not hereafter spring from this lie much greater inconvenience than that from which I now free myself, and as, with all my supposed *cunning*, the

[3] It might be here objected to me that I take refuge behind the word *respect* in an obscure feeling, instead of giving a distinct solution of the question by a concept of the reason. But although respect is a feeling, it is not a feeling *received* through influence, but is *self-wrought* by a rational concept, and, therefore, is specifically distinct from all feelings of the former kind, which may be referred either to inclination or fear. What I recognise immediately as a law for me, I recognise with respect. This merely signifies the consciousness that my will is *subordinate* to a law, without the intervention of other influences of my sense. The immediate determination of the will by the law, and the consciousness of this is called *respect*, so that this is regarded as an *effect* of the law on the subject, and not as the *cause* of it. Respect is properly the conception of a worth which thwarts my self-love. Accordingly it is something which is considered neither as an object of inclination nor of fear, although it has something analogous to both. The *object* of respect is the *law* only, and that, the law which we impose on *ourselves*, and yet recognise as necessary in itself. As a law, we are subjected to it without consulting self-love; as imposed by us on ourselves, it is a result of our will. In the former aspect it has an analogy to fear, in the latter to inclination. Respect for a person is properly only respect for the law (of honesty, & c.), of which he gives us an example. Since we also look on the improvement of our talents as a duty, we consider that we see in a person of talents, as it were, the *example of a law* (viz. to become like him in this by exercise), and this constitutes our respect. All so-called moral *interest* consists simply in *respect* for the law.

consequences cannot be so easily foreseen but that credit once lost may be much more injurious to me than any mischief which I seek to avoid at present, it should be considered whether it would not be more *prudent* to act herein according to a universal maxim, and to make it a habit to promise nothing except with the intention of keeping it. But it is soon clear to me that such a maxim will still only be based on the fear of consequences. Now it is a wholly different thing to be truthful from duty, and to be so from apprehension of injurious consequences. In the first case, the very notion of the action already implies a law for me; in the second case, I must first look about elsewhere to see what results may be combined with it which would affect myself. For to deviate from the principle of duty is beyond all doubt wicked: but to be unfaithful to my maxim of prudence may often by very advantageous to me, although to abide by it is certainly safer. The shortest way, however, and an unerring one, to discover the answer to this question whether a lying promise is consistent with duty, is to ask myself, Should I be content that my maxim (to extricate myself from difficulty by a false promise) should hold good as a universal law, for myself as well as for others? and should I be able to say to myself, "Every one may make a deceitful promise when he finds himself in a difficulty from which he cannot otherwise extricate himself"? Then I presently become aware that while I can will the lie, I can by no means will that lying should be a universal law. For with such a law there would be no promises at all, since it would be in vain to allege my intention in regard to my future actions to those who would not believe this allegation, or if they over-hastily did so would pay me back in my own coin. Hence my maxim, as soon as it should be made a universal law, would necessarily destroy itself.

I do not, therefore, need any far-reaching penetration to discern what I have to do in order that my will may be morally good. Inexperienced in the course of the world, incapable of being prepared for all its contingencies, I only ask myself: Canst thou also will that thy maxim should be a universal law? If not, then it must be rejected, and that not because of a disadvantage accruing from it to myself or even to others, but because it cannot enter as a principle into a possible universal legislation, and reason extorts from me immediate respect for such legislation. I do not indeed as yet *discern* on what this respect is based (this the philosopher may inquire), but at least I understand this, that it is an estimation of the worth which far outweighs all worth of what is recommended by inclination, and that the necessity of acting from *pure* respect for the practical law is what constitutes duty, to which every other motive must give place, because it is the condition of a will being good *in itself*, and the worth of such a will is above everything.

Thus, then, without quitting the moral knowledge of common human reason, we have arrived at its principle. And although, no doubt, common men do not conceive it in such an abstract and univeral form, yet they always have it really before their eyes, and use it as the standard of their decision. Here it would be easy to show how, with this compass in hand, men are well able to distinguish, in every case that occurs, what is good, what bad, conformably to duty or inconsistent with it, if, without in the least teaching them anything new, we only, like Socrates, direct their attention to the principle they themselves employ; and that therefore we do not need science and philosophy to know what we should do to be honest and good, yea, even wise and virtuous. Indeed we might well have conjectured beforehand that the knowledge of what every man is bound to do, and therefore also to know, would be within the reach of every man, even the commonest. . . .

[Laws and Imperatives]

Everything in nature works according to laws. Rational beings alone have the faculty of acting according *to the conception* of laws, that is according to principles, *i.e.* have a *will*. Since the deduction of actions from principles requires *reason*, the will is nothing but practical reason. If reason infallibly determines the will, then the actions of such a being which are recognised as objectively necessary are subjectively necessary also, *i.e.* the will is a faculty to choose *that only* which reason independent of inclination recognises as practically necessary, *i.e.* as good. But if reason of itself does not sufficiently determine the will, if the latter is subject also to subjective conditions (particular impulses) which do not always coincide with the objective conditions; in a word, if the will does not *in itself* completely accord with reason (which is actually the case with men), then the actions which objectively are recognised as necessary are subjectively contingent, and the determination of such a will according to objective laws is *obligation*, that is to say, the relation of the objective laws to a will that is not thoroughly good is conceived as the determination of the will of a rational being by principles of reason, but which the will from its nature does not of necessity follow.

The conception of an objective principle, in so far as it is obligatory for a will, is called a command (of reason), and the formula of the command is called an Imperative.

All imperatives are expressed by the word *ought* [or *shall*], and thereby indicate the relation of an objective law of reason to a will, which from its subjective constitution is not necessarily determined by it (an obligation). They say that something would be good to do or to forbear, but they say it to a will which does not always do a thing because it is conceived to be good to do it. That is practically *good*, however, which determines the will by means of the conceptions of reason, and consequently not from subjective causes, but objectively, that is on principles which are valid for every rational being as such. It is distinguished from the *pleasant*, as that which influences the will only by means of sensation from merely subjective causes, valid only for the sense of this or that one, and not as a principle of reason, which holds for every one.[4]

A perfectly good will would therefore be equally subject to objective laws (viz. laws of good), but could not be conceived as *obliged* thereby to act lawfully, because of itself from its subjective constitution it can only be determined by the conception of good. Therefore no imperatives hold for the Divine will, or in general for a *holy* will; *ought* is here out of place, because the volition is already of itself necessarily in unison with the law. Therefore imperatives are only formulæ to express the relation of objective laws of all volition to the subjective imperfection of the will of this or that rational being, *e.g.* the human will.

[Hypothetical and Categorical Imperatives]

Now all *imperatives* command either *hypothetically* or *categorically*. The former represent the practical necessity of a possible action as means to something else that is willed (or at least which one might possibly will). The categorical imperative would be that which represented an action as necessary of itself without reference to another end, *i.e.* as objectively necessary.

[4] The dependence of the desires on sensations is called inclination, and this accordingly always indicates a *want*. The dependence of a contingently determinable will on principles of reason is called an *interest*. This therefore is found only in the case of a dependent will, which does not always of itself conform to reason; in the Divine will we cannot conceive any interest. But the human will can also *take an interest* in a thing without therefore acting *from interest*. The former signifies the *practical* interest in the action, the latter the *pathological* in the object of the action. The former indicates only dependence of the will on principles of reason in themselves; the second, dependence on principles of reason for the sake of inclination, reason supplying only the practical rules how the requirement of the inclination may be satisfied. In the first case the action interests me; in the second the object of the action (because it is pleasant to me). We have seen in the first section that in an action done from duty we must look not to the interest in the object, but only to that in the action itself, and in its rational principle (viz. the law).

Since every practical law represents a possible action as good, and on this account, for a subject who is practically determinable by reason, necessary, all imperatives are formulæ determining an action which is necessary according to the principle of a will good in some respects. If now the action is good only as a means *to something else*, then the imperative is *hypothetical*; if it is conceived as good *in itself* and consequently as being necessarily the principle of a will which of itself conforms to reason, then it is *categorical*.

Thus the imperative declares what action possible by me would be good, and presents the practical rule in relation to a will which does not forthwith perform an action simply because it is good, whether because the subject does not always know that it is good, or because, even if it know this, yet its maxims might be opposed to the objective principles of practical reason.

Accordingly the hypothetical imperative only says that the action is good for some purpose, *possible* or *actual*. In the first case it is a Problematical, in the second an Assertorial practical principle. The categorical imperative which declares an action to be objectively necessary in itself without reference to any purpose, *i.e.* without any other end, is valid as a (practical) Apodictic principle.

Whatever is possible only by the power of some rational being may also be conceived as a possible purpose of some will; and therefore the principles of action as regards the means necessary to attain some possible purpose are in fact infinitely numerous. All sciences have a practical part, consisting of problems expressing that some end is possible for us, and of imperatives directing how it may be attained. These may, therefore, be called in general imperatives of skill. Here there is no question whether the end is rational and good, but only what one must do in order to attain it. The precepts for the physician to make his patient thoroughly healthy, and for a poisoner to ensure certain death, are of equal value in this respect, that each serves to effect its purpose perfectly. Since in early youth it cannot be known what ends are likely to occur to us in the course of life, parents seek to have their children taught a *great many things*, and provide for their *skill* in the use of means for all sorts of arbitrary ends, of none of which can they determine whether it may not perhaps hereafter be an object to their pupil, but which it is at all events *possible* that he might aim at; and this anxiety is so great that they commonly neglect to form and correct their judgment on the value of the things which may be chosen as ends.

There is *one* end, however, which may be assumed to be actually such to all rational beings (so far as imperatives apply to them, viz. as dependent beings), and therefore, one purpose which they not merely *may* have, but which we may with certainty assume that they all actually *have* by a natural necessity, and this is *happiness*. The hypothetical imperative which expresses the practical necessity of an action as means to the advancement of happiness is Assertorial. We are not to present it as necessary for an uncertain and merely possible purpose, but for a purpose which we may presuppose with certainty and *à priori* in every man, because it belongs to his being. Now skill in the choice of means to his own great well-being may be called *prudence*,[5] in the narrowest sense. And thus the imperative which refers to the choice of means to one's own happiness, *i.e.* the precept of prudence, is still always *hypothetical*; the action is not commanded absolutely, but only as means to another purpose.

Finally, there is an imperative which commands a certain conduct immediately, without having as its condition any other purpose to be attained by it. This imperative is Categorical. It concerns not the matter of action, or its intended result, but its form and the principle of which it is itself a result; and what is essentially good in it consists in the mental disposition, let the consequence be what it may. This imperative may be called that of Morality. . . .

Now arises the question, how are all these imperatives possible? This question does not seek to know how we can conceive the accomplishment of the action which the imperative ordains, but merely how we can conceive the obligation of the will which the imperative expresses. No special explanation is needed to show how an imperative of skill is possible. Whoever wills the end, wills also (so far as reason decides his conduct) the means in his power which are indispensably necessary thereto. This proposition is, as regards the volition, analytical; for, in willing an object as my effect, there is already thought the causality of myself as an acting cause, that is to say, the use of the means; and the imperative educes from the conception of volition of an end the conception of actions necessary to this end. Synthetical propositions must no doubt be employed in defining the means to a proposed end; but they do not concern the principle, the act of the will, but the object and its realization. *Ex. gr.*, that in order to bisect a line on an unerring

[5] The word prudence is taken in two senses: in the one it may bear the name of knowledge of the world, in the other that of private prudence. The former is a man's ability to influence others so as to use them for his own purposes. The latter is the sagacity to combine all these purposes for his own lasting benefit. This latter is properly that to which the value even of the former is reduced, and when a man is prudent in the former sense, but not in the latter, we might better say of him that he is clever and cunning, but, on the whole imprudent.

principle I must draw from its extremities two intersecting arcs; this no doubt is taught by mathematics only in synthetical propositions; but if I know that it is only by this process that the intended operation can be performed, then to say that if I fully will the operation, I also will the action required for it, is an analytical proposition; for it is one and the same thing to conceive something as an effect which I can produce in a certain way, and to conceive myself as acting in this way.

If it were only equally easy to give a definite conception of happiness, the imperatives of prudence would correspond exactly with those of skill, and would likewise be analytical. For in this case as in that, it could be said, whoever wills the end, wills also (according to the dictate of reason necessarily) the indispensable means thereto which are in his power. But, unfortunately, the notion of happiness is so indefinite that although every man wishes to attain it, yet he never can say definitely and consistently what it is that he really wishes and wills. The reason of this is that all the elements which belong to the notion of happiness are altogether empirical, *i.e.* they must be borrowed from experience, and nevertheless the idea of happiness requires an absolute whole, a maximum of welfare in my present and all future circumstances. Now it is impossible that the most clear-sighted, and at the same time most powerful being (supposed finite) should frame to himself a definite conception of what he really wills in this. Does he will riches, how much anxiety, envy, and snares might he not thereby draw upon his shoulders? Does he will knowledge and discernment, perhaps it might prove to be only an eye so much the sharper to show him so much the more fearfully the evils that are now concealed from him and that cannot be avoided, or to impose more wants on his desires, which already give him concern enough. Would he have long life, who guarantees to him that it would not be a long misery? Would he at least have health? how often has uneasiness of the body restrained from excesses into which perfect health would have allowed one to fall? and so on. In short he is unable, on any principle, to determine with certainty what would make him truly happy; because to do so he would need to be omniscient. We cannot therefore act on any definite principles to secure happiness, but only on empirical counsels, *ex.gr.* of regimen, frugality, courtesy, reserve, &c., which experience teaches do, on the average, most promote well-being. Hence it follows that the imperatives of prudence do not, strictly speaking, command at all, that is, they cannot present actions objectively as practically *necessary*; that they are rather to be regarded as counsels (*consilia*) than precepts (*præcepta*) of reason, that the problem to determine certainly and universally what action would promote the happiness of a rational being is completely insoluble, and consequently no imperative respecting it is possible which should, in the strict sense, command to do what makes happy; because happiness is not an ideal of reason but of imagination, resting solely on empirical grounds, and it is vain to expect that these should define an action by which one could attain the totality of a series of consequences which is really endless. This imperative of prudence would however be an analytical proposition if we assume that the means to happiness could be certainly assigned; for it is distinguished from the imperative of skill only by this, that in the latter the end is merely possible, in the former it is given; as however both only ordain the means to that which we suppose to be willed as an end, it follows that the imperative which ordains the willing of the means to him who wills the end is in both cases analytical. Thus there is no difficulty in regard to the possibility of an imperative of this kind either.

On the other hand the question, how the imperative of *morality* is possible, is undoubtedly one, the only one, demanding a solution, as this is not at all hypothetical, and the objective necessity which it presents cannot rest on any hypothesis, as is the case with the hypothetical imperatives. Only here we must never leave out of consideration that we *cannot* make out *by any example*, in other words empirically, whether there is such an imperative at all; but it is rather to be feared that all those which seem to be categorical may yet be at bottom hypothetical. For instance, when the precept is: Thou shalt not promise deceitfully; and it is assumed that the necessity of this is not a mere counsel to avoid some other evil, so that it should mean: thou shalt not make a lying promise, lest if it become known thou shouldst destroy thy credit, but that an action of this kind must be regarded as evil in itself, so that the imperative of the prohibition is categorical; then we cannot show with certainty in any example that the will was determined merely by the law, without any other spring of action, although it may appear to be so. For it is always possible that fear of disgrace, perhaps also obscure dread of other dangers, may have a secret influence on the will. Who can prove by experience the non-existence of a cause when all that experience tells us is that we do not perceive it? But in such a case the so-called moral imperative, which as such appears to be categorical and unconditional, would in reality be only a pragmatic precept, drawing our attention to our own interests, and merely teaching us to take these into consideration.

[The Categorical Imperative]

We shall therefore have to investigate *à priori* the possibility of a categorical imperative, as we have not in this case the advantage of its reality being given in experience, so that [the elucidation of] its possibility should be requisite only for its explanation, not for its establishment. In the meantime it may be discerned beforehand that the categorical imperative alone has the purport of a practical law: all the rest may indeed be called *principles* of the will but not laws, since whatever is only necessary for the attainment of some arbitrary purpose may be considered as in itself contingent, and we can at any time be free from the precept if we give up the purpose: on the contrary, the unconditional command leaves the will no liberty to choose the opposite; consequently it alone carries with it that necessity which we require in a law.

Secondly, in the case of this categorical imperative or law of morality, the difficulty (of discerning its possibility) is a very profound one. It is an *à priori* synthetical practical proposition;[6] and as there is so much difficulty in discerning the possibility of speculative propositions of this kind, it may readily be supposed that the difficulty will be no less with the practical.

In this problem we will first inquire whether the mere conception of a categorical imperative may not perhaps supply us also with the formula of it, containing the proposition which alone can be a categorical imperative; for even if we know the tenor of such an absolute command, yet how it is possible will require further special and laborious study, which we postpone to the last section.

When I conceive a hypothetical imperative in general I do not know beforehand what it will contain until I am given the condition. But when I conceive a categorical imperative I know at once what it contains. For as the imperative contains besides the law only the necessity that the maxim[7] shall conform to this law, while the law contains no conditions

[6] I connect the act with the will without presupposing any condition resulting from any inclination, but *à priori*, and therefore necessarily (though only objectively, *i.e.* assuming the idea of a reason possessing full power over all subjective motives). This is accordingly a practical proposition which does not deduce the willing of an action by mere analysis from another already presupposed (for we have not such a perfect will), but connects it immediately with the conception of the will of a rational being, as something not contained in it.

[7] A MAXIM is a subjective principle of action, and must be distinguished from the *objective principle*, namely, practical law. The former contains the practical rule set by reason according to the conditions of the subject (often its ignorance or its inclinations), so that it is the principle on which the subject *acts*; but the law is the objective principle valid for every rational being, and is the principle on which it *ought to act*, that is, an imperative.

restricting it, there remains nothing but the general statement that the maxim of the action should conform to a universal law, and it is this conformity alone that the imperative properly represents as necessary.

There is therefore but one categorical imperative, namely this: *Act only on that maxim whereby thou canst at the same time will that it should become a universal law.*

Now if all imperatives of duty can be deduced from this one imperative as from their principle, then, although it should remain undecided whether what is called duty is not merely a vain notion, yet at least we shall be able to show what we understand by it and what this notion means.

Since the universality of the law according to which effects are produced constitutes what is properly called *nature* in the most general sense (as to form), that is, the existence of things so far as it is determined by general laws, the imperative of duty may be expressed thus: *Act as if the maxim of thy action were to become by thy will a Universal Law of Nature.*

[Examples]

We will now enumerate a few duties, adopting the usual division of them into duties to ourselves and to others, and into perfect and imperfect duties.[8]

1. A man reduced to despair by a series of misfortunes feels wearied of life, but is still so far in possession of his reason that he can ask himself whether it would not be contrary to his duty to himself to take his own life. Now he inquires whether the maxim of his action could become a universal law of nature. His maxim is: From self-love I adopt it as a principle to shorten my life when its longer duration is likely to bring more evil than satisfaction. It is asked then simply whether this principle founded on self-love can become a universal law of nature. Now we see at once that a system of nature of which it should be a law to destroy life by means of the very feeling whose special nature it is to

---

[8] It must be noted here that I reserve the division of duties for a future *metaphysic of morals;* so that I give it here only as an arbitrary one (in order to arrange my examples). For the rest, I understand by a perfect duty one that admits no exception in favour of inclination, and then I have not merely external, but also internal perfect duties. This is contrary to the use of the word adopted in the schools; but I do not intend to justify it here, as it is all one for my purpose whether it is admitted or not. [*Perfect* duties are usually understood to be those which can be enforced by external law; *imperfect,* those which cannot be enforced. They are also called respectively *determinate* and *indeterminate, officia juris* and *officia virtutis.*]

impel to the improvement of life would contradict itself, and therefore could not exist as a system of nature; hence that maxim cannot possibly exist as a universal law of nature, and consequently would be wholly inconsistent with the supreme principle of all duty.

2. Another finds himself forced by necessity to borrow money. He knows that he will not be able to repay it, but sees also that nothing will be lent to him, unless he promises stoutly to repay it in a definite time. He desires to make this promise, but he has still so much conscience as to ask himself: Is it not unlawful and inconsistent with duty to get out of a difficulty in this way? Suppose however that he resolves to do so, then the maxim of his action would be expressed thus: When I think myself in want of money, I will borrow money and promise to repay it, although I know that I never can do so. Now this principle of self-love or of one's own advantage may perhaps be consistent with my whole future welfare; but the question now is, is it right? I change then the suggestion of self-love into a universal law, and state the question thus: How would it be if my maxim were a universal law? Then I see at once that it could never hold as a universal law of nature but would necessarily contradict itself. For supposing it to be a universal law that everyone when he thinks himself in a difficulty should be able to promise whatever he pleases, with the purpose of not keeping his promise, the promise itself would become impossible, as well as the end that one might have in view in it, since no one would consider that anything was promised to him, but would ridicule all such statements as vain pretences.

3. A third finds in himself a talent which with the help of some culture might make him a useful man in many respects. But he finds himself in comfortable circumstances, and prefers to indulge in pleasure rather than to take pains in enlarging and improving his happy natural capacities. He asks, however, whether his maxim of neglect of his natural gifts, besides agreeing with his inclination to indulgence, agrees also with what is called duty. He sees then that a system of nature could indeed subsist with such a universal law altough men (like the South Sea islanders) should let their talents rust, and resolve to devote their lives merely to idleness, amusement, and propagation of their species—in a word, to enjoyment; but he cannot possibly *will* that this should be a universal law of nature, or be implanted in us as such by a natural instinct. For, as a rational being, he necessarily wills that his faculties be developed, since they serve him, and have been given him, for all sorts of possible purposes.

4. A fourth, who is in prosperity, while he sees that others have to

contend with great wretchedness and that he could help them, thinks: What concern is it of mine? Let everyone be as happy as heaven pleases, or as he can make himself; I will take nothing from him nor even envy him, only I do not wish to contribute anything to his welfare or to his assistance in distress! Now no doubt if such a mode of thinking were a universal law, the human race might very well subsist, and doubtless even better than in a state in which every one talks of sympathy and good-will, or even takes care occasionally to put it into practice, but on the other side, also cheats when he can, betrays the rights of men, or otherwise violates them. But although it is possible that a universal law of nature might exist in accordance with that maxim, it is impossible to *will* that such a principle should have the universal validity of a law of nature. For a will which resolved this would contradict itself, inasmuch as many cases might occur in which one would have need of the love and sympathy of others, and in which, by such a law of nature, sprung from his own will, he would deprive himself of all hope of the aid he desires.

These are a few of the many actual duties, or at least what we regard as such, which obviously fall into two classes on the one principle that we have laid down. We must be *able to will* that a maxim of our action should be a universal law. This is a canon of the moral appreciation of the action generally. Some actions are of such a character that their maxim cannot without contradiction be even *conceived* as a universal law of nature, far from it being possible that we should *will* that it *should* be so. In others this intrinsic impossibility is not found, but still it is impossible to *will* that their maxim should be raised to the universality of a law of nature, since such a will would contradict itself. It is easily seen that the former violate strict or rigorous (inflexible) duty; the latter only laxer (meritorious) duty. Thus it has been completely shown by these examples how all duties depend as regards the nature of the obligation (not the object of the action) on the same principle.

If now we attend to ourselves on occasion of any transgression of duty, we shall find that we in fact do not will that our maxim should be a universal law, for that is impossible for us; on the contrary we will that the opposite should remain a universal law, only we assume the liberty of making an *exception* in our own favour or (just for this time only) in favour of our inclination. Consequently if we considered all cases from one and the same point of view, namely, that of reason, we should find a contradiction in our own will, namely, that a certain principle should be objectively necessary as a universal law, and yet subjectively should not be universal, but admit of exceptions. As however we at one moment regard our action from the point of view of a will wholly conformed to reason, and then again look at the same action from the point of view of a will affected by inclination, there is not really any contradiction, but an antagonism of inclination to the precept of reason, whereby the universality of the principle is changed into a mere generality, so that the practical principle of reason shall meet the maxim half way. Now, although this cannot be justified in our own impartial judgment, yet it proves that we do really recognise the validity of the categorical imperative and (with all respect for it) only allow ourselves a few exceptions, which we think unimportant and forced from us.

We have thus established at least this much, that if duty is a conception which is to have any import and real legislative authority for our actions, it can only be expressed in categorical, and not at all in hypothetical imperatives. We have also, which is of great importance, exhibited clearly and definitely for every practical application the content of the categorical imperative, which must contain the principle of all duty if there is such a thing at all. We have not yet, however, advanced so far as to prove *à priori* that there actually is such an imperative, that there is a practical law which commands absolutely of itself, and without any other impulse, and that the following of this law is duty. . . .

[The Means-End Formulation]

Now I say: man and generally any rational being *exists* as an end in himself, *not merely as a means* to be arbitrarily used by this or that will, but in all his actions, whether they concern himself or other rational beings, must be always regarded at the same time as an end. All objects of the inclinations have only a conditional worth, for if the inclinations and the wants founded on them did not exist, then their object would be without value. But the inclinations themselves being sources of want, are so far from having an absolute worth for which they should be desired, that on the contrary it must be the universal wish of every rational being to be wholly free from them. Thus the worth of any object which is *to be acquired* by our action is always conditional. Beings whose existence depends not on our will but on nature's, have nevertheless, if they are irrational beings, only a relative value as means, and are therefore called *things;* rational beings, on the contrary, are called *persons,* because their very nature points them out as ends in themselves, that is as something which must not be used merely as means, and so far therefore restricts freedom of action (and is an object of respect). These, therefore, are not merely subjective ends whose existence has a worth *for us* as an effect of our action, but *objective ends,* that is things whose existence is an end in itself: an end moreover for which no other can be substituted, which they should subserve *merely* as means, for otherwise nothing whatever would possess *absolute worth;* but if all worth were conditioned and therefore contingent, then there would be no supreme practical principle of reason whatever.

If then there is a supreme practical principle, or, in respect of the human will, a categorical imperative, it must be one which, being drawn from the conception of that which is necessarily an end for every one because it is *an end in itself,* constitutes an *objective* principle of will, and can therefore serve as a universal practical law. The foundation of this principle is: *rational nature exists as an end in itself.* Man necessarily conceives his own existence as being so: so far then this is a *subjective* principle of human actions. But every other rational being regards its existence similarly, just on the same rational principle that holds for me, so that it is at the same time an objective principle, from which as a supreme practical law all laws of the will must be capable of being deduced. Accordingly the practical imperative will be as follows: *So act as to treat humanity, whether in thine own person or in that of any other, in every case as an end withal, never as means only. . . .*

[The Kingdom of Ends]

The conception of every rational being as one which must consider itself as giving in all the maxims of its will universal laws, so as to judge itself and its actions from this point of view—this conception leads to another which depends on it and is very fruitful, namely, that of *a kingdom of ends.*

By a *kingdom* I understand the union of different rational beings in a system by common laws. Now since it is by laws that ends are determined as regards their universal validity, hence, if we abstract from the personal differences of rational beings, and likewise from all the content of their private ends, we shall be able to conceive all ends combined in a systematic whole (including both rational beings as ends in themselves, and also the special ends which each may propose to himself), that is to say, we can conceive a kingdom of ends, which on the preceding principles is possible.

For all rational beings come under the *law* that each of them must treat itself and all others *never merely as means,* but in every case *at the same time as ends in themselves.* Hence results a systematic union of rational beings by common objective laws, *i.e.,* a kingdom which may be called a kingdom of ends, since what these laws have in view is just the relation of these beings to one another as ends and means. It is certainly only an ideal.

A rational being belongs as a *member* to the kingdom of ends when, although giving universal laws in it, he is also himself subject to these laws. He belongs to it *a sovereign* when, while giving laws, he is not subject to the will of any other.

A rational being must always regard himself as giving laws either as member or as sovereign in a kingdom of ends which is rendered possible by the freedom of will. He cannot, however, maintain the latter position merely by the maxims of his will, but only in case he is a completely independent being without wants and with unrestricted power adequate to his will.

Morality consists then in the reference of all action to the legislation which alone can render a kingdom of ends possible. This legislation must be capable of existing in every rational being, and of emanating from his will, so that the principle of this will is, never to act on any maxim which could not without contradiction be also a universal law, and accordingly always so to act *that the will could at the same time regard itself as giving in its maxims universal laws*. . . .

W.D. Ross

The Right and the Good, Chapter II

What Makes Right Acts Right?

The real point at issue between hedonism and utilitarianism on the one hand and their opponents on the other is not whether 'right' means 'productive of so and so'; for it cannot with any plausibility be maintained that it does. The point at issue is that to which we now pass, viz. whether there is any general character which makes right acts right, and if so, what it is. Among the main historical attempts to state a single characteristic of all right actions which is the foundation of their rightness are those made of egoism and utilitarianism. But I do not propose to discuss these, not because the subject is unimportant, but because it has been dealt with so often and so well already, and because there has come to be so much agreement among moral philosophers that neither of these theories is satisfactory. A much more attractive theory has been put forward by Professor Moore: that what makes actions right is that they are productive of more *good* than could have been produced by any other action open to the agent.[1]

This theory is in fact the culmination of all the attempts to base rightness on productivity of some sort of result. The first form this attempt takes is the attempt to base rightness on conduciveness to the advantage or pleasure of the agent. This theory comes to grief over the fact, which stares us in the face, that a great part of duty consists in an observance of the rights and a furtherance of the interests of others, whatever the cost to ourselves may be. Plato and others may be right in holding that a regard for the rights of others never in the long run involves a loss of happiness for the agent, that 'the just life profits a man'. But this, even if true, is irrelevant to the rightness of the act. As soon as a man does an action *because* he thinks he will promote his own interests thereby, he is acting not from a sense of its rightness but from self-interest.

To the egoistic theory hedonistic utilitarianism supplies a much-needed amendment. It points out correctly that the fact that a certain pleasure will be enjoyed by the agent is no reason why he *ought* to bring it into being rather than an equal or greater pleasure to be enjoyed by

[1] I take the theory which, as I have tried to show, seems to be put forward in *Ethics* rather than the earlier and less plausible theory put forward in *Principia Ethica*.

another, though, human nature being what it is, it makes it not unlikely that he *will* try to bring it into being. But hedonistic utilitarianism in its turn needs a correction. On reflection it seems clear that pleasure is not the only thing in life that we think good in itself, that for instance we think the possession of a good character, or an intelligent understanding of the world, as good or better. A great advance is made by the substitution of 'productive of the greatest good' for 'productive of the greatest pleasure'.

Not only is this theory more attractive than hedonistic utilitarianism, but its logical relation to that theory is such that the latter could not be true unless *it* were true, while it might be true though hedonistic utilitarianism were not. It is in fact one of the logical bases of hedonistic utilitarianism. For the view that what produces the maximum pleasure is right has for its bases the views (1) that what produces the maximum good is right, and (2) that pleasure is the only thing good in itself. If they were not assuming that what produces the maximum *good* is right, the utilitarians' attempt to show that pleasure is the only thing good in itself, which is in fact the point they take most pains to establish, would have been quite irrelevant to their attempt to prove that only what produces the maximum *pleasure* is right. If, therefore, it can be shown that productivity of the maximum good is not what makes all right actions right, we shall *a fortiori* have refuted hedonistic utilitarianism.

When a plain man fulfils a promise because he thinks he ought to do so, it seems clear that he does so with no thought of its total consequences, still less with any opinion that these are likely to be the best possible. He thinks in fact much more of the past than of the furture. What makes him think it right to act in a certain way is the fact that he has promised to do so—that and, usually, nothing more. That his act will produce the best possible consequences is not his reason for calling it right. What lends colour to the theory we are examining, then, is not the actions (which form probably a great majority of our actions) in which some such reflection as 'I have promised' is the only reason we give ourselves for thinking a certain action right, but the exceptional cases in which the consequences of fulfilling a promise (for instance) would be so disastrous to others that we judge it right not to do so. It must of course be admitted that such cases exist. If I have promised to meet a friend at a particular time for some trivial purpose, I should certainly think myself justified in breaking my engagement if by doing so I could prevent a serious accident or bring relief to the victims of one. And the supporters of the view we are examining hold that my thinking so is due to my thinking that I shall bring more good into existence by the one action than by the other. A different account may, however, be given of the matter, an account which will, I believe, show itself to be the true one. It may be said that besides the duty of fulfilling promises I have and recognize a duty of relieving distress,[2] and that when I think it right to do the latter at the cost of not doing the former, it is not because I think I shall produce more good thereby but because I think it the duty which is in the circumstances more of a duty. This account surely corresponds much more closely with what we really think in such a situation. If, so far as I can see, I could bring equal amounts of good into being by fulfilling my promise and by helping some one to whom I had made no promise, I should not hesitate to regard the former as my duty. Yet on the view that what is right is right because it is productive of the most good I should not so regard it.

There are two theories, each in its way simple, that offer a solution of such cases of conscience. One is the view of Kant, that there are certain duties of perfect obligation, such as those of fulfilling promises, of paying debts, of telling the truth, which admit of no exception whatever in favour of duties of imperfect obligation, such as that of relieving distress. The other is the view of, for instance, Professor Moore and Dr. Rashdall, that there is only the duty of producing good, and that all 'conflicts of duties' should be resolved by asking 'by which action will most good be produced?' But it is more important that our theory fit the facts than that it be simple, and the account we have given above corresponds (it seems to me) better than either of the simpler theories with what we really think, viz. that normally promise-keeping, for example, should come before benevolence, but that when and only when the good to be produced by the benevolent act is very great and the promise comparatively trivial, the act of benevolence becomes our duty.

In fact the theory of 'ideal utilitarianism', if I may for brevity refer so to the theory of Professor Moore, seems to simplify unduly our relations to our fellows. It says, in effect, that the only morally significant relation in which my neighbours stand to me is that of being possible beneficiaries by my action.[3] They do stand in this relation to me, and this relation is morally significant. But they may also stand to me in the relation of promisee to promiser, of creditor to debtor, of wife to husband, of child

[2] These are not strictly speaking duties, but things that tend to be our duty, or *prima facie* duties.

[3] Some will think it, apart from other considerations, a sufficient refutation of this view to point out that I also stand in that relation to myself, so that for this view the distinction of oneself from others is morally insignificant.

to parent, of friend to friend, of fellow countryman to fellow countryman, and the like; and each of these relations is the foundation of a *prima facie* duty, which is more or less incumbent on me according to the circumstances of the case. When I am in a situation, as perhaps I always am, in which more than one of these *prima facie* duties is incumbent on me, what I have to do is to study the situation as fully as I can until I form the considered opinion (it is never more) that in the circumstances one of them is more incumbent than any other; then I am bound to think that to do this *prima facie* duty is my duty *sans phrase* in the situation.

I suggest '*prima facie* duty' or 'conditional duty' as a brief way of referring to the characteristic (quite distinct from that of being a duty proper) which an act has, in virtue of being of a certain kind (e.g. the keeping of a promise), of being an act which would be a duty proper if it were not at the same time of another kind which is morally significant. Whether an act is a duty proper or actual duty depends on *all* the morally significant kinds it is an instance of. The phrase '*prima facie* duty' must be apologized for, since (1) it suggests that what we are speaking of is a certain kind of duty, whereas it is in fact not a duty, but something related in a special way to duty. Strictly speaking, we want not a phrase in which duty is qualified by an adjective, but a separate noun. (2) '*Prima' facie* suggests that one is speaking only of an appearance which a moral situation presents at first sight, and which may turn out to be illusory; whereas what I am speaking of is an objective fact involved in the nature of the situation, or more strictly in an element of its nature, though not, as duty proper does, arising from its *whole* nature. I can, however, think of no term which fully meets the case. 'Claim' has been suggested by Professor Prichard. The word 'claim' has the advantage of being quite a familiar one in this connexion, and it seems to cover much of the ground. It would be quite natural to say, 'a person to whom I have made a promise has a claim on me', and also, 'a person whose distress I could relieve (at the cost of breaking the promise) has a claim on me'. But (1) while 'claim' is appropriate from *their* point of view, we want a word to express the corresponding fact from the agent's point of view—the fact of his being subject to claims that can be made against him; and ordinary language provides us with no such correlative to 'claim'. And (2) (what is more important) 'claim' seems inevitably to suggest two persons, one of whom might make a claim on the other; and while this covers the ground of social duty, it is inappropriate in the case of that important part of duty which is the duty of cultivating a certain kind of character in oneself. It would be artificial,

I think, and at any rate metaphorical, to say that one's character has a claim on oneself.

There is nothing arbitrary about these *prima facie* duties. Each rests on a definite circumstance which cannot seriously be held to be without moral significance. Of *prima facie* duties I suggest, without claiming completeness or finality for it, the following division.[4]

(1) Some duties rest on previous acts of my own. These duties seem to include two kinds, (*a*) those resting on a promise or what may fairly be called an implicit promise, such as the implicit undertaking not to tell lies which seems to be implied in the act of entering into conversation (at any rate by civilized men), or of writing books that purport to be history and not fiction. These may be called the duties of fidelity. (*b*) Those resting on a previous wrongful act. These may be called the duties of reparation. (2) Some rest on previous acts of other men, i.e. services done by them to me. These may be loosely described as the duties of gratitude.[5] (3) Some rest on the fact or possibility of a distribution of pleasure or happiness (or of the means thereto) which is not in accordance with the merit of the persons concerned; in such cases there arises a duty to upset or prevent such a distribution. These are the duties of justice. (4) Some rest on the mere fact that there are other beings in the world whose condition we can make better in respect of virtue, or of intelligence, or of pleasure. These are the duties of beneficence. (5) Some rest on the fact that we can improve our own condition in respect of virtue or of intelligence. These are the duties of self-improvement. (6) I think that we should distinguish from (4) the duties that may be summed up under the title of 'not injuring others'. No doubt to injure others is incidentally to fail to do them good; but it seems to me clear that non-maleficence is apprehended as a duty distinct from that of beneficence, and as a duty of a more stringent character. It will be noticed that this alone among the types of duty has been stated in a negative way. An attempt might no doubt be made to state this duty,

[4] I should make it plain at this stage that I am *assuming* the correctness of some of our main convictions as to *prima facie* duties, or, more strictly, am claiming that we *know* them to be true. To me it seems as self-evident as anything could be, that to make a promise, for instance, is to create a moral claim on us in someone else. Many readers will perhaps say that they do *not* know this to be true. If so, I certainly cannot prove it to them; I can only ask them to reflect again, in the hope that they will ultimately agree that they also know it to be true. The main moral convictions of the plain man seem to me to be, not opinions which it is for philosophy to prove or disprove, but knowledge from the start; and in my own case I seem to find little difficulty in distinguishing these essential convictions from other moral convictions which I also have, which are merely fallible opinions based on an imperfect study of the working for good or evil of certain institutions or types of action.

[5] For a needed correction of this statement, cf. pp. 90–91.

like the others, in a positive way. It might be said that it is really the duty to prevent ourselves from acting either from an inclination to harm others or from an inclination to seek our own pleasure, in doing which we should incidentally harm them. But on reflection it seems clear that the primary duty here is the duty not to harm others, this being a duty whether or not we have an inclination that if followed would lead to our harming them; and that when we have such an inclination the primary duty not to harm others gives rise to a consequential duty to resist the inclination. The recognition of this duty of non-maleficence is the first step on the way to the recognition of the duty of beneficence; and that accounts for the prominence of the commands 'thou shalt not kill', 'thou shalt not commit adultery', 'thou shalt not steal', 'thou shalt not bear false witness', in so early a code as the Decalogue. But even when we have come to recognize the duty of beneficence, it appears to me that the duty of non-maleficence is recognized as a distinct one, and as *prima facie* more binding. We should not in general consider it justifiable to kill one person in order to keep another alive, or to steal from one in order to give alms to another.

The essential defect of the 'ideal utilitarian' theory is that it ignores, or at least does not do full justice to, the highly personal character of duty. If the only duty is to produce the maximum of good, the question who is to have the good—whether it is myself, or my benefactor, or a person to whom I have made a promise to confer that good on him, or a mere fellow man to whom I stand in no such special relation—should make no difference to my having a duty to produce that good. But we are all in fact sure that it makes a vast difference.

One or two other comments must be made on this provisional list of the divisions of duty. (1) The nomenclature is not strictly correct. For by 'fidelity' or 'gratitude' we mean, strictly, certain states of motivation; and, as I have urged, it is not our duty to have certain motives, but to do certain acts. By 'fidelity', for instance, is meant, strictly, the disposition to fulfil promises and implicit promises *because we have made them*. We have no general word to cover the actual fulfilment of promises and implicit promises *irrespective of motive*; and I use 'fidelity', loosely but perhaps conveniently, to fill this gap. So too I use 'gratitude' for the returning of services, irrespective of motive. The term 'justice' is not so much confined, in ordinary usage, to a certain state of motivation, for we should often talk of a man as acting justly even when we did not think his motive was the wish to do what was just simply for the sake of doing so. Less apology is therefore needed for our use of 'justice' in this sense. And I have used the word 'beneficence' rather than 'benevolence', in order to emphasize the fact that it is our duty to do certain things, and not to do them from certain motives.

(2) If the objection be made, that this catalogue of the main types of duty is an unsystematic one resting on no logical principle, it may be replied, first, that it makes no claim to being ultimate. It is a *prima facie* classification of the duties which reflection on our moral convictions seems actually to reveal. And if these convictions are, as I would claim that they are, of the nature of knowledge, and if I have not misstated them, the list will be a list of authentic conditional duties, correct as far as it goes though not necessarily complete. The list of *goods* put forward by the rival theory is reached by exactly the same method—the only sound one in the circumstances—viz. that of direct reflection on what we really think. Loyalty to the facts is worth more than a symmetrical architectonic or a hastily reached simplicity. If further reflection discovers a perfect logical basis for this or for a better classification, so much the better.

(3) It may, again, be objected that our theory that there are these various and often conflicting types of *prima facie* duty leaves us with no principle upon which to discern what is our actual duty in particular circumstances. But this objection is not one which the rival theory is in a position to bring forward. For when we have to choose between the production of two heterogeneous goods, say knowledge and pleasure, the 'ideal utilitarian' theory can only fall back on an opinion, for which no logical basis can be offered, that one of the goods is the greater; and this is no better than a similar opinion that one of two duties is the more urgent. And again, when we consider the infinite variety of the effects of our actions in the way of pleasure, it must surely be admitted that the claim which *hedonism* sometimes makes, that it offers a readily applicable criterion of right conduct, is quite illusory.

I am unwilling, however, to content myself with an *argumentum ad hominem*, and I would contend that in principle there is no reason to anticipate that every act that is our duty is so for one and the same reason. Why should two sets of circumstances, or one set of circumstances, *not* possess different characteristics, any one of which makes a certain act our *prima facie* duty? When I ask what it is that makes me in certain cases sure that I have a *prima facie* duty to do so and so, I find that it lies in the fact that I have made a promise; when I ask the same question in another case, I find the answer lies in the fact that I have done a wrong. And if on reflection I find (as I think I do) that neither of these reasons is reducible to the other, I must not on any *a priori* ground assume that such a reduction is possible.

An attempt may be made to arrange in a more systematic way the main types of duty which we have indicated. In the first place it seems self-evident that if there are things that are intrinsically good, it is *prima facie* a duty to bring them into existence rather than not to do so, and to bring as much of them into existence as possible. . . . [T]here are three main things that are intrinsically good—virtue, knowledge, and, with certain limitations, pleasure. And since a given virtuous disposition, for instance, is equally good whether it is realized in myself or in another, it seems to be my duty to bring it into existence whether in myself or in another. So too with a given piece of knowledge.

The case of pleasure is difficult; for while we clearly recognize a duty to produce pleasure for others, it is by no means so clear that we recognize a duty to produce pleasure for ourselves. This appears to arise from the following facts. The thought of an act as our duty is one that presupposes a certain amount of reflection about the act; and for that reason does not normally arise in connexion with acts towards which we are already impelled by another strong impulse. So far, the cause of our not thinking of the promotion of our own pleasure as a duty is analogous to the cause which usually prevents a highly sympathetic person from thinking of the promotion of the pleasure of others as a duty. He is impelled so strongly by direct interest in the well-being of others towards promoting their pleasure that he does not stop to ask whether it is his duty to promote it; and we are all impelled so strongly towards the promotion of our own pleasure that we do not stop to ask whether it is a duty or not. But there is a further reason why even when we stop to think about the matter it does not usually present itself as a duty: viz. that, since the performance of most of our duties involves the giving up of some pleasure that we desire, the doing of duty and the getting of pleasure for ourselves come by a natural association of ideas to be thought of as incompatible things. This association of ideas is in the main salutary in its operation, since it puts a check on what but for it would be much too strong, the tendency to pursue one's own pleasure without thought of other considerations. Yet if pleasure is good, it seems in the long run clear that it is right to get it for ourselves as well as to produce it for others, when this does not involve the failure to discharge some more stringent *prima facie* duty. The question is a very difficult one, but it seems that this conclusion can be denied only on one or other of three grounds: (1) that pleasure is not *prima facie* good (i.e. good when it is neither the actualization of a bad disposition nor undeserved), (2) that there is no *prima facie* duty to produce as much that is good as we can, or (3) that though there is a *prima facie* duty to produce other things that are good, there is no *prima facie* duty to produce pleasure which will be enjoyed by ourselves. I give reasons later for not accepting the first contention. The second hardly admits of argument but seems to me plainly false. The third seems plausible only if we hold that an act that is pleasant or brings pleasure to ourselves must for that reason not be a duty; and this would lead to paradoxical consequences, such as that if a man enjoys giving pleasure to others or working for their moral improvement, it cannot be his duty to do so. Yet it seems to be a very stubborn fact, that in our ordinary consciousness we are not aware of a duty to get pleasure for ourselves; and by way of partial explanation of this I may add that though, as I think, one's own pleasure is a good and there is a duty to produce it, it is only if we *think* of our own pleasure not as simply our own pleasure, but as an objective good, something that an impartial spectator would approve, that we can think of the getting it as a duty; and we do not habitually think of it in this way.

If these contentions are right, what we have called the duty of beneficence and the duty of self-improvement rest on the same ground. No different principles of duty are involved in the two cases. If we feel a special responsibility for improving our own character rather than that of others, it is not because a special principle is involved, but because we are aware that the one is more under our control than the other. It was on this ground that Kant expressed the practical law of duty in the form 'seek to make yourself good and other people happy'. He was so persuaded of the internality of virtue that he regarded any attempt by one person to produce virtue in another as bound to produce, at most, only a counterfeit of virtue, the doing of externally right acts not from the true principle of virtuous action but out of regard to another person. It must be admitted that one man cannot compel another to be virtuous; compulsory virtue would just not be virtue. But experience clearly shows that Kant overshoots the mark when he contends that one man cannot do anything to *promote* virtue in another, to bring such influences to bear upon him that his own response to them is more likely to be virtuous than his response to other influences would have been. And our duty to do this is not different in kind from our duty to improve our own characters.

It is equally clear, and clear at an earlier stage of moral development, that if there are things that are bad in themselves we ought, *prima facie*, not to bring them upon others; and on this fact rests the duty of non-maleficence.

The duty of justice is particularly complicated, and the word is used to cover things which are really very different—things such as the payment of debts, the reparation of injuries done by oneself to another, and the bringing about of a distribution of happiness between other people in proportion to merit. I use the word to denote only the last of these three. . . . [B]esides the three (comparatively) simple goods, virtue, knowledge, and pleasure, there is a more complex good, not reducible to these, consisting in the proportionment of happiness to virtue. The bringing of this about is a duty which we owe to all men alike, though it may be reinforced by special responsibilities that we have undertaken to particular men. This, therefore, with beneficence and self-improvement, comes under the general principle that we should produce as much good as possible, though the good here involved is different in kind from any other.

But besides this general obligation, there are special obligations. These may arise, in the first place, incidentally, from acts which were not essentially meant to create such an obligation, but which nevertheless create it. From the nature of the case such acts may be of two kinds—the infliction of injuries on others, and the acceptance of benefits from them. It seems clear that these put us under a special obligation to other men, and that only these acts can do so incidentally. From these arise the twin duties of reparation and gratitude.

And finally there are special obligations arising from acts the very intention of which, when they were done, was to put us under such an obligation. The name for such acts is 'promises'; the name is wide enough if we are willing to include under it implicit promises, i.e. modes of behaviour in which without explicit verbal promise we intentionally create an expectation that we can be counted on to behave in a certain way in the interest of another person.

These seem to be, in principle, all the ways in which *prima facie* duties arise. In actual experience they are compounded together in highly complex ways. Thus, for example, the duty of obeying the laws of one's country arises partly (as Socrates contends in the *Crito*) from the duty of gratitude for the benefits one has received from it; partly from the implicit promise to obey which seems to be involved in permanent residence in a country whose laws we know we are *expected* to obey, and still more clearly involved when we ourselves invoke the protection of its laws (this is the truth underlying the doctrine of the social contract); and partly (if we are fortunate in our country) from the fact that its laws are potent instruments for the general good.

Or again, the sense of a general obligation to bring about (so far as we can) a just apportionment of happiness to merit is often greatly reinforced by the fact that many of the existing injustices are due to a social and economic system which we have, not indeed created, but taken part in and assented to; the duty of justice is then reinforced by the duty of reparation.

It is necessary to say something by way of clearing up the relation between *prima facie* duties and the actual or absolute duty to do one particular act in particular circumstances. If, as almost all moralists except Kant are agreed, and as most plain men think, it is sometimes right to tell a lie or to break a promise, it must be maintained that there is a difference between *prima facie* duty and actual or absolute duty. When we think ourselves justified in breaking, and indeed morally obliged to break, a promise in order to relieve some one's distress, we do not for a moment cease to recognize a *prima facie* duty to keep our promise, and this leads us to feel, not indeed shame or repentance, but certainly compunction, for behaving as we do; we recognize, further, that it is our duty to make up somehow to the promisee for the breaking of the promise. We have to distinguish from the characteristic of being our duty that of tending to be our duty. Any act that we do contains various elements in virtue of which it falls under various categories. In virtue of being the breaking of a promise, for instance, it tends to be wrong; in virtue of being an instance of relieving distress it tends to be right. Tendency to be one's duty may be called a parti-resultant attribute, i.e. one which belongs to an act in virtue of some one component in its nature. *Being* one's duty is a toti-resultant attribute, one which belongs to an act in virtue of its whole nature and of nothing less than this. This distinction between parti-resultant and toti-resultant attributes is one which we shall meet in another context also.

Another instance of the same distinction may be found in the operation of natural laws. *Qua* subject to the force of gravitation towards some other body, each body tends to move in a particular direction with a particular velocity; but its actual movement depends on *all* the forces to which it is subject. It is only by recognizing this distinction that we can preserve the absoluteness of laws of nature, and only by recognizing a corresponding distinction that we can preserve the absoluteness of the general principles of morality. But an important difference between the two cases must be pointed out. When we say that in virtue of gravitation a body tends to move in a certain way, we are referring to a causal influence actually exercised on it by another body or other bodies. When we say that in virtue of being deliberately untrue a certain remark tends to be wrong, we are referring to no causal relation, to no relation that involves succession in time, but to such a relation as connects the various attributes of a mathematical figure. And if the word 'tendency' is thought to suggest too much a causal relation, it is better to talk of certain types of act as being *prima facie* right or wrong (or of different persons as having different and possibly conflicting claims upon us), than of their tending to be right or wrong.

Something should be said of the relation between our apprehension of the *prima facie* rightness of certain types of act and our mental attitude towards particular acts. It is proper to use the word 'apprehension' in the former case and not in the latter. That an act, *qua* fulfilling a promise, or *qua* effecting a just distribution of good, or *qua* returning services rendered, or *qua* promoting the good of others, or *qua* promoting the virtue or insight of the agent, is *prima facie* right, is self-evident; not in the sense that it is evident from the beginning of our lives, or as soon as we attend to the proposition for the first time, but in the sense that when we have reached sufficient mental maturity and have given sufficient attention to the proposition it is evident without any need of proof, or of evidence beyond itself. It is self-evident just as a mathematical axiom, or the validity of a form of inference, is evident. The moral order expressed in these propositions is just as much part of the fundamental nature of the universe (and, we may add, of any possible universe in which there were moral agents at all) as is the spatial or numerical structure expressed in the axioms of geometry or arithmetic. In our confidence that these propositions are true there is involved the same trust in our reason that is involved in our confidence in mathematics; and we should have no justification for trusting it in the latter sphere and distrusting it in the former. In both cases we are dealing with propositions that cannot be proved, but that just as certainly need no proof.

Some of these general principles of *prima facie* duty may appear to be open to criticism. It may be thought, for example, that the principle of returning good for good is a falling off from the Christian principle, generally and rightly recognized as expressing the highest morality, or returning good for evil. To this it may be replied that I do not suggest that there is a principle commanding us to return good for good and forbidding us to return good for evil, and that I do suggest that there is a positive duty to seek the good of all men. What I maintain is that an act in which good is returned for good is recognized as *specially* binding on us just because it is of that character, and that *ceteris paribus* any one would think it his duty to help his benefactors rather than his enemies, if he could not do both; just as it is generally recognized that *ceteris paribus* we should pay our debts rather than give our money in charity, when we cannot do both. A benefactor is not only a man, calling for our effort on his behalf on that ground, but also our benefactor, calling for our *special* effort on *that* ground.

Our judgements about our actual duty in concrete situations have none of the certainty that attaches to our recognition of the general principles of duty. A statement is certain, i.e. is an expression of knowledge, only in one or other of two cases: when it is either self-evident, or a valid conclusion from self-evident premisses. And our judgements about our particular duties have neither of these characters. (1) They are not self-evident. Where a possible act is seen to have two characteristics, in virtue of one of which is a *prima facie* right, and in virtue of the other *prima facie* wrong, we are (I think) well aware that we are not certain whether we ought or ought not to do it; that whether we do it or not, we are taking a moral risk. We come in the long run, after consideration, to think one duty more pressing than the other, but we do not feel certain that it is so. And though we do not always recognize that a possible act has two such characteristics, and though there *may* be cases in which it has not, we are never certain that any particular possible act has not, and therefore never certain that it is right, nor certain that it is wrong. For, to go no further in the analysis, it is enough to point out that any particular act will in all probability in the course of time contribute to the bringing about of good or of evil for many human beings, and thus have a *prima facie* rightness or wrongness of which we know nothing. (2) Again, our judgements about our particular duties are not logical conclusions from self-evident premisses. The only possible premisses would be the general principles stating their *prima facie* rightness or wrongness *qua* having the different characteristics they do have; and even if we could (as we cannot) apprehend the extent to which an act will tend on the one hand, for example, to bring about advantages for our benefactors, and on the other hand to bring about disadvantages for fellow men who are not our benefactors, there is no principle by which we can draw the conclusion that it is on the whole right or on the whole wrong. In this respect the judgement as to the rightness of a particular act is just like the judgement as to the beauty of a particular natural object or work of art. A poem is, for instance, in respect of certain qualities beautiful and in respect of certain others not beautiful; and our judgement as to the degree of beauty it possesses on the whole is never reached by logical reasoning from the apprehension of its particular beauties or particular defects. Both in this and in the moral case we have more or less probable opinions which are not logically justified conclusions from the general principles that are recognized as self-evident.

There is therefore much truth in the description of the right act as a fortunate act. If we cannot be certain that it is right, it is our good fortune if the act we do is the right act. This consideration does not, however, make the doing of our duty a mere matter of chance. There is a parallel here between the doing of duty and the doing of what will be our personal advantage. We never *know* what act will in the long run be to our advantage. Yet it is certain that we are more likely in general to secure our advantage if we estimate to the best of our ability the probable tendencies of our actions in this respect, than if we act on caprice. And similarly we are more likely to do our duty if we reflect to the best of our ability on the *prima facie* rightness or wrongness of various possible acts in virtue of the characteristics we perceive them to have, than if we act without reflection. With this greater likelihood we must be content.

Many people would be inclined to say that the right act for me is not that whose general nature I have been describing, viz. that which if I were omniscient I should see to be my duty, but that which on all the evidence available to me I should think to be my duty. But suppose that from the state of partial knowledge in which I think act *A* to be my duty, I could pass to a state of perfect knowledge in which I saw act *B* to be my duty, should I not say 'act *B* was the right act for me to do'? I should no doubt add 'though I am not to be blamed for doing act *A*'. But in adding this, am I not passing from the question 'what is right' to the question 'what is morally good'? At the same time I am not making the *full* passage from the one notion to the other; for in order that the act should be morally good, or an act I am not be blamed for doing, it must not merely be the act which it is reasonable for me to think my duty; it must also be done for that reason, or from some other morally good motive. Thus the conception of the right act as the act which it is reasonable for me to think my duty is an unsatisfactory compromise between the true notion of the right act and the notion of the morally good action.

The general principles of duty are obviously not self-evident from the beginning of our lives. How do they come to be so? The answer is, that they come to be self-evident to us just as mathematical axioms do. We find by experience that this couple of matches and that couple make four matches, that this couple of balls on a wire and that couple make four balls; and by reflection on these and similar discoveries we come to see that it is of the nature of two and two to make four. In a precisely similar way, we see the *prima facie* rightness of an act which would be the fulfilment of a particular promise, and of another which would be the fulfilment of another promise, and when we have reached sufficient maturity to think in general terms, we apprehend *prima facie* rightness to belong to the nature of any fulfilment of promise. What comes first in time is the apprehension of the self-evident *prima facie* rightness of an individual act of a particular type. From this we come by reflection to apprehend the self-evident general principle of *prima facie* duty. From this, too, perhaps along with the apprehension of the self-evident *prima facie* rightness of the same act in virtue of its having another characteristic as well, and perhaps in spite of the apprehension of its *prima facie* wrongness in virtue of its having some third characteristic, we come to believe something not self-evident at all, but an object of probable opinion, viz. that this particular act is (not *prima facie* but) actually right.

In this respect there is an important difference between rightness and mathematical properties. A triangle which is isosceles necessarily has two of its angles equal, whatever other characteristics the triangle may have—whatever, for instance, be its area, or the size of its third angle. The equality of the two angles is a parti-resultant attribute. And the same is true of all mathematical attributes. It is true, I may add, of *prima facie* rightness. But no act is ever, in virtue of falling under some general description, necessarily actually right; its rightness depends on its whole nature[6] and not on any element in it. The reason is that no mathematical object (no figure, for instance, or angle) ever has two characteristics that tend to give it opposite resultant characteristics, while moral acts often (as every one knows) and indeed always (as on reflection we must admit) have different characteristics that tend to make them at the same time *prima facie* right and *prima facie* wrong; there is probably no act, for instance, which does good to any one without doing harm to some one else, and *vice versa*.

Supposing it to be agreed, as I think on reflection it must, that no one *means* by 'right' just 'productive of the best possible consequences', or 'optimific', the attributes 'right' and 'optimific' might stand in either of two kinds of relation to each other. (1) They might be so related that we could apprehend *a priori*, either immediately or deductively, that any act that is optimific is right and any act that is right is optimific, as we can apprehend that any triangle that is equilateral is equiangular and *vice*

[6] To avoid complicating unduly the statement of the general view I am putting forward, I have here rather overstated it. Any act is the origination of a great variety of things many of which make no difference to its rightness or wrongness. But there are always many elements in its nature (i.e. in what it is the origination of) that make a difference to its rightness or wrongness, and no element in its nature can be dismissed without consideration as indifferent.

versa. Professor Moore's view is, I think, that the coextensiveness of 'right' and 'optimific' is apprehended immediately. He rejects the possibility of any proof of it. Or (2) the two attributes might be such that the question whether they are invariably connected had to be answered by means of an inductive inquiry. Now at first sight it might seem as if the constant connexion of the two attributes could be immediately apprehended. It might seem absurd to suggest that it could be right for any one to do an act which would produce consequences less good than those which would be produced by some other act in his power. Yet a little thought will convince us that this is not absurd. The type of case in which it is easiest to see that this is so is, perhaps, that in which one has made a promise. In such a case we all think that *prima facie* it is our duty to fulfil the promise irrespective of the precise goodness of the total consequences. And though we do not think it is necessarily our actual or absolute duty to do so, we are far from thinking that any, even the slightest, gain in the value of the total consequences will necessarily justify us in doing something else instead. Suppose, to simplify the case by abstraction, that the fulfilment of a promise to *A* would produce 1,000 units of good[7] for him, but that by doing some other act I could produce 1,001 units of good for *B*, to whom I have made no promise, the other consequences of the two acts being of equal value; should we really think it self-evident that it was our duty to do the second act and not the first? I think not. We should, I fancy, hold that only a much greater disparity of value between the total consequences would justify us in failing to discharge our *prima facie* duty to *A*. After all, a promise is a promise, and is not to be treated so lightly as the theory we are examining would imply. What, exactly, a promise is, is not so easy to determine, but we are surely agreed that it constitutes a serious moral limitation to our freedom of action. To produce the 1,001 units of good for *B* rather than fulfil our promise to *A* would be to take, not perhaps our duty as philanthropists too seriously, but certainly our duty as makers of promises too lightly.

Or consider another phase of the same problem. If I have promised to confer on *A* a particular benefit containing 1,000 units of good, is it self-evident that if by doing some different act I could produce 1,001 units of good for *A* himself (the other consequences of the two acts being supposed equal in value), it would be right for me to do so? Again, I

[7] I am assuming that good is objectively quantitative, but not that we can accurately assign an exact quantitative measure to it. Since it is of a definite amount, we can make the *supposition* that its amount is so-and-so, though we cannot with any confidence *assert* that it is.

think not. Apart from my general *prima facie* duty to do *A* what good I can, I have another *prima facie* duty to do him the particular service I have promised to do him, and this is not to be set aside in consequence of a disparity of good of the order of 1,001 to 1,000, though a much greater disparity might justify me in so doing.

Or again, suppose that *A* is a very good and *B* a very bad man, should I then, even when I have made no promise, think it self-evidently right to produce 1,001 units of good for *B* rather than 1,000 for *A*? Surely not. I should be sensible of a *prima facie* duty of justice, i.e. of producing a distribution of goods in proportion to merit, which is not outweighed by such a slight disparity in the total goods to be produced.

Such instances—and they might easily be added to—make it clear that there is no self-evident connexion between the attributes 'right' and 'optimific'. The theory we are examining has a certain attractiveness when applied to our decision that a particular act is our duty (though I have tried to show that it does not agree with our actual moral judgements even here). But it is not even plausible when applied to our recognition of *prima facie* duty. For if it were self-evident that the right coincides with the optimific, it should be self-evident that what is *prima facie* right is *prima facie* optimific. But whereas we are certain that keeping a promise is *prima facie* right, we are not certain that it is *prima facie* optimific (though we are perhaps certain that it is *prima facie* bonific). Our certainty that it is *prima facie* right depends not on its consequences but on its being the fulfilment of a promise. The theory we are examining involves too much difference between the evident ground of our conviction about *prima facie* duty and the alleged ground of our conviction about actual duty.

The coextensiveness of the right and the optimific is, then, not self-evident. And I can see no way of proving it deductively; nor, so far as I know, has any one tried to do so. There remains the question whether it can be established inductively. Such an inquiry, to be conclusive, would have to be very thorough and extensive. We should have to take a large variety of the acts which we, to the best of our ability, judge to be right. We should have to trace as far as possible their consequences, not only for the persons directly affected but also for those indirectly affected, and to these no limit can be set. To make our inquiry thoroughly conclusive, we should have to do what we cannot do, viz. trace these consequences into an unending future. And even to make it reasonably conclusive, we should have to trace them far into the future. It is clear that the most we could possibly say is that a large variety of typical acts that are judged right appear, so far as we can trace their consequences, to produce more good than any other acts possible to the agents in the circumstances. And such a result falls far short of proving the constant connexion of the two attributes. But it is surely clear that no inductive inquiry justifying even this result has ever been carried through. The advocates of utilitarian systems have been so much persuaded either of the identity or of the self-evident connexion of the attributes 'right' and 'optimific' (or 'felicific') that they have not attempted even such an inductive inquiry as is possible. And in view of the enormous complexity of the task and the inevitable inconclusiveness of the result, it is worth no one's while to make the attempt. What, after all, would be gained by it? If, as I have tried to show, for an act to be right and to be optimific are not the same thing, and an act's being optimific is not even the ground of its being right, then if we could ask ourselves (though the question is really unmeaning) which we ought to do, right acts because they are right or optimific acts because they are optimific, our answer must be 'the former'. If they are optimific as well as right, that is interesting but not morally important; if not, we still ought to do them (which is only another way of saying that they *are* the right acts), and the question whether they are optimific has no importance for moral theory. . . .

Part III

Rights

Introduction

Egoists, utilitarians, and nonconsequentialists all agree that morality is concerned with human welfare. But, as we have seen, they disagree about what human welfare is and how best to achieve it. Thus the possibility arises that disagreements about values are unavoidable features of morality, because they cannot be settled by rational arguments. The values people hold ultimately reflect the morality of their society, and different societies have different values. This is the view of *relativism*. If relativism were correct, it would follow that any set of values may constitute the morality of a society, provided only that they are generally accepted in that society.

The first reading in this section is another hypothetical case. It concerns a conflict of values between two societies. One question it raises is whether a society is justified in imposing its values on another society. What complicates matters is that the values one society wants to impose are believed to promote the welfare of the other. Relativists argue that the imposition of values across societies is unjustified, because what counts as welfare in one society is different from what counts as welfare in another. So that if members of a society believe that something is not in their welfare, then their beliefs cannot be overruled on rational grounds.

Contractarianism rejects this view. Contractarians argue that at the foundation of the political institutions of a morally good society there are some objective values, and they are the same for all societies. The protection of these objective values is the social contract upon which morally good societies are based. The claim that objective values derive from human nature, which is the same everywhere, undergirds the position presented in John Locke's (1632–1704) *Second Treatise of Government*, the source of the second reading in this section. Locke's work deeply influenced The Declaration of Independence and the Constitution. Locke argues that it follows from human nature that everyone has certain inalienable rights to life, liberty, and property, to the basic requirements of human welfare in all societies.

The third reading in this section is a contemporary essay by John Rawls, the author of *A Theory of Justice*. This influential work is a development of the contractarian tradition. It goes beyond Locke in attempting to spell out in greater detail what principles must guide a just society. Rawls arrives at these principles by considering what principles would be chosen by self-interested and rational people, if they had no way of knowing what position they would have in the society guided by these principles.

If contractarians are correct, then we can identify the limits, marked by human rights, beyond which it is morally wrong to go even if doing so would be for the common good. Thus contractarianism reinforces the constraints nonconsequentialists placed on the utilitarian pursuit of general happiness. And if there are such constraints, then relativists must be mistaken. The question remains, however, of what motivates reasonable people to conform to the requirements of morality. Why should reasonable people do what morality asks of them, especially in view of the fact that doing so is often very hard? In the next section, we shall consider this question.

Problem Case: Morality and Relativism

There is a small tribe in a distant tropical country. Its members are strongly pro-American, and they have saved the lives of many Americans in the hostilities raging in their country. As a result, they are cruelly persecuted by the vastly more powerful anti-American majority and their lives are in imminent danger. American immigration authorities offer to transport and resettle them in America, if they so wish. Members of the tribe meet, consider the danger and the offer, and unanimously decide to emigrate.

Largely because of their traditional religious beliefs, the tribe is closely knit. Their priests are their moral authorities and also their medicine men. Indeed, they make no distinction between spiritual and physical health. Health and goodness, on the one hand, and illness and evil, on the other hand, are inextricably connected in their minds. The priests know nothing of Western medicine, but they are quite able to deal with such medical matters as arise in their originial tropical context. It is a central part of their religious belief that the body is sacred and interference with it is permissible only for priests who have been ritually purified and who alone possess the required knowledge and authority.

The tribe is flown to America and housed in an area whose climatic conditions resemble most closely their own. But, of course, there are vast differences in a variety of factors, such as diet, bacteria, viruses, the environment, the rhythm of life, and the people surrounding them. Serious illness develops, and American authorities fear that unless drastic medical intervention takes place, the tribe will suffer very high mortality, possibly even extinction. Their priests do what they can, but they are helpless in the face of these new diseases and circumstances.

Members of the tribe unanimously refuse to receive medicine, treatment, or even medical examination from anyone but their priests. To do otherwise would be sacrilegious. Yet whatever the priests do is of no help. When it is pointed out to the priests and to the tribe that new circumstances require adaptation, they respond by attributing their illness to their own immorality, not to new circumstances. They think that their gods are punishing them, and so they do not blame their priests or their new circumstances. Western medical experts agree that unless something is done quickly, the vast majority, and perhaps all, will die.

Does morality require violating the tribe's religious beliefs by forcing medical treatment on them, or does it require respecting their beliefs and allowing them to die?

John Locke

Two Treatises of Government

Of Civil Government

Book II

§ 3. Political power, then, I take to be a right of making laws with penalties of death, and consequently all less penalties, for the regulating and preserving of property, and of employing the force of the community, in the execution of such laws, and in the defence of the commonwealth from foreign injury; and all this only for the public good.

Of the State of Nature

§ 4. To understand political power right, and derive it from its original, we must consider what state all men are naturally in, and that is, a state of perfect freedom to order their actions and dispose of their possessions and persons, as they think fit, within the bounds of law of nature; without asking leave, or depending upon the will of any other man.

A state also of equality, wherein all the power and jurisdiction is reciprocal, no one having more than another; there being nothing more evident than that creatures of the same species and rank, promiscuously born to all the same advantages of nature, and the use of the same faculties, should also be equal one amongst another without subordination or subjection; unless the Lord and Master of them all should, by any manifest declaration of his will, set one above another, and confer on him, by an evident and clear appointment, an undoubted right to dominion and sovereignty.

§ 6. But though this be a state of liberty, yet it is not a state of licence: though man in that state have an uncontrollable liberty to dispose of his person or possessions, yet he has not liberty to destroy himself, or so much as any creature in his possession, but where some nobler use than its bare preservation calls for it. The state of nature has a law of nature to govern it, which obliges every one: and reason, which is that law, teaches all mankind, who will but consult it, that being all equal and independent, no one ought to harm another in his life, health, liberty, or possessions: for men being all the wormanship of one omnipotent and infinitely wise Maker; all the servants of one sovereign Master, sent into the world by his order, and about his business; they are his property, whose workmanship they are, made to last during his, not another's pleasure: and being furnished with like faculties, sharing all in one community of nature, there cannot be supposed any such subordination among us that may authorize us to destroy another, as if we were made for one another's uses, as the inferior ranks of creatures are for ours. Every one, as he is bound to preserve himself, and not to quit his station wilfully, so by the like reason, when his own preservation comes not in competition, ought he, as much as he can, to preserve the rest of mankind, and may not, unless it be to do justice to an offender, take away or impair the life, or what tends to the preservation of life, the liberty, health, limb, or goods of another.

§ 7. And that all men may be restrained from invading others' rights, and from doing hurt to one another, and the law of nature be observed, which willeth the peace and preservation of all mankind, the execution of the law of nature is, in that state, put into every man's hands, whereby every one has a right to punish the transgressors of that law to such a degree as may hinder its violation: for the law of nature would, as all other laws that concern men in this world, be in vain, if there were nobody that in the state of nature had a power to execute that law, and thereby preserve the innocent, and restrain offenders. And if any one in the state of nature may punish another for any evil he has done, every one may do so: for in that state of perfect equality, where naturally there is no superiority or jurisdiction of one over another, what any may do in prosecution of that law every one must needs have a right to do.

§ 8. And thus, in the state of nature, "one man comes by a power over another;" but yet no absolute or arbitrary power to use a criminal, when he has got him in his hands, according to the passionate heats or boundless extravagancy of his own will; but only to retribute to him, so far as calm reason and conscience dictate, what is proportionate to his transgression; which is so much as may serve for reparation and restraint: for these two are the only reasons why one man may lawfully do harm to another, which is that we call punishment. In transgressing the law of nature, the offender declares himself to live by another rule than that of reason and common equity, which is that measure God has set to the actions of men for their mutual security; and so he becomes dangerous to mankind, the tie, which is to secure them from injury and violence, being slighted and broken by him: which being a trespass against the whole species, and the peace and safety of it, provided for by the law of nature; every man upon this score, by the right he hath to preserve mankind in general, may restrain, or, where it is necessary, destroy things noxious to them, and so may bring such evil on any one, who hath transgressed that law, as may make him repent the doing of it, and thereby deter him, and by his example others, from doing the like mischief. And in this case, and upon this ground, "every man hath a right to punish the offender, and be executioner of the law of nature."

§ 10. Besides the crime which consists in violating the law, and varying from the right rule of reason, whereby a man so far becomes degenerate, and declares himself to quit the principles of human nature, and to be a noxious creature, there is commonly injury done to some person or other, and some other man receives damage by his transgression: in which case he who hath received any damage, has, besides the right of punishment common to him with other men, a particular right to seek reparation from him that has done it: and any other person, who finds it just, may also join with him that is injured, and assist him in recovering from the offender so much as may make satisfaction for the harm he has suffered.

§ 11. From these two distinct rights, the one of punishing the crime for restraint, and preventing the like offence, which right of punishing is in every body; the other of taking reparation, which belongs only to the injured party; comes it to pass that the magistrate, who by being magistrate hath the common right of punishing put into his hands, can often, where the public good demands not the execution of the law, remit the punishment of criminal offences by his own authority, but yet cannot remit the satisfaction due to any private man for the damage he has received. That he who has suffered the damage has a right to demand in his own name, and he alone can remit: the damnified person has this power of appropriating to himself the goods or service of the offender, by right of self-preservation, as every man has a power to punish the crime, to prevent its being committed again, "by the right he has of preserving all mankind," and doing all reasonable things he can in order to that end: and thus it is that every man, in the state of nature, has a power to kill a murderer, both to deter others from doing the like injury, which no reparation can compensate, by the example of the punishment that attends it from every body; and also to secure men from the attempts of a criminal, who having renounced reason, the common rule and measure God hath given to mankind, hath, by the unjust violence and slaughter he hath committed upon one, declared war against all mankind; and therefore may be destroyed as a lion or a tiger, one of those wild savage beasts with whom men can have no society nor security: and upon this is grounded that great law of nature,

"Whoso sheddeth man's blood, by man shall his blood be shed." And Cain was so fully convinced that every one had a right to destroy such a criminal, that, after the murder of his brother, he cries out, "Every one that findeth me shall slay me;" so plain was it writ in the hearts of mankind.

§ 12. By the same reason may a man in the state of nature punish the lesser breaches of that law. It will perhaps be demanded, with death? I answer, each transgression may be punished to that degree, and with so much severity, as will suffice to make it an ill bargain to the offender, give him cause to repent, and terrify others from doing the like. Every offence, that can be committed in the state of nature, may in the state of nature be also punished equally, and as far forth, as it may in a commonwealth: for though it would be beside my present purpose to enter here into the particulars of the law of nature, or its measures of punishment, yet it is certain there is such a law, and that too as intelligible and plain to a rational creature, and a studier of that law, as the positive laws of commonwealths; nay, possibly plainer, as much as reason is easier to be understood than the fancies and intricate contrivances of men, following contrary and hidden interests put into words; for so truly are a great part of the municipal laws of countries, which are only so far right, as they are founded on the law of nature, by which they are to be regulated and interpreted.

§ 13. To this strange doctrine, viz. That "in the state of nature every one has the executive power" of the law of nature, I doubt not but it will be objected, that it is unreasonable for men to be judges in their own cases, that self-love will make men partial to themselves and their friends: and, on the other side, that ill-nature, passion, and revenge will carry them too far in punishing others; and hence nothing but confusion and disorder will follow: and that therefore God hath certainly appointed government to restrain the partiality and violence of men. I easily grant, that civil government is the proper remedy for the inconveniencies of the state of nature, which must certainly be great, where men may be judges in their own case; since it is easy to be imagined, that he who was so unjust as to do his brother an injury, will scarce be so just as to condemn himself for it: but I shall desire those who make this objection to remember, that absolute monarchs are but men; and if government is to be the remedy of those evils, which necessarily follow from men's being judges in their own cases, and the state of nature is therefore not to be endured; I desire to know what kind of government that is, and how much better it is than the state of nature, where one man, commanding a multitude, has the liberty to be judge in his own case, and may do to all his subjects whatever he pleases, without the least liberty to any one to question or control those who execute his pleasure? and in whatsoever he doth, whether led by reason, mistake, or passion, must be submitted to? Much better it is in the state of nature, wherein men are not bound to submit to the unjust will of another: and if he that judges, judges amiss in his own, or any other case, he is answerable for it to the rest of mankind.

§ 15. To those that say, there were never any men in the state of nature, I will not only oppose the authority of the judicious Hooker, Eccl. Pol. lib. i. sect. 10, where he says, "The laws which have been hitherto mentioned," *i.e.* the laws of nature, "do bind men absolutely, even as they are men, although they have never any settled fellowship, never any solemn agreement amongst themselves what to do, or not to do: but forasmuch as we are not by ourselves sufficient to furnish ourselves with competent store of things, needful for such a life as our nature doth desire, a life fit for the dignity of man; therefore to supply those defects and imperfections which are in us, as living singly and solely by ourselves, we are naturally induced to seek communion and fellowship with others. This was the cause of man's uniting themselves at first in politic societies." But I moreover affirm, that all men are naturally in that state, and remain so, till by their own consents they make themselves members of some politic society; and I doubt not in the sequel of this discourse to make it very clear.

Of the State of War.

§ 16. The state of war is a state of enmity and destruction: and therefore declaring by word or action, not a passionate and hasty, but a sedate, settled design upon another man's life, puts him in a state of war with him against whom he has declared such an intention, and so has exposed his life to the other's power to be taken away by him, or any one that joins with him in his defence, and espouses his quarrel; it being reasonable and just, I should have a right to destroy that which threatens me with destruction: for, by the fundamental law of nature, man being to be preserved as much as possible, when all cannot be preserved, the safety of the innocent is to be preferred: and one may destroy a man who makes war upon him, or has discovered an enmity to his being, for the same reason that he may kill a wolf or a lion; because such men are not under the ties of the common law of reason, have no other rule but that of force and violence, and so may be treated as beasts of prey, those dangerous and noxious creatures, that will be sure to destroy him whenever he falls into their power.

§ 17. And hence it is, that he who attempts to get another man into his absolute power, does thereby put himself into a state of war with him; it being to be understood as a declaration of a design upon his life: for I have reason to conclude, that he who would get me into his power without my consent, would use me as he pleased when he got me there, and destroy me too when he had a fancy to it; for nobody can desire to have me in his absolute power, unless it be to compel me by force to that which is against the right of my freedom, *i.e.* make me a slave. To be free from such force is the only security of my preservation; and reason bids me look on him as an enemy to my preservation, who would take away that freedom which is the fence to it; so that he who makes an attempt to enslave me, thereby puts himself into a state of war with me. He that, in the state of nature, would take away the freedom that belongs to any one in that state, must necessarily be supposed to have a design to take away every thing else, that freedom being the foundation of all the rest; as he that, in the state of society, would take away the freedom belonging to those of that society or commonwealth, must be supposed to design to take away from them every thing else, and so be looked on as in a state of war.

§ 19. And here we have the plain "difference between the state of nature and the state of war;" which, however some men have confounded, are as far distant as a state of peace, good-will, mutual assistance and preservation, and a state of enmity, malice, violence, and mutual destruction, are one from another. Men living together according to reason, without a common superior on earth, with authority to judge between them, is properly the state of nature. But force, or a declared design of force, upon the person of another, where there is no common superior on earth to appeal to for relief, is the state of war: and it is the want of such an appeal gives a man the right of war even against an aggressor, though he be in society, and a fellow-subject. Thus a thief, whom I cannot harm, but by appeal to the law, for having stolen all that I am worth, I may kill, when he sets on me to rob me but of my horse or coat; because the law, which was made for my preservation, where it cannot interpose to secure my life from present force, which, if lost, is capable of no reparation, permits me my own defence, and the right of war, a liberty to kill the aggressor, because the aggressor allows not time to appeal to our common judge, not the decision of the law, for remedy in a case where the mischief may be irreparable. Want of a common judge with authority puts all men in a state of nature: force without right, upon a man's person, makes a state of war, both where there is, and is not, a common judge.

§ 20. But when the actual force is over, the state of war ceases between those that are in society, and are equally on both sides subjected to the fair determination of the law; because then there lies open the remedy of appeal for the past injury, and to prevent future harm: but where no such appeal is, as in the state of nature, for want of positive laws, and judges with authority to appeal to, the state of war once begun, continues with a right to the innocent party to destroy the other whenever he can, until the aggressor offers peace, and desires reconciliation on such terms as may repair any wrongs he has already done, and secure the innocent for the future; nay, where an appeal to the law, and constituted judges, lies open, but the remedy is denied by a manifest perverting of justice, and a barefaced wresting of the laws to protect or indemnify the violence or injuries of some men, or party of men; there it is hard to imagine any thing but a state of war: for wherever violence is used, and injury done, though by hands appointed to administer justice, it is still violence and injury, however coloured with the name, pretences, or forms of law, the end whereof being to protect and redress the innocent, by an unbiassed application of it, to all who are under it; wherever that is not *bona fide* done, war is made upon the sufferers, who having no appeal on earth to right them, they are left to the only remedy in such cases, an appeal to Heaven.

§ 21. To avoid this state of war (wherein there is no appeal but to Heaven, and wherein every the least difference is apt to end, where there is no authority to decide between the contenders) is one great reason of men's putting themselves into society, and quitting the state of nature: for where there is an authority, a power on earth, from which relief can be had by appeal, there the continuance of the state of war is excluded, and the controversy is decided by that power. . . .

Of Slavery.

§ 22. The natural liberty of man is to be free from any superior power on earth, and not to be under the will or legislative authority of man, but to have only the law of nature for his rule. The liberty of man, in society, is to be under no other legislative power, but that established, by consent, in the commonwealth; nor under the dominion of any will, or restraint of any law, but what that legislative shall enact, according to the trust put in it. Freedom, then, is not what sir Robert Filmer tells us,

O.A. 55, "a liberty for every one to do what he lists, to live as he pleases, and not to be tied by any laws:" but freedom of men under government is, to have a standing rule to live by, common to every one of that society, and made by the legislative power erected in it; a liberty to follow my own will in all things, where the rule prescribes not; and not to be subject to the inconstant, uncertain, unknown, arbitrary will of another man: as freedom of nature is, to be under no other restraint but the law of nature.

§ 23. This freedom from absolute, arbitrary power, is so necessary to, and closely joined with, a man's preservation, that he cannot part with it, but by what forfeits his preservation and life together: for a man, not having the power of his own life, cannot, by compact, or his own consent, enslave himself to any one, nor put himself under the absolute, arbitrary power of another, to take away his life when he pleases. Nobody can give more power than he has himself; and he that cannot take away his own life, cannot give another power over it. Indeed, having by his fault forfeited his own life, by some act that deserves death; he, to whom he has forfeited it, may (when he has him in his power) delay to take it, and make use of him to his own service, and he does him no injury by it: for, whenever he finds the hardship of his slavery outweigh the value of his life, it is in his power, by resisting the will of his master, to draw on himself the death he desires.

§ 24. This is the perfect condition of slavery, which is nothing else but "the state of war continued, between a lawful conqueror and a captive:" for, if once compact enter between them, and make an agreement for a limited power on the one side, and obedience on the other, the state of war and slavery ceases, as long as the compact endures: for, as has been said, no man can, by agreement, pass over to another that which he hath not in himself, a power over his own life.

Of Property.

§ 26. God, who hath given the world to men in common, hath also given them reason to make use of it to the best advantage of life and convenience. The earth, and all that is therein, is given to men for the support and comfort of their being. And though all the fruits it naturally produces, and beasts it feeds, belong to mankind in common, as they are produced by the spontaneous hand of nature; and nobody has originally a private dominion, exclusive of the rest of mankind, in any of them, as they are thus in their natural state: yet being given for the use of men, there must of necessity be a means to appropriate them some way or other before they can be of any use, or at all beneficial to any particular man. The fruit, or venison, which nourishes the wild Indian, who knows no enclosure, and is still a tenant in common, must be his, and so his, *i.e.* a part of him, that another can no longer have any right to it, before it can do him any good for the support of his life.

§ 27. Though the earth, and all inferior creatures, be common to all men, yet every man has a property in his own person: this nobody has any right to but himself. The labour of his body, and the work of his hands, we may say, are properly his. Whatsoever then he removes out of the state that nature hath provided, and left it in, he hath mixed his labour with, and joined to it something that is his own, and therby makes it his property. It being by him removed from the common state nature hath placed it in, it hath by this labour something annexed to it that excludes the common right of other men. For this labour being the unquestionable property of the labourer, no man but he can have a right to what that is once joined to, at least where there is enough, and as good, left in common for others.

§ 28. He that is nourished by the acorns he picked up under an oak, or the apples he gathered from the trees in the wood, has certainly appropriated them to himself. Nobody can deny but the nourishment is his. . . . Though the water running in the fountain be every one's, yet who can doubt but that in the pitcher is his only who drew it out? His labour hath taken it out of the hands of nature, where it was common, and belonged equally to all her children, and hath thereby appropriated it to himself.

§ 30. Thus this law of reason makes the deer that Indian's who hath killed it; it is allowed to be his goods who hath bestowed his labour upon it, though before it was the common right of every one. And amongst those who are counted the civilized part of mankind, who have made and multiplied positive laws to determine property, this original law of nature, for the beginning of property, in what was before common, still takes place; and by virtue thereof, what fish any one catches in the ocean, that great and still remaining common of mankind; or what ambergris any one takes up here, is by the labor that removes it out of that common state nature left it in made his property who takes that pains about it. And even amongst us, the hare that any one is hunting is thought his who pursues her during the chase: for being a beast that is still looked upon as common, and no man's private possession; whoever had employed so much labour about any of that kind, as to find and pursue her, has thereby removed her from the state of nature, wherein she was common, and hath begun a property.

§ 31. It will perhaps be objected to this, that "if gathering the acorns, or other fruits of the earth, &c. makes a right to them, then any one may engross as much as he will." To which I answer, Not so. The same law of nature, that does by this means give us property, does also bound that property too. "God has given us all things richly," 1 Tim. vi. 17, is the voice of reason confirmed by inspiration. But how far has he given it us? To enjoy. As much as any one can make use of to any advantage of life before it spoils, so much he may by his labour fix a property in: whatever is beyond this, is more than his share, and belongs to others. Nothing was made by God for man to spoil or destroy. And thus, considering the plenty of natural provisions there was a long time in the world, and the few spenders; and to how small a part of that provision the industry of one man could extend itself, and engross it to the prejudice of others; especially keeping within the bounds, set by reason, of what might serve for his use; there could be then little room for quarrels or contentions about property so established.

§ 32. But the chief matter of property being now not the fruits of the earth, and the beasts that subsist on it, but the earth itself; as that which takes in, and carries with it all the rest; I think it is plain, that property in that too is acquired as the former. As much land as a man tills, plants, improves, cultivates, and can use the product of, so much is his property. He by his labour does, as it were, enclose it from the common. Nor will it invalidate his right, to say every body else has an equal title to it, and therefore he cannot appropriate, he cannot enclose, without the consent of all his fellow-commoners, all mankind. God, when he gave the world in common to all mankind, commanded man also to labour, and the penury of his condition required it of him. God and his reason commanded him to subdue the earth, *i.e.* improve it for the benefit of life, and therein lay out something upon it that was his own, his labour. He that, in obedience to this command of God, subdued, tilled, and sowed any part of it, thereby annexed to it something that was his property, which another had no title to, nor could without injury take from him.

§ 33. Nor was this appropriation of any parcel of land, by improving it, any prejudice to any other man, since there was still enough, and as good left; and more than the yet unprovided could use. So that, in effect, there was never the less left for others because of his enclosure for himself; for he that leaves as much as another can make use of, does as good as take nothing at all. Nobody could think himself injured by the drinking of another man, though he took a good draught, who had a whole river of the same water left him to quench his thirst; and the case of land and water, where there is enough of both, is perfectly the same.

§ 34. God gave the world to men in common; but since he gave it them for their benefit, and the greatest conveniencies of life they were capable to draw from it, it cannot be supposed he meant it should always remain common and uncultivated. He gave it to the use of the industrious and rational (and labour was to be his title to it), not to the fancy or covetousness of the quarrelsome and contentious. He that had as good left for his improvement as was already taken up, needed not complain, ought not to meddle with what was already improved by another's labour: if he did, it is plain he desired the benefit of another's pains, which he had no right to, and not the ground which God had given him in common with others to labour on, and whereof there was as good left as that already possessed, and more than he knew what to do with, or his industry could reach to.

§ 37. This is certain, that in the beginning, before the desire of having more than man needed had altered the intrinsic value of things, which depends only on their usefulness to the life of man; or had agreed, that a little piece of yellow metal, which would keep without wasting or decay, should be worth a great piece of flesh, or a whole heap of corn; though men had a right to appropriate, by their labour, each one to himself, as much of the things of nature as he could use: yet this could not be much, nor to the prejudice of others, where the same plenty was still left to those who would use the same industry. To which let me add, that he who appropriates land to himself by his labour, does not lessen, but increase the common stock of mankind: for the provisions serving to the support of human life, produced by one acre of enclosed and cultivated land, are (to speak much within compass) ten times more than those which are yielded by an acre of land of an equal richness lying waste in common. And therefore he that encloses land, and has a greater plenty of the conveniencies of life from ten acres, than he could have from an hundred left to nature, may truly be said to give ninety acres to mankind: for his labour now supplies him with provisions out of ten acres, which were by the product of an hundred lying in common. I have here rated the improved land very low, in making its product but as ten to one, when it is much nearer an hundred to one: for I ask, whether in the wild woods and uncultivated waste of America, left to nature, without any improvement, tillage, or husbandry, a thousand acres yield the needy and wretched inhabitants as many conveniencies of life as ten acres equally fertile land do in Devonshire, where they are well cultivated?

Before the appropriation of land, he who gathered as much of the wild fruit, killed, caught, or tamed, as many of the beasts, as he could; he that so employed his pains about any of the spontaneous products of nature, as any way to alter them from thc state which nature put them in, by placing any of his labour on them, did thereby acquire a propriety in them: but if they perished, in his possession, without their due use; if the fruits rotted, or the venison putrefied, before he could spend it; he offended against the common law of nature, and was liable to be punished; he invaded his neighbour's share, for he had no right, farther than his use called for any of them, and they might serve to afford him conveniencies of life.

§ 40. Nor is it so strange, as perhaps before consideration it may appear, that the property of labour should be able to overbalance the community of land: for it is labour indeed that put the difference of value on every thing; and let any one consider what the difference is between an acre of land planted with tobacco or sugar, sown with wheat or barley, and an acre of the same land lying in common, without any husbandry upon it, and he will find, that the improvement of labour makes the far greater part of the value. I think it will be but a very modest computation to say, that of the products of the earth useful to the life of man, nine-tenths are the effects of labour: nay, if we will rightly estimate things as they come to our use, and cast up the several expenses about them, what in them is purely owning to nature, and what to labour, we shall find, that in most of them ninety-nine hundredths are wholly to be put on the account of labour.

§ 42. To make this a little clear, let us but trace some of the ordinary provisions of life, through their several progresses, before they come to our use, and see how much of their value they receive from human industry. Bread, wine, and cloth, are things of daily use, and great plenty; yet notwithstanding, acorns, water, and leaves, or skins, must be our bread, drink, and clothing, did not labour furnish us with these more useful commodities: for whatever bread is more worth than acorns, wine than water, and cloth or silk than leaves, skins, or moss, that is wholly owing to labour and industry; the one of these being the food and raiment which unassisted nature furnishes us with; the other, provisions which our industry and pains prepare for us; which, how much they exceed the other in value, when any one hath computed, he will then see how much labour makes the far greatest part of the value of things we enjoy in this world: and the ground which produces the materials is scarce to be reckoned in as any, or, at most, but a very small part of it; so little, that even amongst us, land that is left wholly to nature, that hath no improvement of pasturage, tillage, or planting, is called, as indeed it is, waste; and we shall find the benefit of it amount to little more than nothing.

This shows how much numbers of men are to be preferred to largeness of dominions; and that the increase of lands, and the right of employing of them, is the great art of government: and that prince, who shall be so wise and godlike, as by established laws of liberty to secure protection and encouragement to the honest industry of mankind, against the oppression of power and narrowness of party, will quickly be too hard for his neighbours: but this by the by. To return to the argument in hand.

§ 44. From all which it is evident, that though the things of nature are given in common, yet man, by being master of himself, and "proprietor of his own person, and the actions or labour of it, had still in himself the great foundation of property;" and that which made up the greater part of what he applied to the support or comfort of his being, when invention and arts had improved the conveniencies of life, was perfectly his own, and did not belong in common to others.

§ 45. Thus labour, in the beginning, gave a right of property wherever any one was pleased to employ it upon what was common, which remained a long while the far greater part, and is yet more than mankind makes use of. Men, at first, for the most part, contented themselves with what unassisted nature offered to their necessities: and though afterwards, in some parts of the world, (where the increase of people and stock, with the use of money, had made land scarce, and so of some value) the several communities settled the bounds of their distinct territories, and by laws within themselves regulated the properties of the private men of their society, and so, by compact and agreement, settled the property which labour and industry began: and the leagues that have been made between several states and kingdoms, either expressly or tacitly disowning all claim and right to the land in the others' possession, have, by common consent, given up their pretences to their natural common right, which originally they had to those countries, and so have, by positive agreement, settled a property amongst themselves, in distinct parts and parcels of the earth; yet there are still great tracts of ground to be found, which (the inhabitants thereof not having joined with the rest of mankind in the consent of the use of their common money) lie waste, and are more than the people who dwell on it do or can make use of, and so still lie in common;

though this can scarce happen amongst that part of mankind that have consented to the use of money.

§ 46. The greatest part of things really useful to the life of man, and such as the necessity of subsisting made the first commoners of the world look after, as it doth the Americans now, are generally things of short duration; such as, if they are not consumed by use, will decay and perish of themselves.

§ 47. And thus came in the use of money, some lasting thing that men might keep without spoiling, and that by mutual consent men would take in exchange for the truly useful, but perishable supports of life.

§ 48. And as different degrees of industry were apt to give men possessions in different proportions, so this invention of money gave them the opportunity to continue and enlarge them: for supposing an island, separate from all possible commerce with the rest of the world, wherein there were but an hundred families, but there were sheep, horses, and cows, with other useful animals, wholesome fruits, and land enough for corn for a hundred thousand times as many, but nothing in the island, either because of its commonness, or perishableness, fit to supply the place of money; what reason could any one have there to enlarge his possessions beyond the use of his family and a plentiful supply to its consumption, either in what their own industry produced, or they could barter for like perishable, useful commodities with others? Where there is not something, both lasting and scarce, and so valuable, to be hoarded up, there men will not be apt to enlarge their possessions of land, were it ever so rich, ever so free for them to take: for I ask, what would a man value ten thousand, or an hundred thousand acres of excellent land, ready cultivated, and well stocked too with cattle, in the middle of the inland parts of America, where he had no hopes of commerce with other parts of the world, to draw money to him by the sale of the product? It would not be worth the enclosing, and we should see him give up again to the wild common of nature, whatever was more than would supply the conveniencies of life to be had there for him and his family.

§ 49. Thus in the beginning all the world was America, and more so than that is now; for no such thing as money was any where known. Find out something that hath the use and value of money amongst his neighbours, you shall see the same man will begin presently to enlarge his possessions.

§ 50. But since gold and silver, being little useful to the life of man in proportion to food, raiment, and carriage, has its value only from the consent of men, whereof labour yet makes, in great part, the measure;

it is plain, that men have agreed to a disproportionate and unequal possession of the earth; they having, by a tacit and voluntary consent, found out a way how a man may fairly possess more land than he himself can use the product of, by receiving, in exchange for the overplus, gold and silver, which may be hoarded up without injury to any one; these metals not spoiling or decaying in the hands of the possessor. This partage of things in an inequality of private possessions, men have made practicable out of the bounds of society, and without compact; only by putting a value on gold and silver, and tacitly agreeing in the use of money: for in governments, the laws regulate the right of property, and the possession of land is determined by positive constitutions.

§ 51. And thus, I think, it is very easy to conceive, "how labour could at first begin a title of property" in the common things of nature, and how the spreading it upon our uses bounded it. So that there could then be no reason of quarrelling about title, nor any doubt about the largeness of possession it gave. Right and conveniency went together; for as a man had a right to all he could employ his labour upon, so he had no temptation to labour for more than he could make use of. This left no room for controversy about the title, nor for encroachment on the right of others; what portion a man carved to himself was easily seen: and it was useless, as well as dishonest, to carve himself too much, or take more than he needed.

Of political or civil Society.

§ 87. Man being born, as has been proved, with a title to perfect freedom, and uncontrolled enjoyment of all the rights and privileges of the law of nature, equally with any other man, or number of men in the world, hath by nature a power, not only to preserve his property, that is, his life, liberty, and estate, against the injuries and attempts of other men; but to judge of and punish the breaches of that law in others, as he is persuaded the offence deserves, even with death itself, in crimes where the heinousness of the fact, in his opinion, requires it. But because no political society can be, nor subsist, without having in itself the power to preserve the property, and, in order thereunto, punish the offences of all those of that society; there, and there only is political society, where every one of the members hath quitted this natural power, resigned it up into the hands of the community in all cases that exclude him not from appealing for protection to the law established by it. And thus all private judgment of every particular member being excluded, the community comes to be umpire, by settled standing rules, indifferent, and the same to all parties; and by men having authority from the community, for the execution of those rules, decides all the differences that may happen between any members of that society concerning any matter of right; and punishes those offences which any member hath committed against the society, with such penalties as the law has established: whereby it is easy to discern who are, and who are not, in political society together. Those who are united into one body, and have a common established law and judicature to appeal to, with authority to decide controversies between them, and punish offenders, are in civil society one with another: but those who have no such common appeal, I mean on earth, are still in the state of nature, each being, where there is no other, judge for himself, and executioner: which is, as I have before showed it, the perfect state of nature.

§ 88. And thus the commonwealth comes by a power to set down what punishment shall belong to the several transgressions which they think worthy of it, committed amongst the members of that society, (which is the power of making laws) as well as it has the power to punish any injury done unto any of its members, by any one that is not of it, (which is the power of war and peace:) and all this for the preservation of the property of all the members of that society, as far as is possible. But though every man who has entered into civil society, and is become a member of any commonwealth, has thereby quitted his power to punish offences against the law of nature, in prosecution of his own private judgment; yet with the judgment of offences, which he has given up to the legislative in all cases, where he can appeal to the magistrate, he has given a right to the commonwealth to employ his force, for the execution of the judgments of the commonwealth, whenever he shall be called to it; which indeed are his own judgments, they being made by himself, or his representative. And herein we have the original of the legislative and executive power of civil society, which is to judge by standing laws, how far offences are to be punished, when committed within the commonwealth; and also to determine, by occasional judgments founded on the present circumstances of the fact, how far injuries from without are to be vindicated; and in both these to employ all the force of all the members, when there shall be need.

§ 89. Whenever therefore any number of men are so united into one society, as to quit every one his executive power of the law of nature, and to resign it to the public, there and there only is a political or civil society. And this is done, wherever any number of men, in the state of nature, enter into society to make one people, one body politic, under one supreme government; or else when any one joins himself to, and incorporates with any government already made: for hereby he authorizes the society, or, which is all one, the legislative thereof, to make laws for him, as the public good of the society shall require; to the execution whereof, his own assistance (as to his own degrees) is due. And this puts men out of a state of nature into that of a commonwealth, by setting up a judge on earth, with authority to determine all the controversies, and redress the injuries that may happen to any member of the commonwealth; which judge is the legislative, or magistrate appointed by it. And wherever there are any number of men, however associated, that have no such decisive power to appeal to, there they are still in the state of nature.

Of the Beginning of Political Societies.

§ 95. Men being, as has been said, by nature all free, equal, and independent, no one can be put out of this estate, and subjected to the political power of another, without his own consent. The only way whereby any one divests himself of his natural liberty, and puts on the bonds of civil society, is by agreeing with other men to join and unite into a community, for their comfortable, safe, and peaceable living one amongst another, in a secure enjoyment of their properties, and a greater security against any that are not of it. This any number of men may do, because it injures not the freedom of the rest; they are left as they were in the liberty of the state of nature. When any number of men have so consented to make one community or government, they are thereby presently incorporated, and make one body politic, wherein the majority have a right to act and conclude the rest.

§ 96. For when any number of men have, by the consent of every individual, made a community, they have thereby made that community one body, with a power to act as one body, which is only by the will and determination of the majority; for that which acts any community being only the consent of the individuals of it, and it being necessary to that which is one body to move one way; it is necessary the body should move that way whither the greater force carries it, which is the consent of the majority: or else it is impossible it should act or continue one body, one community, which the consent of every individual that united into it agreed that it should; and so every one is bound by that consent to be concluded by the majority. And therefore we see that in assemblies, empowered to act by positive laws, where no number is set by that positive law which empowers them, the act of the majority passes for the act of the whole, and of course determines; as having, by the law of nature and reason, the power of the whole.

§ 97. And thus every man, by consenting with others to make one body politic under one government, puts himself under an obligation to every one of that society to submit to the determination of the majority, and to be concluded by it; or else this original compact, whereby he with others incorporate into one society, would signify nothing, and be no compact, if he be left free, and under no other ties than he was in before in the state of nature. For what appearance would there be of any compact? what new engagement, if he were no farther tied by any decrees of the society than he himself thought fit, and did actually consent to? This would be still as great a liberty as he himself had before his compact, or any one else in the state of nature hath, who may submit himself and consent to any acts of it if he thinks fit.

§ 98. For if the consent of the majority shall not, in reason, be received as the act of the whole, and conclude every individual, nothing but the consent of every individual can make any thing to be the act of the whole: but such a consent is next to impossible ever to be had, if we consider the infirmities of health, and avocations of business, which in a number, though much less than that of a commonwealth, will necessarily keep many away from the public assembly. To which if we add the variety of opinions, and contrariety of interests which unavoidably happen in all collections of men, the coming into society upon such terms would be only like Cato's coming into the theatre, only to go out again. Such a constitution as this would make the mighty leviathan of a shorter duration than the feeblest creatures, and not let it outlast the day it was born in: which cannot be supposed, till we can think that rational creatures should desire and constitute societies only to be dissolved: for where the majority cannot conclude the rest, there they cannot act as one body, and consequently will be immediately dissolved again.

§ 99. Whosoever therefore out of a state of nature unite into a community, must be understood to give up all the power necessary to the ends for which they unite into society, to the majority of the community, unless they expressly agreed in any number greater than the majority. And this is done by barely agreeing to unite into one political society, which is all the compact that is, or need be, between the individuals that enter into, or make up a commonwealth. And thus that which begins and actually constitutes any political society, is nothing but the consent of any number of freemen capable of a majority, to unite and incorporate into such a society. And this is that, and that only, which did or could give beginning to any lawful government in the world.

§ 119. Every man being, as has been showed, naturally free, and nothing being able to put him into subjection to any earthly power, but only his own consent; it is to be considered, what shall be understood to be a sufficient declaration of a man's consent, to make him subject to the laws of any government. There is a common distinction of an express and a tacit consent, which will concern our present case. Nobody doubts but an express consent of any man entering into any society, makes him a perfect member of that society, a subject of that government. The difficulty is, what ought to be looked upon as a tacit consent, and how far it binds, *i.e.* how far any one shall be looked on to have consented, and thereby submitted to any government, where he has made no expressions of it at all. And to this I say, that every man, that hath any possessions, or enjoyment of any part of the dominions of any government, doth thereby give his tacit consent, and is as far forth obliged to obedience to the laws of that government, during such enjoyment, as any one under it; whether this his possession be of land, to him and his heirs for ever, or a lodging only for a week; or whether it be barely travelling freely on the highway; and, in effect, it reaches as far as the very being of any one within the territories of that government.

§ 120. To understand this the better, it is fit to consider, that every man, when he at first incorporates himself into any commonwealth, he, by his uniting himself thereunto, annexes also, and submits to the community those possessions which he has, or shall acquire, that do not already belong to any other government: for it would be a direct contradiction for any one to enter into society with others for the securing and regulating of property, and yet to suppose his land, whose property is to be regulated by the laws of the society, should be exempt from the jurisdiction of that government, to which he himself, the proprietor of the land, is a subject.

§ 122. But submitting to the laws of any country, living quietly, and enjoying privileges and protection under them, makes not a man a member of that society: this is only a local protection and homage due to and from all those, who, not being in a state of war, come within the territories belonging to any government, to all parts whereof the force of its laws extends. But this no more makes a man a member of that society, a perpetual subject of that commonwealth, than it would make a man a subject to another, in whose family he found it convenient to abide for some time; though, whilst he continued in it, he were obliged to comply with the laws, and submit to the government he found there. And thus we see, that foreigners, by living all their lives under another government, and enjoying the privileges and protection of it, though they are bound, even in conscience, to submit to its administration, as far forth as any denison; yet do not thereby come to be subjects or members of that commonwealth. Nothing can make any man so, but his actually entering into it by positive engagement, and express promise and compact. This is that which I think concerning the beginning of political societies, and that consent which makes any one a member of any commonwealth.

Of the Ends of political Society and Government

§ 123. If man in the state of nature be so free as has been said; if he be absolute lord of his own person and possessions, equal to the greatest, and subject to nobody, why will he part with his freedom, why will he give up this empire, and subject himself to the dominion and control of any other power? To which it is obvious to answer, that though in the state of nature he hath such a right, yet the enjoyment of it is very uncertain, and constantly exposed to the invasion of others; for all being kings as much as he, every man his equal, and the greater part no strict observers of equity and justice, the enjoyment of the property he has in this state is very unsafe, very unsecure. This makes him willing to quit a condition, which, however free, is full of fears and continual dangers: and it is not without reason that he seeks out, and is willing to join in society with others, who are already united, or have a mind to unite, for the mutual preservation of their lives, liberties, and estates, which I call by the general name property.

§ 124. The great and chief end, therefore, of men's uniting into commonwealths, and putting themselves under government, is the preservation of their property. To which in the state of nature there are many things wanting.

First, There wants an established, settled, known law, received and allowed by common consent to be the standard of right and wrong, and the common measure to decide all controversies between them: for though the law of nature be plain and intelligible to all rational creatures; yet men being biassed by their interest, as well as ignorant for want of studying it, are not apt to allow of it as a law binding to them in the application of it to their particular cases.

§ 125. Secondly, In the state of nature there wants a known and indifferent judge, with authority to determine all differences according to the established law: for every one in that state being both judge and executioner of the law of nature, men being partial to themselves, passion and revenge is very apt to carry them too far, and with too much heat, in their own cases; as well as negligence and unconcernedness, to make them too remiss in other men's.

§ 126. Thirdly, In the state of nature there often wants power to back and support the sentence when right, and to give it due execution. They who by any injustice offend, will seldom fail, where they are able, by force to make good their injustice; such resistance many times makes the punishment dangerous, and frequently destructive to those who attempt it.

§ 127. Thus mankind, notwithstanding all the privileges of the state of nature, being but in an ill condition, while they remain in it, are quickly driven into society. Hence it comes to pass, that we seldom find any number of men live any time together in this state. The inconveniencies that they are therein exposed to, by the irregular and uncertain exercise of the power every man has of punishing the transgressions of others, make them take sanctuary under the established laws of government, and therein seek the preservation of their property. It is this makes them so willingly give up every one his single power of punishing, to be exercised by such alone as shall be appointed to it amongst them; and by such rules as the community, or those authorized by them to that purpose, shall agree on. And in this we have the original right of both the legislative and executive power, as well as of the governments and societies themselves.

§ 128. For in the state of nature, to omit the liberty he has of innocent delights, a man has two powers.

The first is to do whatsoever he thinks fit for the preservation of himself and others within the permission of the law of nature: by which law, common to them all, he and all the rest of mankind are one community, make up one society, distinct from all other creatures. And, were it not for the corruption and viciousness of degenerate men, there would be no need of any other; no necessity that men should separate from this great and natural community, and by positive agreements combine into smaller and divided associations.

The other power a man has in the state of nature, is the power to punish the crimes committed against that law. Both these he gives up when he joins in a private, if I may so call it, or particular politic society, and incorporates into any commonwealth, separate from the rest of mankind.

§ 129. The first power, viz. "of doing whatsoever he thought fit for the preservation of himself" and the rest of mankind, he gives up to be regulated by laws made by the society, so far forth as the preservation of himself and the rest of that society shall require; which laws of the society in many things confine the liberty he had by the law of nature.

§ 130. Secondly, The power of punishing he wholly gives up, and engages his natural force (which he might before employ in the execution of the law of nature, by his own single authority, as he thought fit), to assist the executive power of the society, as the law thereof shall require: for being now in a new state, wherein he is to enjoy many conveniencies, from the labour, assistance, and society of others in the same community, as well as protection from its whole strength; he is to part also with as much of his natural liberty, in providing for himself, as the good, prosperity, and safety of the society shall require; which is not only necessary, but just, since the other members of the society do the like.

§ 131. But though men, when they enter into society, give up the equality, liberty, and executive power they had in the state of nature, into the hands of the society, to be so far disposed of by the legislative as the good of the society shall require; yet it being only with an intention in every one the better to preserve himself, his liberty and property (for no rational creature can be supposed to change his condition with an intention to be worse); the power of the society, or legislative constituted by them, can never be supposed to extend farther than the common good; but is obliged to secure every one's property, by providing against those three defects above-mentioned, that made the state of nature so unsafe and uneasy. And so whoever has the legislative or supreme power of any commonwealth, is bound to govern by established standing laws, promulgated and known to the people, and not by extemporary decrees; by indifferent and upright judges, who are to decide controversies by those laws; and to employ the force of the community at home, only in the execution of such laws; or abroad to prevent or redress foreign injuries, and secure the community from inroads and invasion. And all this to be directed to no other end but the peace, safety, and public good of the people.

Of the Extent of the legislative Power.

§ 134. The great end of men's entering into society being the enjoyment of their properties in peace and safety, and the great instrument and means of that being the laws established in that society; the first and fundamental positive law of all commonwealths is the establishing of the legislative power; as the first and fundamental natural law, which is to govern even the legislative itself, is the preservation of the society, and (as far as will consist with the public good) of every person in it. This legislative is not only the supreme power of the commonwealth, but sacred and unalterable in the hands where the community have once placed it; nor can any edict of any body else, in what form soever conceived, or by what power soever backed, have the force and obligation of a law, which has not its sanction from that legislative which the public has chosen and appointed: for without this the law could not have that which is absolutely necessary to its being a law, the consent of the society; over whom nobody can have a power to make laws, but by their own consent, and by authority received from them. And therefore all the obedience, which by the most solemn ties any one can be obliged to pay, ultimately terminates in this supreme power, and is directed by those laws which it enacts: nor can any oaths to any foreign power whatsoever, or any domestic subordinate power, discharge any member of the society from his obedience to the legislative, acting pursuant to their trust; nor oblige him to any obedience contrary to the laws so enacted, or farther than they do allow; it being ridiculous to imagine one can be tied ultimately to obey any power in the society which is not supreme.

§ 135. Though the legislative, whether placed in one or more, whether it be always in being, or only by intervals, though it be the supreme power in every commonwealth; yet,

First, It is not, nor can possibly be absolutely arbitrary over the lives and fortunes of the people: for it being but the joint power of every member of the society given up to that person or assembly which is legislator; it can be no more than those persons had in a state of nature before they entered into society, and gave up to the community: for nobody can transfer to another more power than he has in himself; and nobody has an absolute arbitrary power over himself, or over any other, to destroy his own life, or take away the life or property of another. A man, as has been proved, cannot subject himself to the arbitrary power of another; and having in the state of nature no arbitrary power over the life, liberty, or possession of another, but only so much as the law of nature gave him for the preservation of himself and the rest of mankind; this is all he doth, or can give up to the commonwealth, and by it to the legislative power, so that the legislative can have no more than this. Their power, in the utmost bounds of it, is limited to the public good of the society. It is a power that hath no other end but preservation, and therefore can never have a right to destroy, enslave, or designedly to impoverish the subjects. The obligations of the law of nature cease not in society, but only in many cases are drawn closer, and have by human laws known penalties annexed to them, to enforce their observation. Thus the law of nature stands as an eternal rule to all men, legislators as well as others. The rules that they make for other men's actions must, as well as their own and other men's actions be conformable to the law of nature, *i.e.* to the will of God, of which that is a declaration; and the "fundamental law of nature being the preservation of mankind," no human sanction can be good or valid against it.

§ 136. Secondly, The legislative or supreme authority cannot assume to itself a power to rule by extemporary, arbitrary decrees; but is bound to dispense justice, and to decide the rights of the subject, by promulgated, standing laws, and known authorized judges. For the law of nature being unwritten, and so nowhere to be found, but in the minds of men, they who, through passion, or interest, shall miscite, or misapply it, cannot so easily be convinced of their mistake, where there is no established judge: and so it serves not, as it ought, to determine the rights, and fence the properties of those that live under it; especially where every one is judge, interpreter, and executioner of it too, and that in his own case: and he that has right on his side, having ordinarily but his own single strength, hath not force enough to defend himself from injuries, or to punish delinquents. To avoid these inconveniencies, which disorder men's properties in the state of nature, men unite into societies, that they may have the united strength of the whole society to secure and defend their properties, and may have standing rules to bound it, by which every one may know what is his. To this end it is that men give up all their natural power to the society which they enter into, and the community put the legislative power into such hands as they think fit; with this trust, that they shall be governed by declared laws, or else their peace, quiet, and property will still be at the same uncertainty as it was in the state of nature.

§ 137. Absolute arbitrary power, or governing without settled standing laws, can neither of them consist with the ends of society and government, which men would not quit the freedom of the state of nature for, and tie themselves up under, were it not to preserve their lives, liberties, and fortunes, and by stated rules of right and property to secure their peace and quiet. It cannot be supposed that they should intend, had they a power so to do, to give to any one, or more, an absolute arbitrary power over their persons and estates, and put a force into the magistrate's hand to execute his unlimited will arbitrarily upon them. This were to put themselves into a worse condition than the state of nature, wherein they had a liberty to defend their right against the injuries of others, and were upon equal terms of force to maintain it, whether invaded by a single man, or many in combination. Whereas by supposing they have given up themselves to the absolute arbitrary power and will of a legislator, they have disarmed themselves, and armed him, to make a prey of them when he pleases; he being in a much worse condition, who is exposed to the arbitrary power of one man, who has the command of 100,000, than he that is exposed to the arbitrary power of 100,000 single men; nobody being secure that his will, who has such a command, is better than that of other men, though his force be 100,000 times stronger. And therefore, whatever form the commonwealth is under, the ruling power ought to govern by declared and received laws, and not by extemporary dictates and undetermined resolutions; for then mankind will be in a far worse condition than in the state of nature, if they shall have armed one or a few men with the joint power of a multitude, to force them to obey at pleasure the exorbitant and unlimited degrees of their sudden thoughts, or unrestrained, and till that moment unknown wills, without having any measures set down which may guide and justify their actions: for all the power the government has being only for the good of the society, as it ought not to be arbitrary and at pleasure, so it ought to be exercised by established and promulgated laws; that both the people may know their duty, and be safe and secure within the limits of the law; and the rulers too kept within their bounds, and not be tempted, by the power they have in their hands, to employ it to such purposes, and by such measures, as they would not have known, and own not willingly.

§ 138. Thirdly, The supreme power cannot take from any man part of his property without his own consent: for the preservation of property being the end of government, and that for which men enter into society, it necessarily supposes and requires, that the people should have property, without which they must be supposed to lose that, by entering into society, which was the end for which they entered into it; too gross an absurdity for any man to own. Men therefore in society having property, they have such right to the goods, which by the law of the community are theirs, that nobody hath a right to take their substance or any part of it from them, without their own consent: without this they have no property at all; for I have truly no property in that, which another can by right take from me, when he pleases, against my consent. Hence it is a mistake to think, that the supreme or legislative power of any commonwealth can do what it will, and dispose of the estates of the subject arbitrarily, or take any part of them at pleasure. This is not much to be feared in governments where the legislative consists, wholly or in part, in assemblies which are variable, whose members, upon the dissolution of the assembly, are subjects under the common laws of their country, equally with the rest. But in governments where the legislative is in one lasting assembly always in being, or in one man, as in absolute monarchies, there is danger still that they will think themselves to have a distinct interest from the rest of the community; and so will be apt to increase their own riches and power, by taking what they think fit from the people: for a man's property is not at all secure, though there be good and equitable laws to set the bounds of it between him and his fellow-subjects, if he who commands those subjects have power to take from any private man what part he pleases of his property, and use and dispose of it as he thinks good.

§ 139. But government, into whatsoever hands it is put, being, as I have before showed, entrusted with this condition, and for this end, that men might have and secure their properties; the prince, or senate, however it may have power to make laws for the regulating of property between the subjects one amongst another, yet can never have a power to take to themselves the whole or any part of the subject's property without their own consent: for this would be in effect to leave them no property at all. And to let us see, that even absolute power, where it is necessary, is not arbitrary by being absolute, but is still limited by that reason, and confined to those ends, which required it in some cases to be absolute, we need look no farther than the common practice of martial discipline: for the preservation of the army, and in it of the whole commonwealth, requires an absolute obedience to the command of every superior officer, and it is justly death to disobey or dispute the most dangerous or unreasonable of them; but yet we see, that neither the serjeant, that could command a soldier to march up to the mouth of a cannon, or stand in a breach, where he is almost sure to perish, can command that soldier to give him one penny of his money; nor the general, that can condemn him to death for deserting his post, or for not obeying the most desperate orders, can yet, with all his absolute power of life and death, dispose of one farthing of that soldier's estate, or seize one jot of his goods; whom yet he can command any thing, and hang for the least disobedience; because such a blind obedience is necessary to that end for which the commander has his power, viz. the preservation of the rest; but the disposing of his goods has nothing to do with it.

§ 140. It is true, governments cannot be supported without great charge, and it is fit every one who enjoys his share of the protection, should pay out of his estate his proportion for the maintenance of it. But still it must be with his own consent, *i.e.* the consent of the majority, giving it either by themselves, or their representatives chosen by them: for if any one shall claim a power to lay and levy taxes on the people by his own authority, and without such consent of the people, he thereby invades the fundamental law of property, and subverts the end of government: for what property have I in that which another may by right take, when he pleases, to himself?

§ 141. Fourthly, The legislative cannot transfer the power of making laws to any other hands: for it being but a delegated power from the people, they who have it cannot pass it over to others. The people alone can appoint the form of the commonwealth, which is by constituting the legislative, and appointing in whose hands that shall be. And when the people have said, we will submit to rules, and be governed by laws made by such men, and in such forms, nobody else can say other men shall make laws for them; nor can the people be bound by any laws but such as are enacted by those whom they have chosen, and authorized to make laws for them.

John Rawls

Justice As Fairness[1]

The fundamental idea in the concept of justice is that of fairness. It is the aspect of justice for which utilitarianism, in its classical form, is unable to account, but which is represented, even if misleadingly so, in the idea of the social contract. To establish these propositions I shall develop, but of necessity only very briefly, a particular conception of justice by stating two principles which specify it and by considering how they may be thought to arise. The parts of this conception are familiar; but perhaps it is possible by using the notion of fairness as a framework to assemble and to look at them in a new way.

1. Throughout I discuss justice as a virtue of institutions constituting restrictions as to how they may define offices and powers, and assign rights and duties; and not as a virtue of particular actions, or persons. Justice is but one of many virtues of institutions, for these may be inefficient, or degrading, or any of a number of things, without being unjust. Essentially justice is the elimination of arbitrary distinctions and the establishment, within the structure of a practice, of a proper balance between competing claims. I do not argue that the principles given below are *the* principles of justice. It is sufficient for my purposes that they be typical of the family of principles which might reasonably be called principles of justice as shown by the background against which they may be thought to arise.

The first principle is that each person participating in a practice, or affected by it, has an equal right to the most extensive liberty compatible with a like liberty for all; and the second is that inequalities are arbitrary unless it is reasonable to expect that they will work out for everyone's advantage and unless the offices to which they attach, or from which they may be gained, are open to all. These principles express justice as a complex of three ideas: liberty, equality, and reward for contributions to the common advantage.

The first principle holds, of course, only *ceteris paribus*: while there must always be a justification for departing from the initial position of equal liberty (which is defined by the pattern of rights and duties), and

[1] Considerations of space have made it impossible to give appropriate references. I must, however, mention that in the second paragraph of section 3 I am indebted to H. L. A. Hart. See his paper "Are There Any Natural Rights?," *Philosophical Review*, LXIV (1955), pp. 185 f.

the burden of proof is placed upon him who would depart from it, nevertheless, there can be, and often there is, a justification for doing so. One can view this principle as containing the principle that similar cases be judged similarly, or if distinctions are made in the handling of cases, there must be some relevant difference between them (a principle which follows from the concept of a judgment of any kind). It could be argued that justice requires only an equal liberty; but if a greater liberty were possible for all without loss or conflict, then it would be irrational to settle on a lesser liberty. There is no reason for circumscribing rights until they mutually interfere with one another. Therefore no serious distortion of the concept of justice is likely to follow from including within it the concept of the greatest equal liberty instead of simply equal liberty.

The second principle specifies what sorts of inequalities are permissible, where by inequalities it seems best to understand not any difference between offices and positions, since structural differences are not usually an issue (people do not object to there being different offices as such, and so to there being the offices of president, senator, governor, judge, and so on), but differences in the benefits and burdens attached to them either directly or indirectly, such as prestige and wealth, or liability to taxation and compulsory service. An inequality is allowed only if there is reason to believe that the practice with the inequality will work to the advantage of *every* party. This is interpreted to require, first, that there must normally be evidence acceptable to common sense and based on a common fund of knowledge and belief which shows that this is in fact likely to be the case. The principle does not rule out, however, arguments of a theological or metaphysical kind to justify inequalities (e.g., a religious basis for a caste system) provided they belong to common belief and are freely acknowledged by people who may be presumed to know what they are doing.

Secondly, an inequality must work for the common advantage; and since the principle applies to practices, this implies that the representative man in *every* office or position of the practice, when he views it as a going institution, must find it reasonable to prefer his condition and prospects with the inequality to what they would be without it. And finally, the various offices to which special benefits and burdens attach are required to be open to all; and so if, for example, it is to the common advantage to attach benefits to offices (because by doing so not only is the requisite talent attracted to them, but encouraged to give its best efforts once there), they must be won in a fair competition in which contestants are judged on their merits. If some offices were not open, those excluded would normally be justified in feeling wronged, even if they benefited from the greater efforts of those who were allowed to compete for them. Assuming that offices are open, it is necessary only to consider the design of the practices themselves and how they jointly, as a system, work together. It is a mistake to fix attention on the varying relative positions of particular persons and to think that each such change, as a once-for-all transaction, must be in itself just. The system must be judged from a general point of view: unless one is prepared to criticize it from the standpoint of a representative man holding some particular office, one has no complaint against it.

2. Given these principles, one might try to derive them from *a priori* principles of reason, or offer them as known by intuition. These are familiar steps, and, at least in the case of the first principle, might be made with some success. I wish, however, to look at the principles in a different way.

Consider a society where certain practices are already established, and whose members are mutually self-interested: their allegiance to the established practices is founded on the prospect of self-advantage. It need not be supposed that they are incapable of acting from any other motive: if one thinks of the members of this society as families, the individuals thereof may be bound by ties of sentiment and affection. Nor must they be mutually self-interested under all circumstances, but only under those circumstances in which they ordinarily participate in their common practices. Imagine also that the persons in this society are rational: they know their own interests more or less accurately; they are capable of tracing out the likely consequences of adopting one practice rather than another and of adhering to a decision once made; they can resist present temptations and attractions of immediate gain; and the knowledge, or the perception, of the difference between their condition and that of others is not, in itself, a source of great dissatisfaction. Finally, they have roughly similar needs and interests and are sufficiently equal in power and ability to assure that in normal circumstances none is able to dominate the others.

Now suppose that on some particular occasion several members of this society come together to discuss whether any of them has a legitimate complaint against their established institutions. They try first to arrive at the principles by which complaints, and so practices themselves, are to be judged. Their procedure for this is the following: each is to propose the principles upon which he wishes his complaints to be tried with the understanding that, if acknowledged, the complaints of others will be similarly tried, and that no complaints will be heard at all until everyone is roughly of one mind as to how complaints are to be judged. They understand further that the principles proposed and acknowledged on this occasion are to be binding on future occasions. Thus each will be wary of proposing principles which give him a peculiar advantage, supposing them to be accepted, in his present circumstances, since he will be bound by it in future cases the circumstances of which are unknown and in which the principle might well be to his detriment. Everyone is, then, forced to make in advance a firm commitment, which others also may reasonably be expected to make, and no one is able to tailor the canons of a legitimate complaint to fit his own special condition. Therefore each person will propose principles of a general kind which will, to a large degree, gain their sense from the various applications to be made of them. These principles will express the conditions in accordance with which each is least unwilling to have his interests limited in the design of practices on the supposition that the interests of others will be limited likewise. The restrictions which would so arise might be thought of as those a person would keep in mind if he were designing a practice in which his enemy were to assign him his place.

In this account of a hypothetical society the character and respective situations of the parties reflect the circumstances in which questions of justice may be said to arise, and the procedure whereby principles are proposed and acknowledged represents constraints, analogous to those of having a morality, whereby rational and mutually self-interested parties are brought to act reasonably. Given all conditions as described, it would be natural to accept the two principles of justice. Since there is no way for anyone to win special advantage for himself, each might consider it reasonable to acknowledge equality as an initial principle. There is, however, no reason why they should regard this position as final; for if there are inequalities which satisfy the second principle, the immediate gain which equality would allow can be considered as intelligently invested in view of its future return. If, as is quite likely, these inequalities work as incentives to draw out better efforts, the members of this society may look upon them as concessions to human nature: they, like us, may think that people ideally should want to serve one another. But as they are mutually self-interested, their acceptance of these inequalities is merely the acceptance of the relations in which they actually stand. They have no title to complain of one another. And so, provided the conditions of the principle are met, there is no reason why they should reject such inequalities in the design of their social practices. Indeed, it would be short-sighted of them to do so, and could result, it seems, only from their being dejected by the bare knowledge, or perception, that others are better situated. Each person will, however, insist on a common advantage, for none is willing to sacrifice anything for the others.

These remarks are not, of course, offered as a proof that persons so circumstanced would settle upon the two principles, but only to show that the principles of justice could have such a background; and so can be viewed as those principles which mutually self-interested and rational persons, when similarly situated and required to make in advance a firm commitment, could acknowledge as restrictions governing the assignment of rights and duties in their common practices, and thereby accept as limiting their rights against one another.

3. That the principles of justice can be regarded in this way is an important fact about them. It brings out the idea that fundamental to justice is the concept of fairness which relates to right dealing between persons who are coöperating with or competing against one another, as when one speaks of fair games, fair competition, and fair bargains. The question of fairness arises when free persons, who have no authority over one another, are engaging in a joint activity and amongst themselves settling or acknowledging the rules which define it and which determine the respective shares in its benefits and burdens. A practice will strike the parties as fair if none feels that, by participating in it, he, or any of the others, is taken advantage of, or forced to give in to claims which he does not regard as legitimate. This implies that each has a conception of legitimate claims which he thinks it reasonable that others as well as himself should acknowledge. If one thinks of the principles of justice as arising in the way described, then they do define this sort of conception. A practice is just, then, when it satisfies the principles which those who participate in it could propose to one another for mutual acceptance under the aforementioned circumstances. Persons engaged in a just, or fair, practice can face one another honestly, and support their respective positions, should they appear questionable, by reference to principles which it is reasonable to expect each to accept. It is this notion of the possibility of mutual acknowledgement which makes the concept of fairness fundamental to justice. Only if such acknowledgment is possible, can there be true community between persons in their common practices; otherwise their relations will appear to them as founded to some extent on force and violence. If, in ordinary speech, fairness applies more particularly to practices in which there is a choice whether to engage or not, and justice to practices in which there is no choice and one must play, the element of necessity does not alter

the basic conception of the possibility of mutual acceptance, although it may make it much more urgent to change unjust than unfair institutions.

Now if the participants in a practice accept its rules as fair, and so have no complaint to lodge against it, there arises a prima facie duty (and a corresponding prima facie right) of the parties to each other to act in accordance with the practice when it falls upon them to comply. When any number of persons engage in a practice, or conduct a joint undertaking, according to rules, and thus restrict their liberty, those who have submitted to these restrictions when required have a right to a similar acquiescence on the part of those who have benefited by their submission. These conditions will, of course, obtain if a practice is correctly acknowledged to be fair, for in this case, all who participate in it will benefit from it. The rights and duties so arising are special rights and duties in that they depend on previous voluntary actions—in this case, on the parties' having engaged in a common practice and accepted its benefits. It is not, however, an obligation which presupposes a deliberate performative act in the sense of a promise, or contract, and the like. It is sufficient that one has knowingly participated in a practice acknowledged to be fair and accepted the resulting benefits. This prima facie obligation may, of course, be overridden: it may happen, when it comes one's turn to follow a rule, that other considerations will justify not doing so. But one cannot, in general, be released from this obligation by denying the justice of the practice only when it falls on one to obey. If a person rejects a practice, he should, as far as possible, declare his intention in advance, and avoid participating in it or accepting its benefits.

This duty may be called that of fair play, which is, perhaps, to extend the ordinary notion; for acting unfairly is usually not so much the breaking of any particular rule, even if the infraction is difficult to detect (cheating), but taking advantage of loop-holes or ambiguities in rules, availing oneself of unexpected or special circumstances which make it impossible to enforce them, insisting that rules be enforced when they should be suspended, and, more generally, acting contrary to the intention of a practice. (Thus one speaks of the sense of fair play: acting fairly is not simply following rules; what is fair must be felt or perceived.) Nevertheless, it is not an unnatural extension of the duty of fair play to have it include the obligation which participants in a common practice owe to each other to act in accordance with it when their performance falls due. Consider the tax dodger, or the free rider.

The duty of fair play stands beside those of fidelity and gratitude as a fundamental moral notion; and like them it implies a constraint on self-interest in particular cases. I make this point to avoid a misunderstanding: the conception of the mutual acknowledgment of principles under special circumstances is used to analyze the concept of justice. I do not wish to imply that the acceptance of justice in actual conduct depends solely on an existing equality of conditions. My own view, which is perhaps but one of several compatible with the preceding analysis, and which I can only suggest here, is that the acknowledgment of the duty of fair play, as shown in acting on it, and wishing to make amends and the like when one has been at fault, is one of the forms of conduct in which participants in a common practice show their recognition of one another as persons. In the same way that, failing a special explanation, the criterion for the recognition of suffering is helping him who suffers, acknowledging the duty of fair play is the criterion for recognizing another as a person with similar capacities, interests, and feelings as oneself. The acceptance by participants in a common practice of this duty is a reflection in each of the recognition of the aspirations of the others to be realized by their joint activity. Without this acceptance they would recognize one another as but complicated objects in a complicated routine. To recognize another as a person one must respond to him and act towards him as one; and these forms of action and response include, among other things, acknowledging the duty of fair play. These remarks are unhappily obscure; their purpose here is to forestall the misunderstanding mentioned above.

The conception at which we have arrived, then, is that the principles of justice may be thought of as arising once the constraints of having a morality are imposed upon rational and mutually self-interested parties who are related and situated in a special way. A practice is just if it is in accordance with the principles which all who participate in it might reasonably be expected to propose or to acknowledge before one another when they are similarly circumstanced and required to make a firm commitment in advance; and thus when it meets standards which the parties could accept as fair should occasion arise for them to debate its merits. Once persons knowingly engage in a practice which they acknowledge to be fair and accept the benefits of doing so, they are bound by the duty of fair play which implies a limitation of self-interest in particular cases.

Now if a claim fails to meet this conception of justice there is no moral value in granting it, since it violates the conditions of reciprocity and community amongst persons: he who presses it, not being willing to acknowledge it when pressed by another, has no grounds for complaint when it is denied; whereas him against whom it is pressed can complain. As it cannot be mutually acknowledged, it is a resort to coercion: granting the claim is only possible if one party can compel what the other will not admit. Thus in deciding on the justice of a practice it is not enough to ascertain that it answers to wants and interest in the fullest and most effective manner. For if any of these be such that they conflict with justice, they should not be counted; their satisfaction is no reason for having a practice. It makes no sense to concede claims the denial of which gives rise to no complaint in preference to claims the denial of which can be objected to. It would be irrelevant to say, even if true, that it resulted in the greatest satisfaction of desire.

4. This conception of justice differs from that of the stricter form of utilitarianism (Bentham and Sidgwick), and its counterpart in welfare economics, which assimilates justice to benevolence and the latter in turn to the most efficient design of institutions to promote the general welfare. Now it is said occasionally that this form of utilitarianism puts no restrictions on what might be a just assignment of rights and duties. But this is not so. Beginning with the notion that the general happiness can be represented by a social utility function consisting of the sum of individual utility functions with identical weights (this being the meaning of the maxim that each counts for one and no more than one), it is commonly assumed that the utility functions of individuals are similar in all essential respects. Differences are laid to accidents of education and upbringing, and should not be taken into account; and this assumption, coupled with that of diminishing marginal utility, results in a prima facie case for equality. But even if such restrictions are built into the utility function, and have, in practice, much the same result as the application of the principles of justice (and appear, perhaps, to be ways of expressing these principles in the language of mathematics and psychology), the fundamental idea is very different from the conception of justice as reciprocity. Justice is interpreted as the contingent result of a higher order administrative decision whose form is similar to that of an entrepreneur deciding how much to produce of this or that commodity in view of its marginal revenue, or to that of someone distributing goods to needy persons according to the relative urgency of their wants. The choice between practices is thought of as being made on the basis of the allocation of benefits and burdens to individuals (measured by the present capitalized value of the utility of these benefits over the full period of the practice's existence) which results from the distribution of rights and duties established by a practice. The individuals receiving the benefits are not thought of as related in any way: they represent so

many different directions in which limited resources may be allocated. Preferences and interest are taken as given; and their satisfaction has value irrespective of the relations between persons which they represent and the claims which the parties are prepared to make on one another. This value is properly taken into account by the (ideal) legislator who is conceived as adjusting the rules of the system from the center so as to maximize the present capitalized value of the social utility function. The principles of justice will not be violated by a legal system so conceived provided these executive decisions are correctly made; and in this fact the principles of justice are said to find their derivation and explanation.

Some social decisions are, of course, of an administrative sort; namely, when the decision turns on social utility in the ordinary sense: on the efficient use of common means for common ends whose benefits are impartially distributed, or in connection with which the question of distribution is misplaced, as in the case of maintaining public order, or national defense. But as an interpretation of the basis of the principles of justice the utilitarian conception is mistaken. It can lead one to argue against slavery on the grounds that the advantages to the slaveholder do not counter-balance the disadvantages to the slave and to society at large burdened by a comparatively inefficient system of labor. The conception of justice as fairness, when applied to the offices of slaveholder and slave, would forbid counting the advantages of the slaveholder at all. These offices could not be founded on principles which could be mutually acknowledged, so the question whether the slaveholder's gains are great enough to counter-balance the losses to the slave and society cannot arise in the first place.

The difference between the two conceptions is whether justice is a fundamental moral concept arising directly from the reciprocal relations of persons engaging in common practices, and its principles those which persons similarly circumstanced could mutually acknowledge; or whether justice is derivative from a kind of higher order executive decision as to the most efficient design of institutions conceived as general devices for distributing benefits to individuals the worth of whose interests is defined independently of their relations to each other. Now even if the social utility function is constructed so that the practices chosen by it would be just, at least under normal circumstances, there is still the further argument against the utilitarian conception that the various restrictions on the utility function needed to get this result are borrowed from the conception of justice as fairness. The notion that individuals have similar utility functions, for example, is really the first principle of justice under the guise of a psychological law. It is assumed not in the manner of an empirical hypothesis concerning actual desires and interests, but from sensing what must be laid down if justice is not to be violated. There is, indeed, irony in this conclusion; for utilitarians attacked the notion of the original contract not only as a historical fiction but as a superfluous hypothesis: they thought that utility alone provides sufficient grounds for all social obligation, and is in any case the real basis of contractual obligations. But this is not so unless one's conception of social utility embodies within it restrictions whose basis can be understood only if one makes reference to one of the ideas of contractarian thought: that persons must be regarded as possessing an original and equal liberty, and their common practices are unjust unless they accord with principles which persons so circumstanced and related could freely accept.

Part IV

Individual and Society

Introduction

We have begun with the utilitarian claim that the purpose of morality is to promote general happiness. But, as nonconsequentialists argued, this claim must be restricted, because there are some limits which it is morally impermissible to cross even if doing so would promote general happiness. The next step was the examination of the contractarian approach to the establishment of social and political institutions which guarantee that these limits are not violated and which protect the rights of individuals.

The combination of these three moral theories gives the content of *social morality.* Individuals cannot have satisfactory lives unless the requirements of social morality are met. But meeting these requirements does not guarantee satisfactory lives, for people can put their rights to destructive, inconsistent, shortsighted, and ill-considered uses. Thus social morality must be combined with *personal morality*, whose task is to examine what makes lives satisfactory beyond the conditions established by social morality. This raises the questions considered in this and the next section: what is the relation between social and personal morality? how do we resolve conflicts between them? where does one end and the other begin? how far can social morality go in restricting personal morality? what are the morally permissible limits of personal morality?

The first reading in this section is again a hypothetical case study. It concerns a conflict between social morality and personal morality. Members of a society have to decide whether to tolerate a group of people whose personal morality they find repulsive. It sharpens the conflict that although the people with objectionable personal morality have not broken any laws and have not violated anyone's rights, it is reasonable to suppose that they may do so in the future. The case raises the difficult question of how far the social morality of a society can go in determining the content of the personal morality of its members.

The excerpt following the case study is from David Hume's (1711–1776) *An Enquiry Concerning the Principles of Morals.* Hume argues that morality depends on the development of virtuous character-traits. Some virtues are natural; they are found in all human beings. The most important natural virtue is benevolence, the disposition to care about the welfare of at least some other people. Other virtues are acquired through moral education which teaches people about the customs and institutions of their society. The primary concern of social morality is with the development of virtues essential to the welfare of society, while the function of personal morality is to foster virtues people need for living whatever kinds of lives they have chosen within the framework established by social morality. Hume would approach our problem case by considering whether the objectionable personal morality threatens social morality; only if it does would he be in favor of interference.

In the third reading in this section, "Social Morality and Individual Ideal," Peter Strawson presents an influential contemporary approach to drawing the distinction between social and personal morality. He argues that a society is justified in establishing a social morality whose requirements all members must meet. But, he goes on, the justification for this is that it establishes the conditions in which individuals can go on to live many different forms of life. In a society thus arranged, conflict is bound to occur among the diverse forms of life, but Strawson believes that such moral diversity is a benefit, not a defect. He would approach our problem case by asking whether the conflict is within the sphere of personal morality, between popular and unpopular forms of life, or whether it is between social morality and personal morality. If the first, he would encourage it; if the second, he would regard interference as justified.

Problem Case: Rights and Consequences

Paedophilia is a sexual perversion directed toward pre-adolescent children. Paedophiliacs' sexual interests are centered on the very young; they are aroused by them, fantasize about them, often have strong desires to fondle and to be fondled by them, and to have sexual intercourse with them. Acting on this desire is a criminal offense. Every year many people are convicted for this crime. It is supposed, however, that the vast majority of such offenses goes undetected, because the children do not report them; if they report them, they are often not taken seriously; and even if investigated, reasonable conclusions are very difficult to draw, due to lack of evidence.

Paedophiliacs have formed an organization: the American Paedophiliac Association (APA). The aim of APA is to protect and to promote the interests of its members. This involves discussion of public pressures, private desires, the difficulties of living in a society hostile to paedophilia, the attempt to change the law, the establishment of a legal defense fund for poor members, hiring a public relations firm to improve their image, the presentation of films depicting paedophiliac practices, and publishing and distributing similar books and picture magazines.

Some paedophiliacs wish to change, others do not; some receive psychotherapy, others do not; some have been convicted and served sentences, others have not; some act on their desires, others have never done so.

The APA has several very rich and generous members who provide ample funding. At an annual meeting, the membership decides to build a national headquarters, hire a permanent staff, hold frequent meetings, and establish a film, book, and magazine library. After some search, the executive committee selects the town of Middlesex, population 150,000, as the proposed site for their headquarters. For the building and operating of the headquarters, the APA requires various permits from the municipal authorities of Middlesex.

The population of Middlesex is deeply opposed to the whole idea. They regard paedophilia as immoral, they fear for the safety of their children if a large number of paedophiliacs come regularly to their town, and they do not want Middlesex to get a bad name. The municipal authorities agree with the population.

People representing the APA argue that denying their permit application would violate the fundamental rights of APA members. They point out that their organization is lawful; that their members are to be presumed innocent until proven guilty; that the reaction to them comes from an outdated and ignorant view of human sexuality; that there was a time when pre-marital sex was as much condemned as paedophilia is now; and that tolerance, individual freedom, and pluralism are supposed to characterize our society. They protest that such values should apply equally to all persons, and so to them as well.

Does morality require granting the permits to the APA, regardless of the likely consequences, or does it require excluding paedophiliacs, in order to protect the children of Middlesex?

David Hume

An Enquiry Concerning the Principles of Morals

Section I.

OF THE GENERAL PRINCIPLES OF MORALS

Disputes with men, pertinaciously obstinate in their principles, are, of all others, the most irksome; except, perhaps, those with persons, entirely disingenuous, who really do not believe the opinions they defend, but engage in the controversy, from affectation, from a spirit of opposition, or from a desire of showing wit and ingenuity, superior to the rest of mankind. The same blind adherence to their own arguments is to be expected in both; the same contempt of their antagonists; and the same passionate vehemence, in inforcing sophistry and falsehood. And as reasoning is not the source, whence either disputant derives his tenets; it is in vain to expect, that any logic, which speaks not to the affections, will ever engage him to embrace sounder principles.

Those who have denied the reality of moral distinctions, may be ranked among the disingenuous disputants; nor is it conceivable, that any human creature could ever seriously believe, that all characters and actions were alike entitled to the affection and regard of everyone. The difference, which nature has placed between one man and another, is so wide, and this difference is still so much farther widened, by education, example, and habit, that, where the opposite extremes come at once under our apprehension, there is no scepticism so scrupulous, and scarce any assurance so determined, as absolutely to deny all distinction between them. Let a man's insensibility be ever so great, he must often be touched with the images of Right and Wrong; and let his prejudices be ever so obstinate, he must observe, that others are susceptible of like impressions. The only way, therefore, of converting an antagonist of this kind, is to leave him to himself. For, finding that nobody keeps up the controversy with him, it is probable he will, at last, of himself, from mere weariness, come over to the side of common sense and reason.

There has been a controversy started of late, much better worth examination, concerning the general foundation of Morals; whether they be derived from Reason, or from Sentiment; whether we attain the knowledge of them by a chain of argument and induction, or by an immediate feeling and finer internal sense; whether, like all sound judgement of truth and falsehood, they should be the same to every rational intelligent being; or whether, like the perception of beauty and deformity, they be founded entirely on the particular fabric and constitution of the human species. . . .

These arguments on each side (and many more might be produced) are so plausible, that I am apt to suspect, they may, the one as well as the other, be solid and satisfactory, and that *reason* and *sentiment* concur in almost all moral determinations and conclusions. The final sentence, it is probable, which pronounces characters and actions amiable or odious, praise-worthy or blameable; that which stamps on them the mark of honour or infamy, approbation or censure; that which renders morality an active principle and constitutes virtue our happiness, and vice our misery: it is probable, I say, that this final sentence depends on some internal sense or feeling, which nature has made universal in the whole species. For what else can have an influence of this nature? But in order to pave the way for such a sentiment, and give a proper discernment of its object, it is often necessary, we find, that much reasoning should precede, that nice distinctions be made, just conclusions drawn, distant comparisons formed, complicated relations examined, and general facts fixed and ascertained. . . .

Section II.

Of Benevolence

Part I.

It may be esteemed, perhaps, a superfluous task to prove, that the benevolent or softer affections are estimable; and wherever they appear, engage the approbation and good-will of mankind. The epithets *sociable, good-natured, humane, merciful, grateful, friendly, generous, beneficent,* or their equivalents, are known in all languages, and universally express the highest merit, which *human nature* is capable of attaining. Where these amiable qualities are attended with birth and power and eminent abilities, and display themselves in the good government or useful instruction of mankind, they seem even to raise the possessors of them above the rank of *human nature,* and make them approach in some measure to the divine. Exalted capacity, undaunted courage, prosperous success; these may only expose a hero or politician to the envy and ill-will of the public: but as soon as the praises are added of humane and beneficent; when instances are displayed of lenity, tenderness or friendship; envy itself is silent, or joins the general voice of approbation and applause. . . .

Our object here being more the speculative, than the practical part of morals, it will suffice to remark, (what will readily, I believe, be allowed) that no qualities are more intitled to the general good-will and approbation of mankind than beneficence and humanity, friendship and gratitude, natural affection and public spirit, or whatever proceeds from a tender sympathy with others, and a generous concern for our kind and species. These wherever they appear, seem to transfuse themselves, in a manner, into each beholder, and to call forth, in their own behalf, the same favourable and affectionate sentiments, which they exert on all around.

Part II.

We may observe that, in displaying the praises of any humane, beneficent man, there is one circumstance which never fails to be amply insisted on, namely, the happiness and satisfaction, derived to society from his intercourse and good offices. To his parents, we are apt to say, he endears himself by his pious attachment and duteous care still more than by the connexions of nature. His children never feel his authority, but when employed for their advantage. With him, the ties of love are consolidated by beneficence and friendship. The ties of friendship approach, in a fond observance of each obliging office, to those of love and inclination. His domestics and dependants have in him a sure resource; and no longer dread the power of fortune, but so far as she exercises it over him. From him the hungry receive food, the naked clothing, the ignorant and slothful skill and industry. Like the sun, an inferior minister of providence he cheers, invigorates, and sustains the surrounding world.

If confined to private life, the sphere of his activity is narrower; but his influence is all benign and gentle. If exalted into a higher station, mankind and posterity reap the fruit of his labours.

As these topics of praise never fail to be employed, and with success, where we would inspire esteem for any one; may it not thence be concluded, that the utility, resulting from the social virtues, forms, at least, a *part* of their merit, and is one source of that approbation and regard so universally paid to them? . . .

Upon the whole, then, it seems undeniable, *that* nothing can bestow more merit on any human creature than the sentiment of benevolence in an eminent degree; and *that* a *part*, at least, of its merit arises from its tendency to promote the interests of our species, and bestow happiness on human society. We carry our view into the salutary consequences of such a character and disposition; and whatever has so benign an influence, and forwards so desirable an end, is beheld with complacency and pleasure. The social virtues are never regarded without their beneficial tendencies, nor viewed as barren and unfruitful. The happiness of mankind, the order of society, the harmony of families, the mutual support of friends, are always considered as the result of their gentle dominion over the breasts of men.

How considerable a *part* of their merit we ought to ascribe to their utility, will better appear from future disquisitions;[1] as well as the reason, why this circumstance has such a command over our esteem and approbation.[2]

Section III.

Of Justice

Part I.

That Justice is useful to society, and consequently that *part* of its merit, at least, must arise from that consideration it would be a superfluous undertaking to prove. That public utility is the *sole* origin of justice, and that reflections on the beneficial consequences of this virtue are the *sole* foundation of its merit; this proposition, being more curious and important, will better deserve our examination and enquiry.

Let us suppose that nature has bestowed on the human race such profuse *abundance* of all *external* conveniencies, that, without any uncertainty in the event, without any care or industry on our part, every individual finds himself fully provided with whatever his most voracious appetites can want, or luxurious imagination wish or desire. His natural beauty, we shall suppose, surpasses all acquired ornaments: the perpetual clemency of the seasons renders useless all clothes or covering: the raw herbage affords him the most delicious fare; the clear fountain, the richest beverage. No laborious occupation required: no

[1] Sect. III and IV.
[2] Sect. V.

tillage: no navigation. Music, poetry, and contemplation form his sole business: conversation, mirth, and friendship his sole amusement.

It seems evident that, in such a happy state, every other social virtue would flourish, and receive tenfold increase; but the cautious, jealous virtue of justice would never once have been dreamed of. For what purpose make a partition of goods, where every one has already more than enough? Why give rise to property, where there cannot possibly be any injury? Why call this object *mine*, when upon the seizing of it by another, I need but stretch out my hand to possess myself to what is equally valuable? Justice, in that case, being totally useless, would be an idle ceremonial, and could never possibly have place in the catalogue of virtues. . . .

Again; suppose, that, though the necessities of human race continue the same as at present, yet the mind is so enlarged, and so replete with friendship and generosity, that every man has the utmost tenderness for every man, and feels no more concern for his own interest than for that of his fellows; it seems evident, that the use of justice would, in this case, be suspended by such an extensive benevolence, nor would the divisions and barriers of property and obligation have ever been thought of. Why should I bind another, by a deed or promise, to do me any good office, when I know that he is already prompted, by the strongest inclination, to seek my happiness, and would, of himself, perform the desired service; except the hurt, he thereby receives, be greater than the benefit accruing to me? in which case, he knows, that, from my innate humanity and friendship, I should be the first to oppose myself to his imprudent generosity. Why raise land-marks between my neighbour's field and mine, when my heart has made no division between our interests; but shares all his joys and sorrows with the same force and vivacity as if originally my own? Every man, upon this supposition, being a second self to another, would trust all his interests to the discretion of every man; without jealousy, without partition, without distinction. And the whole human race would form only one family; where all would lie in common, and be used freely, without regard to property; but cautiously too, with as entire regard to the necessities of each individual, as if our own interests were most intimately concerned.

In the present disposition of the human heart, it would, perhaps, be difficult to find complete instances of such enlarged affections; but still we may observe, that the case of families approaches towards it; and the stronger the mutual benevolence is among the individuals, the nearer it approaches; till all distinction of property be, in a great measure, lost and confounded among them. Between married persons, the cement of friendship is by the laws supposed so strong as to abolish all division of possessions; and has often, in reality, the force ascribed to it. And it is observable, that, during the ardour of new enthusiasms, when every principle is inflamed into extravagance, the community of goods has frequently been attempted; and nothing but experience of its inconveniencies, from the returning or disguised selfishness of men, could make the imprudent fanatics adopt anew the ideas of justice and of separate property. So true is it, that this virtue derives its existence entirely from its necessary *use* to the intercourse and social state of mankind.

To make this truth more evident, let us reverse the foregoing suppositions; and carrying everything to the opposite extreme, consider what would be the effect of these new situations. Suppose a society to fall into such want of all common necessaries, that the utmost frugality and industry cannot preserve the greater number from perishing, and the whole from extreme misery; it will readily, I believe, be admitted, that the strict laws of justice are suspended, in such a pressing emergence, and give place to the stronger motives of necessity and self-preservation. Is it any crime, after a shipwreck, to seize whatever means or instrument of safety one can lay hold of, without regard to former limitations of property? Or if a city besieged were perishing with hunger; can we imagine, that men will see any means of preservation before them, and lose their lives, from a scrupulous regard to what, in other situations, would be the rules of equity and justice? The use and tendency of that virtue is to procure happiness and security, by preserving order in society: but where the society is ready to perish from extreme necessity, no greater evil can be dreaded from violence and injustice; and every man may now provide for himself by all the means, which prudence can dictate, or humanity permit. The public, even in less urgent necessities, opens granaries, without the consent of proprietors; as justly supposing, that the authority of magistracy may, consistent with equity, extend so far: but were any number of men to assemble, without the tie of laws or civil jurisdiction; would an equal partition of bread in a famine, though effected by power and even violence, be regarded as criminal or injurious?

Suppose likewise, that it should be a virtuous man's fate to fall into the society of ruffians, remote from the protection of laws and government; what conduct must he embrace in that melancholy situation? He sees such a desperate rapaciousness prevail; such a disregard to equity, such contempt of order, such stupid blindness to future consequences, as must immediately have the most tragical conclusion, and must terminate in destruction to the greater number, and in a total dissolution of society to the rest. He, meanwhile, can have no other expedient than to arm himself, to whomever the sword he seizes, or the buckler, may belong: To make provision of all means of defence and security: And his particular regard to justice being no longer of use to his own safety or that of others, he must consult the dictates of self-preservation alone, without concern for those who no longer merit his care and attention.

When any man, even in political society, renders himself by his crimes, obnoxious to the public, he is punished by the laws in his goods and person; that is, the ordinary rules of justice are, with regard to him, suspended for a moment, and it becomes equitable to inflict on him, for the *benefit* of society, what otherwise he could not suffer without wrong or injury.

The rage and violence of public war; what is it but a suspension of justice among the warring parties, who perceive, that this virtue is now no longer of any *use* or advantage to them? The laws of war, which then succeed to those of equity and justice, are rules calculated for the *advantage* and *utility* of that particular state, in which men are now placed. And were a civilized nation engaged with barbarians, who observed no rules even of war, the former must also suspend their observance of them, where they no longer serve to any purpose; and must render every action or rencounter as bloody and pernicious as possible to the first aggressors.

Thus, the rules of equity or justice depend entirely on the particular state and condition in which men are placed, and owe their origin and existence to that utility, which results to the public from their strict and regular observance. Reverse, in any considerable circumstance, the condition of men: Produce extreme abundance or extreme necessity: Implant in the human breast perfect moderation and humanity, or perfect rapaciousness and malice: By rendering justice totally *useless*, you thereby totally destroy its essence, and suspend its obligation upon mankind.

The common situation of society is a medium amidst all these extremes. We are naturally partial to ourselves, and to our friends; but are capable of learning the advantage resulting from a more equitable conduct. Few enjoyments are given us from the open and liberal hand of nature; but by art, labour, and industry, we can extract them in great abundance. Hence the ideas of property become necessary in all civil society: Hence justice derives its usefulness to the public: And hence alone arises its merit and moral obligation.

These conclusions are so natural and obvious, that they have not escaped even the poets, in their descriptions of the felicity attending the golden age or the reign of Saturn. The seasons, in that first period of nature, were so temperate, if we credit these agreeable fictions, that there was no necessity for men to provide themselves with clothes and houses, as a security against the violence of heat and cold: The rivers flowed with wine and milk: The oaks yielded honey; and nature spontaneously produced her greatest delicacies. Nor were these the chief advantages of that happy age. Tempests were not alone removed from nature; but those more furious tempests were unknown to human breasts, which now cause such uproar, and engender such confusion. Avarice, ambition, cruelty, selfishness, were never heard of: Cordial affection, compassion, sympathy, were the only movements with which the mind was yet acquainted. Even the punctilious distinction of *mine* and *thine* was banished from among that happy race of mortals, and carried with it the very notion of property and obligation, justice and injustice.

This *poetical* fiction of the *golden age* is, in some respects, of a piece with the *philosophical* fiction of the *state of nature*; only that the former is represented as the most charming and most peaceable condition, which can possibly be imagined; whereas the latter is painted out as a state of mutual war and violence, attended with the most extreme necessity. On the first origin of mankind, we are told, their ignorance and savage nature were so prevalent, that they could give no mutual trust, but must each depend upon himself and his own force or cunning for protection and security. No law was heard of: No rule of justice known: No distinction of property regarded: Power was the only measure of right; and a perpetual war of all against all was the result of men's untamed selfishness and barbarity. . . .

Whether such a condition of human nature could ever exist, or if it did, could continue so long as to merit the appellation of a *state*, may justly be doubted. Men are necessarily born in a family-society, at least; and are trained up by their parents to some rule of conduct and behaviour. But this must be admitted, that, if such a state of mutual war and violence was ever real, the suspension of all laws of justice, from their absolute inutility, is a necessary and infallible consequence.

The more we vary our views of human life, and the newer and more unusual the lights are in which we survey it, the more shall we be convinced, that the origin here assigned for the virtue of justice is real and satisfactory.

Were there a species of creatures intermingled with men, which, though rational, were possessed of such inferior strength, both of body and mind, that they were incapable of all resistance, and could never, upon the highest provocation, make us feel the effects of their resentment; the necessary consequence, I think, is that we should be bound by the laws of humanity to give gentle usage to these creatures, but should not, properly speaking, lie under any restraint of justice with regard to them, nor could they possess any right or property, exclusive of such arbitrary lords. Our intercourse with them could not be called society, which supposes a degree of equality; but absolute command on the one side, and servile obedience on the other. Whatever we covet, they must instantly resign: Our permission is the only tenure, by which they hold their possessions: Our compassion and kindness the only check, by which they curb our lawless will: And as no inconvenience ever results from the exercise of a power, so firmly established in nature, the restraints of justice and property, being totally *useless*, would never have place in so unequal a confederacy.

This is plainly the situation of men, with regard to animals; and how far these may be said to possess reason, I leave it to others to determine. The great superiority of civilized Europeans above barbarous Indians, tempted us to imagine ourselves on the same footing with regard to them, and made us throw off all restraints of justice, and even of humanity, in our treatment of them. In many nations, the female sex are reduced to like slavery, and are rendered incapable of all property, in opposition to their lordly masters. But though the males, when united, have in all countries bodily force sufficient to maintain this severe tyranny, yet such are the insinuation, address, and charms of their fair companions, that women are commonly able to break the confederacy, and share with the other sex in all the rights and privileges of society.

Were the human species so framed by nature as that each individual possessed within himself every faculty, requisite both for his own preservation and for the propagation of his kind: Were all society and intercourse cut off between man and man, by the primary intention of the supreme Creator: It seems evident, that so solitary a being would be as much incapable of justice, as of social discourse and conversation. Where mutual regards and forbearance serve to no manner of purpose, they would never direct the conduct of any reasonable man. The headlong course of the passions would be checked by no reflection on future consequences. And as each man is here supposed to love himself alone, and to depend only on himself and his own activity for safety and happiness, he would, on every occasion, to the utmost of his power, challenge the preference above every other being, to none of which he is bound by any ties, either of nature or of interest.

But suppose the conjunction of the sexes to be established in nature, a family immediately arises; and particular rules being found requisite for its subsistence, these are immediately embraced; though without comprehending the rest of mankind within their prescriptions. Suppose that several families unite together into one society, which is totally disjoined from all others, the rules, which preserve peace and order, enlarge themselves to the utmost extent of that society; but becoming then entirely useless, lose their force when carried one step further. But again suppose, that several distinct societies maintain a kind of intercourse for mutual convenience and advantage, the boundaries of justice still grow larger, in proportion to the largeness of men's views, and the force of their mutual connexions. History, experience, reason sufficiently instruct us in this natural progress of human sentiments, and in the gradual enlargement of our regards to justice, in proportion as we become acquainted with the extensive utility of that virtue.

Part II.

If we examine the *particular* laws, by which justice is directed, and property determined; we shall still be presented with the same conclusion. The good of mankind is the only object of all these laws and regulations. Not only it is requisite, for the peace and interest of society, that men's possessions should be separated; but the rules, which we follow, in making the separation, are such as can best be contrived to serve farther the interests of society.

We shall suppose that a creature, possessed of reason, but unacquainted with human nature, deliberates with himself what rules of justice or property would best promote public interest, and establish peace and security among mankind: His most obvious thought would be, to assign the largest possessions to the most extensive virtue, and give every one the power of doing good, proportioned to his inclination. In a perfect theocracy, where a being, infinitely intelligent, governs by particular volitions, this rule would certainly have place, and might serve to the wisest purposes: But were mankind to execute such a law; so great is the uncertainty of merit, both from its natural obscurity, and from the self-conceit of each individual, that no determinate rule of conduct would ever result from it; and the total dissolution of society must be the immediate consequence. . . .

It must, indeed, be confessed, that nature is so liberal to mankind, that, were all her presents equally divided among the species, and improved by art and industry, every individual would enjoy all the necessaries, and even most of the comforts of life; nor would ever be liable to any ills, but such as might accidentally arise from the sickly frame and constitution of his body. It must also be confessed, that, wherever we depart from this equality, we rob the poor of more satisfaction than we add to the rich, and that the slight gratification of a frivolous vanity, in one individual, frequently costs more than bread to many families, and even provinces. It may appear withal, that the rule of equality, as it would be highly *useful*, is not altogether *impracticable*; but has taken place, at least in an imperfect degree, in some republics; particularly that of Sparta; where it was attended, it is said, with the most beneficial consequences. Not to mention that the Agrarian laws, so frequently claimed in Rome, and carried into execution in many Greek cities, proceeded, all of them, from a general idea of the utility of this principle.

But historians, and even common sense, may inform us, that, however specious these ideas of *perfect* equality may seem, they are really, at bottom, *impracticable*; and were they not so, would be extremely *pernicious* to human society. Render possessions ever so equal, men's different degrees of art, care, and industry will immediately break that equality. Or if you check these virtues, you reduce society to the most extreme indigence; and instead of preventing want and beggary in a few, render it unavoidable to the whole community. The most rigorous inquisition too is requisite to watch every inequality on its first appearance; and the most severe jurisdiction, to punish and redress it. But besides, that so much authority must soon degenerate into tyranny, and be exerted with great partialities; who can possibly be possessed of it, in such a situation as is here supposed? Perfect equality of possessions, destroying all subordination, weakens extremely the authority of magistracy, and must reduce all power nearly to a level, as well as property.

We may conclude, therefore, that, in order to establish laws for the regulation of property, we must be acquainted with the nature and situation of man; must reject appearances, which may be false, though specious; and must search for those rules, which are, on the whole, most *useful* and *beneficial*. Vulgar sense and slight experience are sufficient for this purpose; where men give not way to too selfish avidity, or too extensive enthusiasm.

Who sees not, for instance, that whatever is produced or improved by a man's art or industry ought, for ever, to be secured to him, in order to give encouragement to such *useful* habits and accomplishments? That the property ought also to descend to children and relations, for the same *useful* purpose? That it may be alienated by consent, in order to beget that commerce and intercourse, which is so *beneficial* to human society? And that all contracts and promises ought carefully to be fulfilled, in order to secure mutual trust and confidence, by which the general *interest* of mankind is so much promoted?

Examine the writers on the laws of nature; and you will always find, that, whatever principles they set out with, they are sure to terminate here at last, and to assign, as the ultimate reason for every rule which they establish, the convenience and necessities of mankind. A concession thus extorted, in opposition to systems, has more authority than if it had been made in prosecution of them.

What other reason, indeed, could writers ever give, why this must be *mine* and that *yours*; since uninstructed nature surely never made any such distinction? The objects which receive those appellations are, of themselves, foreign to us; they are totally disjoined and separated from us; and nothing but the general interests of society can form the connexion.

Sometimes the interests of society may require a rule of justice in a particular case; but may not determine any particular rule, among several, which are all equally beneficial. In that case, the slightest *analogies* are laid hold of, in order to prevent that indifference and ambiguity, which would be the source of perpetual dissension. Thus possession alone, and first possession, is supposed to convey property, where no body else has any preceding claim and pretension. Many of the reasonings of lawyers are of this analogical nature, and depend on very slight connexions of the imagination.

Does any one scruple, in extraordinary cases, to violate all regard to the private property of individuals, and sacrifice to public interest a distinction, which had been established for the sake of that interest? The safety of the people is the supreme law: All other particular laws are subordinate to it, and dependent on it: And if, in the *common* course of things, they be followed and regarded; it is only because the public safety and interest *commonly* demand so equal and impartial an administration.

Sometimes both *utility* and *analogy* fail, and leave the laws of justice in total uncertainty. Thus, it is highly requisite, that prescription or long possession should convey property; but what number of days or months or years should be sufficient for that purpose, it is impossible for reason alone to determine. *Civil laws* here supply the place of the natural *code*, and assign different terms for prescription, according to the different *utilities*, proposed by the legislator. Bills of exchange and promissory notes, by the laws of most countries, prescribe sooner than bonds, and mortgages, and contracts of a more formal nature.

In general we may observe that all questions of property are subordinate to the authority of civil laws, which extend, restrain, modify, and alter the rules of natural justice, according to the particular *convenience* of each community. The laws have, or ought to have, a constant reference to the constitution of government, the manners, the climate, the religion, the commerce, the situation of each society. A late author of genius, as well as learning, has prosecuted this subject at large, and has established, from these principles, a system of political knowledge, which abounds in ingenious and brilliant thoughts, and is not wanting in solidity. . . .

What is a man's property? Anything which it is lawful for him, and for him alone, to use. *But what rule have we, by which we can distinguish these objects?* Here we must have recourse to statutes, customs, precedents, analogies, and a hundred other circumstances; some of which are constant and inflexible, some variable and arbitrary. But the ultimate point, in which they all professedly terminate, is the interest and happiness of human society. Where this enters not into consideration, nothing can appear more whimsical, unnatural, and even superstitious, than all or most of the laws of justice and of property. . . .

But there is this material difference between *superstition* and *justice*, that the former is frivolous, useless, and burdensome; the latter is absolutely requisite to the well-being of mankind and existence of society. When we abstract from this circumstance (for it is too apparent ever to be overlooked) it must be confessed, that all regards to right and property, seem entirely without foundation, as much as the grossest and most vulgar superstition. Were the interests of society nowise concerned, it is as unintelligible why another's articulating certain sounds implying consent, should change the nature of my actions with regard to a particular object, as why the reciting of a liturgy by a priest, in a certain habit and posture, should dedicate a heap of brick and timber, and render it, thenceforth and for ever, sacred. . . .

These reflections are far from weakening the obligations of justice, or diminishing anything from the most sacred attention to property. On the contrary, such sentiments must acquire new force from the present reasoning. For what stronger foundation can be desired or conceived for any duty, than to observe, that human society, or even human nature, could not subsist without the establishment of it; and will still arrive at greater degrees of happiness and perfection, the more inviolable the regard is, which is paid to that duty? . . .

What alone will beget a doubt concerning the theory, on which I insist, is the influence of education and acquired habits, by which we are so accustomed to blame injustice, that we are not, in every instance, conscious of any immediate reflection on the pernicious consequences of it. The views the most familiar to us are apt, for that very reason, to escape us; and what we have very frequently performed from certain motives, we are apt likewise to continue mechanically, without recalling, on every occasion, the reflections, which first determined us. The convenience, or rather necessity, which leads to justice is so universal, and everywhere points so much to the same rules, that the habit takes place in all societies; and it is not without some scrutiny, that we are able to ascertain its true origin. The matter, however, is not so obscure, but that even in common life we have every moment recourse to the principle of public utility, and ask, *What must become of the world, if such practices prevail? How could society subsist under such disorders?* Were the distinction or separation of possessions entirely useless, can any one conceive, that it ever should have obtained in society?

Thus we seem, upon the whole, to have attained a knowledge of the force of that principle here insisted on, and can determine what degree of esteem or moral approbation may result from reflections on public interest and utility. The necessity of justice to the support of society is the sole foundation of that virtue; and since no moral excellence is more highly esteemed, we may conclude that this circumstance of usefulness has, in general, the strongest energy, and most entire commands over our sentiments. It must, therefore, be the source of a considerable part of the merit ascribed to humanity, benevolence, friendship, public spirit, and other social virtues of that stamp; as it is the sole source of the moral approbation paid to fidelity, justice, veracity, integrity, and those other estimable and useful qualities and principles. . . .

Section V.

Why Utility Pleases.

Part I.

It seems so natural a thought to ascribe to their utility the praise, which we bestow on the social virtues, that one would expect to meet with this principle everywhere in moral writers, as the chief foundation of their reasoning and enquiry. In common life, we may observe, that the circumstance of utility is always appealed to; nor is it supposed, that a greater eulogy can be given to any man, than to display his usefulness to the public, and enumerate the services, which he has performed to mankind and society. . . .

From the apparent usefulness of the social virtues, it has readily been inferred by sceptics, both ancient and modern, that all moral distinctions arise from education, and were, at first, invented, and afterwards encouraged, by the art of politicians, in order to render men tractable, and subdue their natural ferocity and selfishness, which incapacitated them for society. This principle, indeed, of precept and education, must so far be owned to have a powerful influence, that it may frequently increase or diminish, beyond their natural standard, the sentiments of approbation or dislike; and may even, in particular instances, create, without any natural principle, a new sentiment of this kind; as is evident in all superstitious practices and observances: But that *all* moral affection or dislike arises from this origin, will never surely be allowed by any judicious enquirer. Had nature made no such distinction, founded on the original constitution of the mind, the words, *honourable* and *shameful*, *lovely* and *odious*, *noble* and *despicable*, had never had place in any language; nor could politicians, had they invented these terms, ever have been able to render them intelligible, or make them convey any idea to the audience. So that nothing can be more superficial than this paradox of the sceptics; and it were well, if, in the abstruser studies of logic and metaphysics, we could as easily obviate the cavils of that sect, as in the practical and more intelligible sciences of politics and morals.

The social virtues must, therefore, be allowed to have a natural beauty and amiableness, which, at first, antecedent to all precept or education, recommends them to the esteem of uninstructed mankind, and engages their affections. And as the public utility of these virtues is the chief circumstance, whence they derive their merit, it follows, that the end, which they have a tendency to promote, must be some way agreeable to us, and take hold of some natural affection. It must please, either from considerations of self-interest, or from more generous motives and regards.

It has often been asserted, that, as every man has a strong connexion with society, and perceives the impossibility of his solitary subsistence, he becomes, on that account, favourable to all those habits or principles, which promote order in society, and insure to him the quiet possessions of so inestimable a blessing. As much as we value our own happiness and welfare, as much must we applaud the practice of justice and humanity, by which alone the social confederacy can be maintained, and every man reap the fruits of mutual protection and assistance.

This deduction of morals from self-love, or a regard to private interest, is an obvious thought, and has not arisen wholly from the wanton sallies and sportive assaults of the sceptics. . . . [Y]et . . . the voice of nature and experience seems plainly to oppose the selfish theory.

We frequently bestow praise on virtuous actions, performed in very distant ages and remote countries; where the utmost subtilty of imagination would not discover any appearance of self-interest, or find any connexion of our present happiness and security with events so widely separated from us.

A generous, a brave, a noble deed, performed by an adversary, commands our approbation; while in its consequences it may be acknowledged prejudicial to our particular interest.

Where private advantage concurs with general affection for virtue, we readily perceive and avow the mixture of these distinct sentiments, which have a very different feeling and influence on the mind. We praise, perhaps, with more alacrity, where the generous humane action contributes to our particular interest: But the topics of praise, which we insist on, are very wide of this circumstance. And we may attempt to bring over others to our sentiments, without endeavouring to convince them, that they reap any advantage from the actions which we recommend to their approbation and applause.

Frame the model of a praiseworthy character, consisting of all the most amiable moral virtues: Give instances, in which these display themselves after an eminent and extraordinary manner: You readily engage the esteem and approbation of all your audience, who never so much as enquire in what age and country the person lived, who possessed these noble qualities: A circumstance, however, of all others, the most material to self-love, or a concern for our own individual happiness. . . .

It is but a weak subterfuge, when pressed by these facts and arguments, to say, that we transport ourselves, by the force of imagination, into distant ages and countries, and consider the advantage, which we should have reaped from these characters, had we been contemporaries, and had any commerce with the persons. It is not conceivable, how a *real* sentiment or passion can ever arise from a known *imaginary* interest; especially when our *real* interest is still kept in view, and is often acknowledged to be entirely distinct from the imaginary, and even sometimes opposite to it. . . .

Usefulness is agreeable, and engages our approbation. This is a matter of fact, confirmed by daily observation. But, *useful*? For what? For somebody's interest, surely. Whose interest then? Not our own only: For our approbation frequently extends farther. It must, therefore, be the interest of those, who are served by the character or action approved of; and these we may conclude, however remote, are not totally indifferent to us. By opening up this principle, we shall discover one great source of moral distinctions.

Part II.

Self-love is a principle in human nature of such extensive energy, and the interest of each individual is, in general, so closely connected with that of the community, that those philosophers were excusable, who fancied that all our concern for the public might be resolved into a concern for our own happiness and preservation. They saw every moment, instances of approbation or blame, satisfaction or displeasure towards characters and actions; they denominated the objects of these sentiments, *virtues*, or *vices*; they observed, that the former had a tendency to increase the happiness, and the latter the misery of mankind; they asked, whether it were possible that we could have any general concern for society, or any disinterested resentment of the welfare or injury of others; they found it simpler to consider all these sentiments as modifications of self-love; and they discovered a pretence, at least, for this unity of principle, in that close union of interest, which is so observable between the public and each individual.

But notwithstanding this frequent confusion of interests, it is easy to attain what natural philosophers, after Lord Bacon, have affected to call the *experimentum crucis*, or that experiment which points out the right way in any doubt or ambiguity. We have found instances, in which private interest was separate from public; in which it was even contrary: And yet we observed the moral sentiment to continue, notwithstanding this disjunction of interests. And wherever these distinct interests sensibly concurred, we always found a sensible increase of the sentiment, and a more warm affection to virtue, and detestation of vice, or what we properly call, *gratitude* and *revenge*. Compelled by these instances, we must renounce the theory, which accounts for every moral sentiment by the principle of self-love. We must adopt a more public affection, and allow, that the interests of society are not, even on their own account, entirely indifferent to us. Usefulness is only a tendency to a certain end; and it is a contradiction in terms, that anything pleases as means to an end, where the end itself no wise affects us. If usefulness, therefore, be a source of moral sentiment, and if this usefulness be not always considered with a reference to self; it follows, that everything, which contributes to the happiness of society, recommends itself directly to our approbation and good-will. Here is a principle, which accounts, in great part, for the origin of morality: And what need we seek for abstruse and remote systems, when there occurs one so obvious and natural?[3] . . .

If any man from a cold insensibility, or narrow selfishness of temper, is unaffected with the images of human happiness or misery, he must be equally indifferent to the images of vice and virtue: As, on the other hand, it is always found, that a warm concern for the interests of our species is attended with a delicate feeling of all moral distinctions; a strong resentment of injury done to men; a lively approbation of their welfare. In this particular, though great superiority is observable of one man above another; yet none are so entirely indifferent to the interest of their fellow-creatures, as to perceive no distinctions of moral good and evil, in consequence of the different tendencies of actions and principles. How, indeed, can we suppose it possible in any one, who wears a human heart, that if there be subjected to his censure, one character or system of conduct, which is beneficial, and another which is pernicious to his species or community, he will not so much as give a cool preference to the former, or ascribe to it the smallest merit or regard? Let us suppose such a person ever so selfish; let private interest have ingrossed ever so much his attention; yet in instances, where that is not concerned, he must unavoidably feel *some* propensity to the good of mankind, and make it an object of choice, if everything else be equal. Would any man, who is walking along, tread as willingly on another's gouty toes, whom he has no quarrel with, as on the hard flint and pavement? There is here surely a difference in the case. We surely take into consideration the happiness and misery of others, in weighing the several motives of action, and incline to the former, where no private regards draw us to seek our own promotion or advantage by the injury

[3] It is needless to push our researches so far as to ask, why we have humanity or a fellow-feeling with others. It is sufficient, that this is experienced to be a principle in human nature. We must stop somewhere in our examination of causes; and there are, in every science, some general principles, beyond which we cannot hope to find any principle more general. No man is absolutely indifferent to the happiness and misery of others. The first has a natural tendency to give pleasure; the second, pain. This every one may find in himself. It is not probable, that these principles can be resolved into principles more simple and universal, whatever attempts may have been made to that purpose. But if it were possible, it belongs not to the present subject; and we may here safely consider these principles as original: happy, if we can render all the consequences sufficiently plain and perspicuous!

of our fellow-creatures. And if the principles of humanity are capable, in many instances, of influencing our actions, they must, at all times, have *some* authority over our sentiments, and give us a general approbation of what is useful to society, and blame of what is dangerous or pernicious. The degrees of these sentiments may be the subject of controversy; but the reality of their existence, one should think, must be admitted in every theory or system. . . .

Section IX.

Conclusion.

Part I.

It may justly appear surprising that any man in so late an age, should find it requisite to prove, by elaborate reasoning, that Personal Merit consists altogether in the possession of mental qualities, *useful* or *agreeable* to the *person himself* or to *others*. It might be expected that this principle would have occurred even to the first rude, unpractised enquirers concerning morals, and been received from its own evidence, without any argument or disputation. Whatever is valuable in any kind, so naturally classes itself under the division of *useful* or *agreeable*, the *utile* or the *dulce*, that it is not easy to imagine why we should ever seek further, or consider the question as a matter of nice research or inquiry. And as every thing useful or agreeable must possess these qualities with regard either to the *person himself* or to *others*, the complete delineation or description of merit seems to be performed as naturally as a shadow is cast by the sun, or an image is reflected upon water. If the ground, on which the shadow is cast, be not broken and uneven; nor the surface from which the image is reflected, disturbed and confused; a just figure is immediately presented, without any art or attention. And it seems a reasonable presumption, that systems and hypotheses have perverted our natural understanding, when a theory, so simple and obvious, could so long have escaped the most elaborate examination.

But however the case may have fared with philosophy, in common life these principles are still implicitly maintained; nor is any other topic of praise or blame ever recurred to, when we employ any panegyric or satire, any applause or censure of human action and behaviour. If we observe men, in every intercourse of business or pleasure, in every discourse and conversation, we shall find them nowhere, except in the schools, at any loss upon this subject. . . .

And as every quality which is useful or agreeable to ourselves or others is, in common life, allowed to be a part of personal merit; so no other will ever be received, where men judge of things by their natural, unprejudiced reason, without the delusive glosses of superstition and false religion. Celibacy, fasting, penance, mortification, self-denial, humility, silence, solitude, and the whole train of monkish virtues; for what reason are they everywhere rejected by men of sense, but because they serve to no manner of purpose; neither advance a man's fortune in the world, nor render him a more valuable member of society; neither qualify him for the entertainment of company, nor increase his power of self-enjoyment? We observe, on the contrary, that they cross all these desirable ends; stupify the understanding and harden the heart, obscure the fancy and sour the temper. We justly, therefore, transfer them to the opposite column, and place them in the catalogue of vices; nor has any superstition force sufficient among men of the world, to pervert entirely these natural sentiments. A gloomy, hair-brained enthusiast, after his death, may have a place in the calendar; but will scarcely ever be admitted, when alive, into intimacy and society, except by those who are as delirious and dismal as himself.

It seems a happiness in the present theory, that it enters not into that vulgar dispute concerning the *degrees* of benevolence or self-love, which prevail in human nature; a dispute which is never likely to have any issue, both because men, who have taken part, are not easily convinced, and because the phenomena, which can be produced on either side, are so dispersed, so uncertain, and subject to so many interpretations, that it is scarcely possible accurately to compare them, or draw from them any determinate inference or conclusion. It is sufficient for our present purpose, if it be allowed, what surely, without the greatest absurdity cannot be disputed, that there is some benevolence, however small, infused into our bosom; some spark of friendship for human kind; some particle of the dove kneaded into our frame, along with the elements of the wolf and serpent. Let these generous sentiments be supposed ever so weak; let them be insufficient to move even a hand or finger of our body, they must still direct the determinations of our mind, and where everything else is equal, produce a cool preference of what is useful and serviceable to mankind, above what is pernicious and dangerous. A *moral distinction*, therefore, immediately arises; a general sentiment of blame and approbation; a tendency, however faint, to the objects of the one, and a proportionable aversion to those of the other. Nor will those reasoners, who so earnestly maintain the predominant selfishness of human kind, be any wise scandalized at hearing of the weak sentiments of virtue implanted in our nature. On the contrary, they are found as ready to maintain the one tenet as the other; and their spirit of satire (for such it appears, rather than of corruption) naturally gives rise to both opinions; which have, indeed, a great and almost an indissoluble connexion together.

Avarice, ambition, vanity, and all passions vulgarly, though improperly, comprised under the denomination of *self-love*, are here excluded from our theory concerning the origin of morals, not because they are too weak, but because they have not a proper direction for that purpose. The notion of morals implies some sentiment common to all mankind, which recommends the same object to general approbation, and makes every man, or most men, agree in the same opinion or decision concerning it. It also implies some sentiment, so universal and comprehensive as to extend to all mankind, and render the actions and conduct, even of the persons the most remote, an object of applause or censure, according as they agree or disagree with that rule of right which is established. These two requisite circumstances belong alone to the sentiment of humanity here insisted on. The other passions produce in every breast, many strong sentiments of desire and aversion, affection and hatred; but these neither are felt so much in common, nor are so comprehensive, as to be the foundation of any general system and established theory of blame or approbation.

When a man denominates another his *enemy*, his *rival*, his *antagonist*, his *adversary*, he is understood to speak the language of self-love, and to express sentiments, peculiar to himself, and arising from his particular circumstances and situation. But when he bestows on any man the epithets of *vicious* or *odious* or *depraved*, he then speaks another language, and expresses sentiments, in which he expects all his audience are to concur with him. He must here, therefore, depart from his private and particular situation, and must choose a point of view, common to him with others; he must move some universal principle of the human frame, and touch a string to which all mankind have an accord and symphony. If he mean, therefore, to express that this man possesses qualities, whose tendency is pernicious to society, he has chosen this common point of view, and has touched the principle of humanity, in which every man, in some degree, concurs. While the human heart is compounded of the same elements as at present, it will never be wholly indifferent to public good, nor entirely unaffected with the tendency of characters and manners. And though this affection of humanity may not generally be esteemed so strong as vanity or ambition, yet, being common to all men, it can alone be the foundation of morals, or of any general system of blame or praise. One man's ambition is not another's ambition, nor will the same event or object satisfy both; but the humanity of one man is the humanity of every one, and the same object touches this passion in all human creatures.

But the sentiments, which arise from humanity, are not the same in all human creatures, and produce the same approbation or censure; but they also comprehend all human creatures; nor is there any one whose conduct or character is not, by their means, an object to every one of censure or approbation. On the contrary, those other passions, commonly denominated selfish, both produce different sentiments in each individual, according to his particular situation; and also contemplate the greater part of mankind with the utmost indifference and unconcern. Whoever has a high regard and esteem for me flatters my vanity; whoever expresses contempt mortifies and displeases me; but as my name is known but to a small part of mankind, there are few who come within the sphere of this passion, or excite, on its account, either my affection or disgust. But if you represent a tyrannical, insolent, or barbarous behaviour, in any country or in any age of the world, I soon carry my eye to the pernicious tendency of such a conduct, and feel the sentiment of repugnance and displeasure towards it. No character can be so remote as to be, in this light, wholly indifferent to me. What is beneficial to society or to the person himself must still be preferred. And every quality or action, of every human being, must, by this means, be ranked under some class or denomination, expressive of general censure or applause.

What more, therefore, can we ask to distinguish the sentiments, dependent on humanity, from those connected with any other passion, or to satisfy us, why the former are the origin of morals, not the latter? Whatever conduct gains my approbation, by touching my humanity, procures also the applause of all mankind, by affecting the same principle in them; but what serves my avarice or ambition pleases these passions in me alone, and affects not the avarice and ambition of the rest of mankind. There is no circumstance of conduct in any man, provided it have a beneficial tendency, that is not agreeable to my humanity, however remote the person; but every man, so far removed as neither to cross nor serve my avarice and ambition, is regarded as wholly indifferent by those passions. The distinction, therefore, between these species of sentiment being so great and evident, language must soon be moulded upon it, and must invent a peculiar set of terms, in order to express those universal sentiments of censure or approbation, which arise from humanity, or from views of general usefulness and its contrary. Virtue and Vice become then known; morals are recognized; certain general ideas are framed of human conduct and behaviour; such measures are expected from men in such situations. This action is determined to be conformable to our abstract rule; that other, contrary. And by such universal principles are the particular sentiments of self-love frequently controlled and limited. . . .

But these principles, we must remark, are social and universal; they form, in a manner, the *party* of humankind against vice or disorder, its common enemy. And as the benevolent concern for others is diffused, in a greater or less degree, over all men, and is the same in all, it occurs more frequently in discourse, is cherished by society and conversation, and the blame and approbation, consequent on it, are thereby roused from that lethargy into which they are probably lulled, in solitary and uncultivated nature. Other passions, though perhaps originally stronger, yet being selfish and private, are often overpowered by its force, and yield the dominion of our breast to those social and public principles.

Another spring of our constitution, that brings a great addition of force to moral sentiments, is the love of fame; which rules, with such uncontrolled authority, in all generous minds, and is often the grand object of all their designs and undertakings. By our continual and earnest pursuit of a character, a name, a reputation in the world, we bring our own deportment and conduct frequently in review, and consider how they appear in the eyes of those who approach and regard us. This constant habit of surveying ourselves, as it were, in reflection, keeps alive all the sentiments of right and wrong, and begets, in noble natures, a certain reverence for themselves as well as others, which is the surest guardian of every virtue. The animal conveniencies and pleasures sink gradually in their value; while every inward beauty and moral grace is studiously acquired, and the mind is accomplished in every perfection, which can adorn or embellish a rational creature.

Here is the most perfect morality with which we are acquainted: here is displayed the force of many sympathies. Our moral sentiment is itself a feeling chiefly of that nature, and our regard to a character with others seems to arise only from a care of preserving a character with ourselves; and in order to attain this end, we find it necessary to prop our tottering judgement on the correspondent approbation of mankind.

But, that we may accommodate matters, and remove if possible every difficulty, let us allow all these reasonings to be false. Let us allow that, when we resolve the pleasure, which arises from views of utility, into the sentiments of humanity and sympathy, we have embraced a wrong hypothesis. Let us confess it necessary to find some other explication of that applause, which is paid to objects, whether inanimate, animate, or rational, if they have a tendency to promote the welfare and advantage of mankind. However difficult it be to conceive that an object is approved of on account of its tendency to a certain end, while the end itself is totally indifferent: let us swallow this absurdity, and consider what are the consequences. The preceding delineation or definition of Personal Merit must still retain its evidence and authority: it must still be allowed that every quality of the mind, which is *useful* or *agreeable* to the *person himself* or to *others*, communicates a pleasure to the spectator, engages his esteem, and is admitted under the honourable denomination of virtue or merit. Are not justice, fidelity, honour, veracity, allegiance, chastity, esteemed solely on account of their tendency to promote the good of society? Is not that tendency inseparable from humanity, benevolence, lenity, generosity, gratitude, moderation, tenderness, friendship, and all the other social virtues? Can it possibly be doubted that industry, discretion, frugality, secrecy, order, perseverance, forethought, judgement, and this whole class of virtues and accomplishments, of which many pages would not contain the catalogue; can it be doubted, I say, that the tendency of these qualities to promote the interest and happiness of their possessor, is the sole foundation of their merit? Who can dispute that a mind, which supports a perpetual serenity and cheerfulness, a noble dignity and undaunted spirit, a tender affection and good-will to all around; as it has more enjoyment within itself, is also a more animating and rejoicing spectacle, than if dejected with melancholy, tormented with anxiety, irritated with rage, or sunk into the most abject baseness and degeneracy? And as to the qualities, immediately *agreeable to others*, they speak sufficiently for themselves; and he must be unhappy, indeed, either in his own temper, or in his situation and company, who has never perceived the charms of a facetious wit or flowing affability, of a delicate modesty or decent genteelness of address and manner. . . .

Part II.

Having explained the moral *approbation* attending merit or virtue, there remains nothing but briefly to consider our interested *obligation* to it, and to inquire whether every man, who has any regard to his own happiness and welfare, will not best find his account in the practice of every moral duty. If this can be clearly ascertained from the foregoing theory, we shall have the satisfaction to reflect, that we have advanced principles, which not only, it is hoped, will stand the test of reasoning and inquiry, but may contribute to the amendment of men's lives, and their improvement in morality and social virtue. And though the philosophical truth of any proposition by no means depends on its tendency to promote the interests of society; yet a man has but a bad grace, who delivers a theory, however true, which, he must confess, leads to a practice dangerous and pernicious. Why rake into those corners of nature which spread a nuisance all around? Why dig up the pestilence from the pit in which it is buried? The ingenuity of your researches may be admired, but your systems will be detested; and mankind will agree, if they cannot refute them, to sink them, at least, in eternal silence and oblivion. Truths which are *pernicious* to society, if any such there be, will yield to errors which are salutary and *advantageous.*

But what philosophical truths can be more advantageous to society, than those here delivered, which represent virtue in all her genuine and most engaging charms, and makes us approach her with ease, familiarity, and affection? The dismal dress falls off, with which many divines, and some philosophers, have covered her; and nothing appears but gentleness, humanity beneficence, affability; nay, even at proper intervals, play, frolic, and gaiety. She talks not of useless austerities and rigours, suffering and self-denial. She declares that her sole purpose is to make her votaries and all mankind, during every instant of their existence, if possible, cheerful and happy; nor does she ever willingly part with any pleasure but in hopes of ample compensation in some other period of their lives. The sole trouble which she demands, is that of just calculation, and a steady preference of the greater happiness. And if any austere pretenders approach her, enemies to joy and pleasure, she either rejects them as hypocrites and deceivers; or, if she admit them in her train, they are ranked, however, among the least favoured of her votaries.

And, indeed, to drop all figurative expression, what hopes can we ever have of engaging mankind to a practice which we confess full of austerity and rigour? Or what theory of morals can ever serve any useful purpose, unless it can show, by a particular detail, that all the duties which it recommends, are also the true interest of each individual? The peculiar advantage of the foregoing system seems to be, that it furnishes proper mediums for that purpose.

That the virtues which are immediately *useful* or *agreeable* to the person possessed of them, are desirable in a view to self-interest, it would surely be superfluous to prove. Moralists, indeed, may spare themselves all the pains which they often take in recommending these duties. To what purpose collect arguments to evince that temperance is advantageous, and the excesses of pleasure hurtful, when it appears that these excesses are only denominated such, because they are hurtful; and that, if the unlimited use of strong liquors, for instance, no more impaired health or the faculties of mind and body than the use of air or water, it would not be a whit more vicious or blameable?

It seems equally superfluous to prove, that the *companionable* virtues of good manners and wit, decency and genteelness, are more desirable than the contrary qualities. Vanity alone, without any other consideration, is a sufficient motive to make us wish for the possession of these accomplishments. No man was ever willingly deficient in this particular. All our failures here proceed from bad education, want of capacity, or a perverse and unpliable disposition. Would you have your company coveted, admired, followed; rather than hated, despised, avoided? Can any one seriously deliberate in the case? As no enjoyment is sincere, without some reference to company and society; so no society can be agreeable, or even tolerable, where a man feels his presence unwelcome, and discovers all around him symptoms of disgust and aversion.

But why, in the greater society or confederacy of mankind, should not the case be the same as in particular clubs and companies? Why is it more doubtful, that the enlarged virtues of humanity, generosity, beneficence, are desirable with a view of happiness and self-interest, than the limited endowments of ingenuity and politeness? Are we apprehensive lest those social affections interfere, in a greater and more immediate degree than any other pursuits, with private utility, and cannot be gratified, without some important sacrifice of honour and advantage? If so, we are but ill-instructed in the nature of the human passions, and are more influenced by verbal distinctions than by real differences.

Whatever contradiction may vulgarly be supposed between the *selfish* and *social* sentiments or dispositions, they are really no more opposite than selfish and ambitious, selfish and revengeful, selfish and vain. It is requisite that there be an original propensity of some kind, in order to be a basis to self-love, by giving a relish to the objects of its pursuit; and none more fit for this purpose than benevolence or humanity. The goods of fortune are spent in one gratification or another: the miser who accumulates his annual income, and lends it out at interest, has really spent it in the gratification of his avarice. And it would be difficult to show why a man is more a loser by a generous action, than by any other method of expense; since the utmost which he can attain by the most elaborate selfishness, is the indulgence of some affection.

Now if life, without passion, must be altogether insipid and tiresome; let a man suppose that he has full power of modelling his own disposition, and let him deliberate what appetite or desire he would choose for the foundation of his happiness and enjoyment. Every affection, he would observe, when gratified by success, gives a satisfaction proportioned to its force and violence; but besides this advantage, common to all, the immediate feeling of benevolence and friendship, humanity and kindness, is sweet, smooth, tender, and agreeable, independent of all fortune and accidents. These virtues are besides attended with a pleasing consciousness or remembrance, and keep us in humour with ourselves as well as others; while we retain the agreeable reflection of having done our part towards mankind and society. And though all men show a jealousy of our success in the pursuits of avarice and ambition; yet are we almost sure of their good-will and good wishes, so long as we persevere in the paths of virtue, and employ ourselves in the execution of generous plans and purposes. What other passion is there where we shall find so many advantages united; an agreeable sentiment, a pleasing consciousness, a good reputation? But of these truths, we may observe, men are, of themselves, pretty much convinced; nor are they deficient in their duty to society, because they would not wish to be generous, friendly, and humane; but because they do not feel themselves such.

Treating vice with the greatest candour, and making it all possible concessions, we must acknowledge that there is not, in any instance, the smallest pretext for giving it the preference above virtue, with a view of self-interest; except, perhaps, in the case of justice, where a man, taking things in a certain light, may often seem to be a loser by his integrity. And though it is allowed that, without a regard to property, no society could subsist; yet according to the imperfect way in which human affairs are conducted, a sensible knave, in particular incidents, may think that an act of iniquity or infidelity will make a considerable addition to his fortune, without causing any considerable breach in the social union and confederacy. That *honesty is the best policy*, may be a good general rule, but is liable to many exceptions; and he, it may perhaps be thought, conducts himself with most wisdom, who observes the general rule, and takes advantage of all the exceptions.

I must confess that, if a man think that this reasoning much requires an answer, it would be a little difficult to find any which will to him appear satisfactory and convincing. If his heart rebel not against such pernicious maxims, if he feel no reluctance to the thoughts of villainy or baseness, he has indeed lost a considerable motive to virtue; and we may expect that this practice will be answerable to his speculation. But in all ingenuous natures, the antipathy to treachery and roguery is too strong to be counterbalanced by any views of profit or pecuniary advantage. Inward peace of mind, consciousness of integrity, a satisfactory review of our own conduct; these are circumstances, very requisite to happiness, and will be cherished and cultivated by every honest man, who feels the importance of them.

Such a one has, besides, the frequent satisfaction of seeing knaves, with all their pretended cunning and abilities, betrayed by their own maxims; and while they purpose to cheat with moderation and secrecy, a tempting incident occurs, nature is frail, and they give into the snare; whence they can never extricate themselves, without a total loss of reputation, and the forfeiture of all future trust and confidence with mankind.

But were they ever so secret and successful, the honest man, if he has any tincture of philosophy, or even common observation and reflection, will discover that they themselves are, in the end, the greatest dupes, and have sacrificed the invaluable enjoyment of a character, with themselves at least, for the acquisition of worthless toys and gewgaws. How little is requisite to supply the *necessities* of nature? And in a view to *pleasure*, what comparison between the unbought satisfaction of conversation, society, study, even health and the common beauties of nature, but above all the peaceful reflection on one's own conduct; what comparison, I say, between these and the feverish, empty amusements of luxury and expense? These natural pleasures, indeed, are really without price; both because they are below all price in their attainment, and above it in their enjoyment.

P. F. Strawson

Social Morality and Individual Ideal

Men make for themselves pictures of ideal forms of life. Such pictures are various and may be in sharp opposition to each other; and one and the same individual may be captivated by different and sharply conflicting pictures at different times. At one time it may seem to him that he should live—even that *a man* should live—in such-and-such a way; at another that the only truly satisfactory form of life is something totally different, incompatible with the first. In this way, his outlook may vary radically, not only at different periods of his life, but from day to day, even from one hour to the next. It is a function of so many variables: age, experiences, present environment, current reading, current physical state are some of them. As for the ways of life that may thus present themselves at different times as each uniquely satisfactory, there can be no doubt about their variety and opposition. The ideas of self-obliterating devotion to duty or to the service of others; of personal honor and magnanimity; of asceticism, contemplation, retreat; of action, dominance, and power; of the cultivation of "an exquisite sense of the luxurious"; or simple human solidarity and cooperative endeavor; of a refined complexity of social existence; of a constantly maintained and renewed affinity with natural things—any of these ideas, and a great many others too, may form the core and substance of a personal ideal. At some times such a picture may present itself as merely appealing or attractive; at others it may offer itself in a stronger light, as, perhaps, an image of the only sane or nonignoble human reaction to the situation in which we find ourselves. "The nobleness of life is to do thus" or, sometimes, "The sanity of life is to do thus": such may be the devices with which these images present themselves.

Two quite different things may be urged against, or in mitigation of, this picture of a multiplicity of pictures. First, it might be said that the many, apparently conflicting pictures are really different parts or aspects, coming momentarily into misleading prominence, of a single picture; this latter being the composite ideal image of our coolest hours, in which every god is given his due and conflict is avoided by careful arrangement and proper subordination of part to part. And it may be true of some exceptional individuals that they entertain ideal images which exhibit just such a harmonious complexity. I believe this to be rarer than we sometimes pretend; but in any case to describe this situation is not to redescribe the situation I have spoken of, but to describe a different situation. The other mitigating point has more weight. It is that, however great the variety of images which dominate, at one time or another, our ethical imaginations, our individual lives do not, as a matter of fact, exhibit a comparable internal variety. Indeed they scarcely could. Something approaching consistency, some more or less unsteady balance, is usually detectable in the pattern of an individual person's decisions and actions. There are, so to speak, empirical grounds for ordering his ideal images in respect to practical efficacy, even, perhaps, for declaring one of them to be practically dominant. This point I shall grant. I think it is easy to exaggerate it; easy to exaggerate the unity of the personalities of those we say we know, when we really know them only in one or two particular connections; easy to dismiss as phases or moods whatever lacks conformity with our only partly empirical pictures of each other. But I shall not dwell on this. What I shall dwell on is precisely this readiness, which a great many people have, to identify themselves imaginatively at different times with different and conflicting visions of the ends of life, even though these visions may receive the scantiest expression in their actual behaviour and would call for the most upsetting personal revolutions if they received more.

This fact about many people—a fact which partly explains, among other things, the enormous charm of reading novels, biographies, histories—this fact, I say, has important consequences. One consequence is that when some ideal image of a form of life is given striking expression in the words or actions of some person, its expression may evoke a response of the liveliest sympathy from those whose own patterns of life are as remote as possible from conformity to the image expressed. It is indeed impossible that one life should realize all the ideal pictures which may at one time or another attract or captivate the individual imagination. But the owner of one life may with perfect practical consistency wish that his conflicting images should all be realized in different lives. The steadiest adherence to one image may coexist with the strongest desire that other and incompatible images should have their steady adherents too. To one who has such a desire, any doctrine that the pattern of the ideal life should be the same for all is intolerable; as it is to me. The way in which I have just expressed the position makes its practical consistency look more simple than it is. One cannot simply escape the conflict between different ideal images by diffusing their realization over different lives. For different lives interact and one's own is one of them; and there may be conflict in the areas of interaction. One is not forced to welcome this, though one may; it is simply something that in fact goes with the fulfillment of the wish for this kind of diversity in the pursuit of ends. Equally one is not precluded from taking one side in a conflict because one has wished that both sides should exist and has some sympathy with both.

I think there can be no doubt that what I have been talking about falls within the region of the ethical. I have been talking about evaluations such as *can* govern choices and decisions which are of the greatest importance to men. Whether it falls within the region of the moral, however, is something that may be doubted. Perhaps the region of the moral falls within it. Or perhaps there are no such simple inclusion-relations between them. The question is one I shall come back to later. I should like first to say something more about this region of the ethical. It could also be characterized as a region in which there are truths which are incompatible with each other. There exist, that is to say, many profound general statements which are capable of capturing the ethical imagination in the same way as it may be captured by those ideal images of which I spoke. They often take the form of general descriptive statements about man and the world. They can be incorporated into a metaphysical system, or dramatized in a religious or historical myth. Or they can exist—their most persuasive form for many—as isolated statements such as, in France, there is a whole literature of, the literature of the maxim. I will not give examples, but I will mention names. One cannot read Pascal or Flaubert, Nietzsche or Goethe, Shakespeare or Tolstoy, without encountering these profound truths. It is certainly possible, in a coolly analytical frame of mind, to mock at the whole notion of the profound truth; but we are guilty of mildly bad faith if we do. For in most of us the ethical imagination succumbs again and again to *these* pictures of man, and it is precisely as truths that we wish to characterize them while they hold us captive. But these truths have the same kind of relation to each other as those ideal images of which I have already spoken. For pictures of the one kind reflect and are reflected by pictures of the other. They capture our imagination in the same way. Hence it is as wholly futile to think that we could, without destroying their character, systematize these truths into one coherent body of truth as it is to suppose that we could, without destroying their character, form a coherent composite image from these images. This may be expressed by saying that the region of the ethical is the region where there are truths but no truth; or, in other words, that the injunction to see life steadily *and* see it whole is absurd, for one cannot do both. I said I would give no examples, but I will allude to one near contemporary one. Many will remember the recorded encounter between Russell and Lawrence, the attempt at sympathy and the failure to find it. That failure is recorded in such words as "I thought there might be something in what he said, but in the end I saw there was nothing" on the one hand; and "Get back to mathematics where you can do some good; leave talk about human beings alone" on the other. The clash was a clash of two irreconcilable views of man, two irreconcilable attitudes. The spectator familiar with both may say: Russell is right; he tells the truth; he speaks for civilization. He may also say: Lawrence is right; he tells the truth; he speaks for life. The point is that he may say both things. It would be absurd to hope for a reconcilation of the two conflicting attitudes. It is not absurd to desire that both should exist, in conflict.

The region of the ethical, then, is a region of diverse, certainly incompatible and possibly practically conflicting ideal images or pictures of a human life, or of human life; and it is a region in which many such incompatible pictures may secure at least the imaginative, though doubtless not often the practical, allegiance of a single person. Moreover this statement itself may be seen not merely as a description of what is the case, but as a positive evaluation of evaluative diversity. Any diminution in this variety would impoverish the human scene. The multiplicity of conflicting pictures is itself the essential element in one of one's pictures of man.

Now what are the relations between the region of the ethical and the sphere of morality? One widely accepted account of the latter is in terms of the idea of rules or principles governing human behavior which apply universally within a community or class. The class may be variously thought of as a definite social group or the human species as a whole or even the entire class of rational beings. It is not obvious how these contrasting conceptions, of diversity of ideal and of community of rule, are related to each other; and in fact, I think, the relationship is complicated. One way of trying to harmonize the ideals would be as follows. This way is extremely crude and inadequate, but it may serve as a starting point. It is obvious that many, if not all, of the ideal images of which I spoke demand for their realization the existence of some form of social organization. The demand is in varying degrees logical or empirical. Some ideals only make sense in a complex social context, and even in a particular kind of complex social context. For others, some complexity of social organization seems, rather, a practically necessary condition of the ideal's being realized in any very full or satisfactory way. Now it is a condition of the existence of any form of social organization, of any human community, that certain expectations of behavior on the part of its members should be pretty regularly fulfilled: that some duties, one might say, should be performed, some obligations acknowledged, some rules observed. We might begin by locating the sphere of morality here. It is the sphere of the observance of rules, such that the existence of some such set of rules is a condition of the existence of a society. This is a minimal interpretation of morality. It represents it as what might literally be called a kind of public convenience: of the first importance as a condition of everything that matters, but only as a condition of everything that matters, not as something that matters in itself.

I am disposed to see considerable merit in this minimal conception of morality. By this I mean not that it is really, or nearly, an adequate conception—only that it is a useful analytical idea. There would be objections to claiming that it was an adequate conception. One objection might be simply expressed by saying that, after all, being moral is something that does matter in itself, that it is not simply an affair of complying with rules in a situation where the observance of some such rules is an indirect condition of approximating to ideal forms of life. There is a lot in this objection. But it is not an objection to *using* the minimal idea of morality. We might for example argue that there was an intricate interplay between ideal pictures of man on the one hand and the rule requirements of social organization on the other; and that one's ordinary and vague conception of morality was the product of this interplay. This would be one way—I do not say the right way—of using the minimal idea of morality to try to get clearer about the ordinary idea. I shall come back later to this question too.

Meanwhile there is another objection to be considered. I think there is something in it as well, but that what there is in it is not at all straightforward. It turns on the idea of the universal applicability of moral rules. The idea is that it is a necessary requirement of a *moral* rule that it should at least be regarded as applying to all human beings whatever. Moral behavior is what is demanded of men as such. But we can easily imagine, and even find, different societies held together by the observance of sets of rules which are very different from each other. Moreover we can find or imagine a single society held together by a set of rules which by no means make the same demands on all its members, but make very different demands on different classes or groups within the society. Insofar as the rules which give cohesiveness to a society are acknowledged to have this limited and sectional character, they cannot, in the sense of this objection, be seen as moral rules. But the rules which do give cohesiveness to a society may well have this character, whether acknowledged or not. So the prospect of explaining true morality in terms of what I called the minimal conception of morality is a poor one. Now it is possible to admit the principle of this objection, and then meet it with a formal maneuver. Thus a rule which governs the professional behavior of Samoan witch doctors can be said to apply to all men under the condition that they are witch doctor members of a society with the general characteristics of Samoan society. Or again, a rule which might be held to apply to ten-year old children, namely that they should obey their parents in domestic matters, could be represented as applying to all men without exception, under the condition that they were ten-year old children. Obviously there is a certain futility about this maneuver, and equally obviously there is no compulsion to execute it. We might simply drop the idea of moral rules as universally binding on men as men. Or we might say that though there was something in this idea, it was absurd to try to apply it directly and in detail to the question of what people were required to do in particular situations in particular societies. And here we might be tempted by another maneuver, which we should note as a possible one even if we do not think that it, either, is altogether satisfactory. We might be tempted to say that the relevant universally applicable, and hence moral, rule, was that a human being should conform to the rules which apply to him in a particular situation in a particular society. Here universality is achieved by stepping up an order. A man should perform the duties of his station in his society. This allows for an indefinite variety of societies and of stations within them; and would also seem to allow us, in so far as we regarded the universal rule as a truly moral one, to see at least part of true morality as resting upon and presupposing what I called the minimal social interpretation of morality.

Enough, for the moment, of objections to this minimal idea. Let me set out some of its merits. First we must be clearer about what this minimal interpretation is. The fundamental idea is that of a socially sanctioned demand made on an individual in virtue merely of his membership of the society in question, or in virtue of a particular position which he occupies within it or a particular relation in which he stands to other members of it. I spoke of rules in this connection; and the rules I meant would simply be the generalized statements of demands of this type. The formula I employ for the fundamental idea is deliberately flexible, the notions of a society and of social sanctioning deliberately vague. This flexibility is necessary to do justice to the complexities of social organization and social relationships. For instance, we can regard ourselves as members of many different social groups or communities, some of which fall within others; or again, when I speak of the social sanctioning of a demand which is made on an individual member of a group in virtue of his position in the group, we may think of the social sanction of that demand sometimes as arising only within the limited group in question, sometimes as arising also within a wider group which includes that limited group. A position in a society may or may not also be, so to speak, a position in society. Thus a position in a family generally gives rise to certain demands upon the holder of that position which are recognized both within the family and within some wider group or groups within which the family falls. The same may be true of membership of a profession or even of a professional association. On the other hand, some of the demands of certain class or caste moralities receive little or no extraneous reinforcement from the wider social groupings to which the members of the limited class also belong. Or again what one might call the internal morality of an intimate personal relationship may be as private as the relationship itself. One of the merits I should claim for this approach to morality is precisely that it so easily makes room for many concepts which we habitually employ, but which tend to be neglected in moral philosophy. Thus we talk of medical ethics, of the code of honor of a military caste, of bourgeois morality and of working-class morality. Such ideas fit more easily into an account of morality which sees it as essentially, or at any rate fundamentally, a function of social groupings than they do into the more apparently individualistic approaches which are generally current.

Another merit which I shall claim for the present approach is that it makes it relatively easy to understand such notions as those of conscientiousness, duty and obligation in a concrete and realistic way. These notions have been treated almost entirely abstractly in moral philosophy in the recent past, with the result that they have come to some of our contemporaries[1] to seem to be meaningless survivals of discarded ideas about the government of the universe. But as most ordinarily employed I do not think they are that at all. There is nothing in the least mysterious or metaphysical in the fact that duties and obligations go with offices, positions, and relationships to others. The demands to be made on somebody in virtue of his occupation of a certain position may indeed be, and often are, quite explicitly listed in considerable detail. And when we call someone conscientious or say that he has a strong sense of his obligations or of duty, we do not ordinarily mean that he is haunted by the ghost of the idea of supernatural ordinances; we mean rather such

[1] Cf. G. E. M. Anscombe, "Modern Moral Philosophy", *Philosophy* (January, 1958).

things as this, that he can be counted on for sustained efforts to do what is required of him in definite capacities, to fulfil the demand made on him as student or teacher or parent or soldier or whatever he may be. A certain professor once said: "For me to be moral is to behave like a professor".

Suppose we now raise that old philosophical question: What interest has the individual in morality? The question may force us to a more adequate conception of morality than the minimal interpretation offers by itself. It certainly forces us to strike, or to try to strike, some delicate balances. The only answer to the question so far suggested is this: that the individual's ethical imagination may be captured or fired by one or more ideal pictures of life which require for their realization the existence of social groupings and social organizations such as could not exist in the absence of a system of social demands made on individual members of these groups or organizations. I have already hinted that this answer is too crude, that the interplay between ethical ideal and social obligation is more intricate than it suggests. The answer is also not crude enough. The picture of the ideal form of life and the associated ethical vision of the world tend to be the products of the refined mind and relatively comfortable circumstances. But when we ask what the interest of the individual is in morality, we mean to ask about all those individuals on whom socially sanctioned demands are made; not just about the imaginatively restless and materially cozy. We need not, perhaps, insist upon just the same answer for all; but, if we take the question seriously, we must insist on *some* answer for all. There may seem to be a broader answer which does not altogether depart from the form of the over-refined answer. For who could exist at all, or pursue any aim, except in some form of society? And there is no form of society without rules, without some system of socially sanctioned demands on its members. Here at least is a common interest in morality as minimally conceived, an interest which can be attributed to all those about whom the question can be raised. Still we may feel that it is not enough. And in this feeling is the germ of the reason why the minimal conception of morality is inadequate to the ordinary notion, at least in its contemporary form: and perhaps, in uncovering the reason for this inadequacy, we may discover too what there is in the notion of the universal applicability of moral rules.

We have arrived at the fact that everyone on whom some form of socially sanctioned demand is made has an interest in the existence of some system of socially sanctioned demands. But this fact seems inadequate to answer the question what the individual's interest in morality is. We can begin to understand this inadequacy by thinking of the different things that might be meant by the social sanctioning of a demand. "Sanction" is related to "permission" and "approval"; and also to "power" and to "penalty". A socially sanctioned demand is doubtless a demand made with the permission and approval of a society; and backed, in some form and degree, with its power. But the idea of a society as the totality of individuals subject to demands may here come apart from the idea of society as the source of sanction of those demands. The sanctioning society may simply be a subgroup of the total society, the dominant subgroup, the group in which power resides. Mere membership of the total society does not guarantee membership of the sanctioning part of the society. Nor does a mere interest in the existence of some system of socially sanctioned demands guarantee an interest in the particular system of socially sanctioned demands to which one is subjected. But unless at least one, and perhaps both, of these nonguaranteed conditions is satisfied, it does not seem that the fulfillment of a socially sanctioned demand comes anywhere near being what we should regard as the fulfillment of a moral obligation. That is to say, if I have no foothold at all in the sanctioning part of society, and if no interest of mine is safeguarded by the system of demands to which I am subject, then, in fulfilling a demand made upon me, I may indeed, in one sense, be doing what I am obliged to do; but scarcely what I am *morally* obliged to do. No wonder, then, that the question "What is the individual's interest in morality"? is not answered by mentioning the general interest in the existence of some system of socially sanctioned demands. The answer now scarcely appears to touch the question.

Suppose, then, that we consider the idea of a society such that all its members have *some* interest, not merely in there being a system of socially sanctioned demands, but in the actual system of demands which obtains in that society. It seems that we can ensure such an interest even to the powerless and enslaved by stipulating that the system includes not only demands made on them in the interest of their masters, but also demands made on their masters in their interests. We might be tempted to say that by thus securing to them an interest in the system of demands, we secure to them also some sort of position or foothold in the sanctioning part of society. Certainly, when the master recognizes moral obligations to his slave, we shall be at least one step nearer to allowing that the slave is not merely subject to the demands of his master, but may recognize a moral obligation to fulfill them. Even in this extreme case, then, we can approach the situation which everyone would agree to regard as characteristically moral, the situation in which there is reciprocal acknowledgement of rights and duties.

Still I think we must admit a distinction of two stages in this approach to the characteristically moral situation. Interest in claims on others and acknowledgement of claims on oneself are connected but not identical. It is a tautology, though not an easy one, that everyone subject to moral demands has some interest in morality. For a demand made on an individual is to be regarded as a moral demand only if it belongs to a system of demands which includes demands made on others in his interest. It would be agreeable, as I just now suggested, to be able to argue strictly that this fact carries with it the conclusion that mere self-conscious membership of a moral community implies at least in some degree extending one's sanction to its system of demands, to the extent of genuinely acknowledging as obligations at least some of the claims which others have on one, even if only provisionally and with the strongest desire that the system should be different. But to argue so would be to equivocate with the phrase "membership of a moral community". There would be nothing self-contradictory about the idea of one who recognized his interest in the system of moral demands and resolved merely to profit by it as much as he could, fulfilling its demands on himself only in so far as his interest calculably required it. He might get away with it successfully if he were subtle enough in his practice of the hypocrisy which this policy would necessarily involve. But it is an important fact that hypocrisy would be necessary. It is connected with the further fact, a fact of human nature which can probably be explained in a number of ways, that quite thoroughgoing egotism of this kind is rare. But for this fact there could be no such thing as a system of moral demands. We cannot argue that it is a tautology that *anyone* subject to moral demands who recognizes his interest in the system of demands must also genuinely acknowledge some obligations under the system. But we can argue that it is a tautology that the *generality* of those subject to moral demands must genuinely recognize some obligations under the system of demands. For if this were not so, there would be no such thing as a system of moral demands and hence no such thing as being subject to a moral demand.

These steps from a minimal to a more adequate conception of morality (i.e. to a conception which at least begins to square with what we nowadays vaguely understand by the word) may easily encourage abstract exaggerations and distortions in moral philosophy. For instance, the necessary truth that the members of a moral community in general acknowledge some moral claims upon them may be exaggerated into the idea of a self-conscious choice or adoption of the principle of those claims. So everyone appears, grandly but implausibly, as a moral self-legislator. This is an exaggeration which has appealed, in different forms, to more than one philosopher. Again these steps reveal something genuinely universal in morality: the necessary acceptance of reciprocity of claim. And *one* way in which a demand made on one individual in the interest of others can be balanced by a demand made on others in his interest is through the operation of a general rule or principle having application to all alike. But it does not follow from this that *all* moral claims have, or are seen by those who acknowledge them as having, the character of applications of universal principles holding for all men. There is no reason why a system of moral demands characteristic of one community should, or even could, be found in every other. And even within a single system of reciprocal claims, the moral demand may essentially *not* relate to a situation in which any member of the system could find himself *vis-à-vis* any other. Here are two reasons why it is misleading to say that moral behavior is what is demanded of men as men. It might, in some cases, be essentially what is demanded of Spartans by other Spartans, or of a king by his subjects. What is universally demanded of the members of a moral community is something like the abstract virtue of justice: a man should not insist on a particular claim while refusing to acknowledge any reciprocal claim. But from this formally universal feature of morality no consequences follow as to the universality of application of the particular rules in the observance of which, in particular situations and societies, justice consists.

One must beware, however, of meeting exaggeration with counter-exaggeration. It is important to recognize the diversity of possible systems of moral demands, and the diversity of demands which may be made within any system. But it is also important to recognize that certain human interests are so fundamental and so general that they must be universally acknowledged in some form and to some degree in any conceivable moral community. Of some interests, one might say: a system could scarcely command *sufficient* interest in those subject to its demands for these demands to be acknowledged as obligations, unless it secured to them *this* interest. Thus some claim on human succor, some obligation to abstain from the infliction of physical injury, seem to be necessary features of almost any system of moral demands. Here at least we have types of moral behavior which are demanded *of* men as men because they are demanded *for* and *by* men as men. Another interest which is fundamental to many types of social relation and social grouping is the interest in not being deceived. In most kinds of social grouping for which there obtains any system of moral demand and claim at all this interest is acknowledged as a claim which any member of the group has on any other; and perhaps most such groupings could scarcely exist without this acknowledgement. When all allowance has been made, then, for the possible diversity of moral systems and the possible diversity of demands within a system, it remains true that the recognition of certain general virtues and obligations will be a logically or humanly necessary feature of almost any conceivable moral system: these will include the abstract virtue of justice, some form of obligation to mutual aid and to mutual abstention from injury and, in some form and in some degree, the virtue of honesty. This guarded recognition of the necessary universal applicability of some relatively vague and abstract moral principles is itself a corrective to the idea of unbounded freedom of choice of such principles on the part of the individual.

I spoke earlier of the need for striking some delicate balances, and I hope that the nature of some of these is now apparent. Constant checks are required if these balances are not to be lost. We have seen in what sense it is true that everyone on whom a moral demand is made must have an interest in morality. But we have also seen that the existence of a system of moral demands (at least as we now understand this concept) requires some degree of general readiness to recognize claims made upon one even when this recognition cannot plausibly be said to be in one's own interest. The existence of some such readiness needs no more to be argued for than the existence of morality in general. But it is necessary to emphasize it in order to correct another exaggeration, the exaggeration which would represent all morality as prudential.[2] To say that this readiness to acknowledge the claims of others does not need to be argued for is not to say that it does not need to be explained. We may discuss its natural sources; and the terms in which we do so will change with the state of our psychological knowledge: the appeal to the concept of sympathy, for example, will scarcely now seem adequate. But, however we explain it, there is no need to sophisticate ourselves into denying altogether the existence or fundamental importance of this recognition of others' claims. Again, we have seen that the fact of acknowledgement of claims may be blown up into the picture of the self-legislating moral agent; and here we should do well to scale down our pretensions to freedom by remembering, if nothing else, the importance of the training we receive and the limited choice we exercise

[2] Cf. P. R. Foot, "Moral Beliefs", *Proceedings of the Aristotelian Society* (1958–59).

of the moral communities to which we belong. Finally, we have acknowledged some force in the idea of universally applicable principles of moral demand and claim. But to keep within bounds the pretensions of this idea, we must insist again on the flexibility of the concept of a social group, upon the diversity of groups and upon the absurdity of the idea that detailed demands could be shifted indifferently from group to group or apply to all members alike within a group.

There are further important moral phenomena of which the account I have given makes little or no explicit mention. Some of these it might even seem, at first sight, to exclude. Is there not such a thing as moral criticism, from within a society, of the existing moral forms of that society? Cannot different systems of socially sanctioned demand, under which those subject to demands genuinely acknowledge obligations, be the subject of relative moral evaluation? Cannot there be situations in which men may or should recognize moral obligations to each other, although there is no common society of which they are members and there is no concept of a "social" relationship which can be at all plausibly represented as applying to their situation? Any acceptable account of morality must certainly allow an affirmative answer to these questions; and there are others which will suggest themselves. But they no more yield a reason for mistrusting the approach I have adopted than the inadequacy of what I called the minimal interpretation of morality gave a reason for wholly discarding that idea. By enriching the minimal interpretation with certain applications of the notions of interest, and of acknowledgement of obligation, we obtained what was recognizably a concept of social morality. It is necessary only to draw out the significance of certain elements in *this* conception in order to make room for the ideas of moral criticism, and of a morality which transcends standard forms of social relationship. I have remarked already that, because certain human needs and interests are as fundamental and as general as they are, we shall find correspondingly general types of virtue and obligation acknowledged in some form and in some degree in almost any conceivable moral system. Now it is characteristically by analogy with, and extension of, acknowledged forms of these, that moral development proceeds, and that these ideas themselves assume more refined and generous shapes. And moral criticism at its most self-conscious proceeds characteristically by appeal to, and interpretation of, such general moral ideas as those of justice, integrity, and humanity: existing institutions, systems of demand and claim, are criticized as unjust, inhumane, or corrupt. We may say that so far from excluding the idea of moral criticism, the concept of social morality, as I have outlined it, makes fully intelligible the nature and possibility of such criticism. For we can perceive how the seeds of criticism lie in the morality itself; and we may even hope, on this basis, to achieve some understanding of the complex interrelationships between social and economic change, the critical insights of individual moralists, and the actual course of moral evolution. (It is, for instance, an easy consequence of our principles that moral *formalism*—i.e. a rigid adherence to the letter, with no appeal to the spirit, of the rules—will tend to be at a maximum in a static and isolated society, and that moral *disorientation* will tend to be at a maximum when such a morality is suddenly exposed to radical change.) Just as a social morality contains the seeds of moral criticism, so the two together contain the seeds of a morality transcending standard social relationships. It is easy to see how the tendency of at least one type of self-conscious and critical morality is generalizing and antiparochial, as it is antiformalist. Some moralists would maintain that a true concept of morality emerges only at the limit of this generalizing process. This is a judgment in which, as it seems to me, the sense of reality has become quite subordinated to zeal. But wherever we choose to say that "true morality" begins, I have no doubt whatever that our understanding of the concept of morality in general is best served by the kind of approach that I have sketched. Where what we are dealing with is a developing human institution, it is no reproach to any explanation that it may be described as at least partially genetic.

But now it is time to return to the question of the relation between social moralities and those ideal pictures of forms of life which I spoke of at the outset. All I have so far explicitly said about this is that the realization of any such ideal requires the existence of forms of social grouping or organization which in turn require the existence of a system of socially sanctioned demands on their members. We have since remarked that a system of socially sanctioned demands would fall short of being a system of moral demands unless those demands were not merely enforced as demands, but also at least in some degree generally acknowledged as claims by those subject to them; and it follows from this that to be a member of a moral community cannot merely be a matter of convenience, except perhaps for those who can practice a sustained hypocrisy of which few are in fact capable. Yet it may still be true in general to say that the possibility of the pursuit of an ideal form of life quite pragmatically requires membership of a moral community or of moral communities; for it is extremely unlikely in fact that the minimal social conditions for the pursuit of any ethical ideal which anyone is likely to entertain could in practice be fulfilled except through membership of such communities. But of course the relations between these two things are much more intricate and various than this formulation by itself suggests. The possibilities of collision, absorption, and interplay are many. The way I have just expressed the matter perhaps makes most obvious the possibility of collision; and this possibility is worth stressing. It is worth stressing that what one acknowledges or half-acknowledges as obligation may conflict not only, crudely, with interest and, weakly, with inclination but also with ideal aspiration, with the vision that captures the ethical imagination. On the other hand, it may be that a picture of the ideal life is precisely one in which the interests of morality are dominant, are given an ideal, overriding value. To one dominated temporarily or permanently by such a picture the "consciousness of duty faithfully performed" will appear as the supremely satisfactory state, and being moral not merely as something that matters but as the thing that supremely matters. Or again the ideal picture may be, not that in which the interests of morality in general are dominant, but rather one in which the dominating idea operates powerfully to reinforce some, but not perhaps others, of a system of moral demands. So it is with that ideal picture in which obedience to the command to love one another appears as the supreme value.

This is still to draw too simple a picture. Let us remember the diversity of communities to which we may be said to belong, and the diversity of systems of moral demand which belong to them. To a certain extent, though to an extent which we must not exaggerate, the systems of moral relationships into which we enter are a matter of choice—or at least a matter in which there are alternative possibilities; and different systems of moral demand are variously well or ill adapted to different ideal pictures of life. The ideal picture, moreover, may call for membership not merely of communities in which certain interests are safeguarded by a system of moral demands, but for membership of a community or of a system of relationships in which the system of demands reflects in a positive way the nature of the ideal. For one crude instance of this, we may think again of the morality of a military caste in connection with the ideal of personal honor. In general, in a society as complex as ours, it is obvious that there are different moral environments, different subcommunities within the community, different systems of moral relationships, interlocking indeed and overlapping with one another, but offering some possibilities of choice, some possibilities of adjustment of moral demand and individual aspiration. But here again, at least in our time and place, it is the limits of the direct relevance of each to the other that must finally be stressed. Inside a single political human society one may indeed find different, and perhaps widely different, moral environments, social groupings in which different systems of moral demand are recognized. But if the one grouping is to form part of the wider society, its members must be subject to a wider system of reciprocal demand, a wider common morality; and the relative significance of the wider common morality will grow in proportion as the subgroups of the society are closely interlocked, in proportion as each individual is a member of a plurality of subgroups and in proportion as the society is not rigidly stratified, but allows of relatively free access to, and withdrawal from, its subgroups. In a political society which thus combines a wide variety of social groupings with complex interlocking and freedom of movement between them the dissociation of idiosyncratic ideal and common moral demand will doubtless tend to be at its maximum. On the other hand an ideal picture of man *may* tend, in fact or in fancy, to demand the status of a comprehensive common morality. Thus Coleridgean or Tolstoyan dreamers may play with the thought of self-enclosed ideal communities in which the system of moral demands shall answer exactly, or as exactly as possible, to an ideal picture of life held in common by all their members. Such fancies are bound to strike many as weak and futile; for the price of preserving the purity of such communities is that of severance from the world at large. More seriously, there may be some attempt to make the whole moral climate of an existing national state reflect some ideal image of human solidarity or religious devotion or military honor. In view of the natural diversity of human ideals—to mention only that—such a state (or its members) will evidently be subject to at least some stresses from which a liberal society is free.

To conclude. I have spoken of those ideal images of life of which one individual may sympathize with many, and desire to see many realized in some degree. I have spoken also of those systems—though the word is too strong—of recognized reciprocal claim that we have on one another as members of human communities, or as terms of human relationships, many of which could scarcely exist or have the character they have but for the existence of such systems of reciprocal claim. I have said something, though too little, of the complex and various relations which may hold between these two things, viz. our conflicting visions of the ends of life and the systems of moral demand which make social living possible. Finally I have glanced at the relations of both to the political societies in which we necessarily live. The field of phenomena over which I have thus loosely ranged is, I think, very much more complex and many-sided than I have been able to suggest; but I have been concerned to suggest something of its complexity. Some implications for moral philosophy I have hinted at in passing, mainly by way of an attempt to correct some typical exaggerations of contemporary theory. But the main practical implications for moral and political philosophy are, I think, that more attention should be concentrated on types of social structure and social relation, and on those complex interrelationships which I have mentioned as well as others which I have not. For instance, it is hard not to believe that understanding of our secular morality would be enhanced by considering the historical role that religion has played in relation to morality. Or again, I doubt if the nature of morality can be properly understood without some consideration of its relationship to law. It is not merely that the spheres of morality and law are largely overlapping, or that their demands often coincide. It is also that in the way law functions to give cohesiveness to the most important of all social groupings we may find a coarse model of the way in which systems of moral demand function to give cohesiveness to social groupings in general. Similarly, in the complexity of our attitudes towards existing law we may find a model of the complexity of our attitude towards the systems of moral demand which impinge upon us in our social relations at large—or upon others, in theirs.

Finally, I do not think there is any very definite invitation to moral or political commitment implicit in what I have said. But perhaps one question can be raised, and in part answered. What will be the attitude of one who experiences sympathy with a variety of conflicting ideals of life? It seems that he will be most at home in a liberal society, in a society in which there are variant moral environments but in which no ideal endeavors to engross, and determine the character of, the common morality. He will not argue in favor of such a society that it gives the best chance for the truth about life to prevail, for he will not consistently believe that there is such a thing as the truth about life. Nor will he argue in its favor that it has the best chance of producing a harmonious kingdom of ends, for he will not think of ends as necessarily capable of being harmonized. He will simply welcome the ethical diversity which the society makes possible, and in proportion as he values that diversity he will note that he is the natural, though perhaps the sympathetic, enemy of all those whose single intense vision of the ends of life drives them to try to make the requirements of the ideal coextensive with those of common social morality.

Part V

Happiness and Virtues

Introduction

The interpretation of moral theories we have been presenting rests on a distinction between moral necessity and moral freedom. Social morality is the sphere of moral necessity. It is defined by the requirements of human welfare which do not differ from person to person. Personal morality is the sphere of moral freedom. Within it, individuals are encouraged to follow their preferences and try to make satisfying lives for themselves within the limits imposed by social morality. In this section, we shall continue to consider the questions raised in the introduction to the previous section about the distinction between these two spheres.

The case study which is the first reading in this section is concerned with a conflict between social and personal morality. We find a person believing that he is in an extreme situation which permits murder, the violation of a basic prohibition of social morality. What should someone who loves this person do when he acts on his belief? Social morality dictates that one should stop him by any means necessary, while personal morality calls for allowing him to do what he thinks is right even if one disagrees with him.

The classic defense of individual freedom and personal morality is John Stuart Mill's *On Liberty*, the second reading in this section. Mill argues that there is a principle on the basis of which we can draw the line between social and personal morality, between moral necessity and moral freedom. This principle is that interference with personal morality and individual freedom is justified only if harm to others is being done. In the absence of harm, interference is always illegitimate. Thus, for Mill, the relevant question to ask about the conflict between social and personal morality is whether the agent is harming anyone.

In the last selection, we return to the ancient Greeks, the source of so many of our fundamental moral and political concepts. Aristotle's (384–322 B.C.) *Nicomachean Ethics* identifies the goal of morality as individual well-being. This is a life in which individuals aim to realize their full potential in accordance with reason. Aristotle believes that if we are indeed guided by reason, then there is no conflict between social and personal morality. Thus he would argue that the conflict in our case study is only apparent, not real. Aristotle develops an extremely influential account of human virtues and argues that truly virtuous people harmoniously combine in their lives respect for the welfare of others with the pursuit of their own well-being. It will be remembered that this answer was first given by Socrates to the egoist. Thus we end as we began, but with better understanding of the nature of the answer.

Problem Case: Social Morality and Personal Morality

Peter and Paul are very close friends of many years standing. They were born and raised in Northern Ireland, and they emigrated to America together after finishing high school there. They are both Catholics and in their opinion Northern Ireland should be part of Ireland. But as they live here, the troubles of the Irish affect their lives less and less. They attend university, become successful lawyers, marry, have children, and work hard while enjoying the lives they have made for themselves. Through all this, they remain the best of friends. They meet often, and they are in the habit of talking to each other about what really matters to them: their feelings, doubts, problems, hopes, and successes.

But Peter gradually comes to believe that Paul is changing. Paul seems to be less involved in the friendship, he talks less openly, he has cancelled several of their regular meetings, he seems to be preoccupied, worried, concerned with something else. Of course, Peter tries to talk to Paul about it, but Paul will not be engaged in such a conversation. Finally, Peter really insists, puts their friendship on the line, and Paul tells the truth. The truth is that Paul has become a middleman, supplying explosives to a group whose aim is to unite Ireland by any means necessary. Paul knows the intended use of the explosives, he knows that what he is doing is illegal, and he knows also that in all likelihood innocent people will be killed. But he thinks that the unification of Ireland and the past oppression of the Irish justify breaking the law and the likely killings.

Peter now has to think through the situation. As a Catholic, an American citizen, and a lawyer, it is clear to him that what Paul is doing violates the requirements of social morality. Peter is convinced that no matter how worthy the ends, terrorism is wrong. He is horrified by what Paul is doing. He sees his friend directly contributing to murder, and he also sees that Paul is ruining his life. He will have to live with the guilt of what he is doing and the chances are that he will be caught, sent to jail, disbarred as a lawyer, or killed in retaliation by the terrorists of the other side.

On the other hand, Peter feels as keenly as Paul about the political issue, he loves Paul deeply, and he understands perfectly well what motivates Paul. Sympathy, friendship, loyalty, Peter's personal morality—all certainly dictate condoning what Peter's social morality condemns as very serious immorality, involving murder.

Naturally, Peter talks to Paul about it and explains to him exactly his own point of view. Paul understands it, but disagrees. Paul says that his conscience dictates doing what he does, that he thought long and deeply about it, and that he is willing to be involved in murder for the cause he believes in. There are times, he says, when personal morality must take precedence over social morality, and this is one of those times.

Peter knows that Paul will stick to his decision, yet he thinks that Paul's decision is morally very wrong, because it will hurt innocent people, his own family, and himself. So Peter faces a serious moral conflict: should he act as social morality dictates and do what is necessary to prevent Paul from continuing in his murderous conduct, or should he condone what horrifies him as deeply immoral out of loyalty for Paul? What does morality require that Paul should do?

John Stuart Mill

On Liberty

Introductory

. . . The object of this essay is to assert one very simple principle, as entitled to govern absolutely the dealings of society with the individual in the way of compulsion and control, whether the means used be physical force in the form of legal penalties or the moral coercion of public opinion. That principle is that the sole end for which mankind are warranted, individually or collectively, in interfering with the liberty of action of any of their number is self-protection. That the only purpose for which power can be rightfully exercised over any member of a civilized community, against his will, is to prevent harm to others. His own good, either physical or moral, is not a sufficient warrant. He cannot rightfully be compelled to do or forbear because it will be better for him to do so, because it will make him happier, because, in the opinions of others, to do so would be wise or even right. These are good reasons for remonstrating with him, or reasoning with him, or persuading him, or entreating him, but not for compelling him or visiting him with any evil in case he do otherwise. To justify that, the conduct from which it is desired to deter him must be calculated to produce evil to someone else. The only part of the conduct of anyone for which he is amenable to society is that which concerns others. In the part which merely concerns himself, his independence is, of right, absolute. Over himself, over his own body and mind, the individual is sovereign.

It is, perhaps, hardly necessary to say that this doctrine is meant to apply only to human beings in the maturity of their faculties. We are not speaking of children or of young persons below the age which the law may fix as that of manhood or womanhood. Those who are still in a state to require being taken care of by others must be protected against their own actions as well as against external injury. For the same reason we may leave out of consideration those backward states of society in which the race itself may be considered as in its nonage. The early difficulties in the way of spontaneous progress are so great that there is seldom any choice of means for overcoming them; and a ruler full of the spirit of improvement is warranted in the use of any expedients that will attain an end perhaps otherwise unattainable. Despotism is a legitimate mode of government in dealing with barbarians, provided the end be their improvement and the means justified by actually effecting that end. Liberty, as a principle, has no application to any state of things anterior to the time when mankind have become capable of being improved by free and equal discussion. Until then, there is nothing for them but implicit obedience to an Akbar or a Charlemagne if they are so fortunate as to find one. But as soon as mankind have attained the capacity of being guided to their own improvement by conviction or persuasion (a period long since reached in all nations with whom we need here concern ourselves), compulsion, either in the direct form or in that of pains and penalties for noncompliance, is no longer admissible as a means to their own good, and justifiable only for the security of others.

It is proper to state that I forego any advantage which could be derived to my argument from the idea of abstract right as a thing independent of utility. I regard utility as the ultimate appeal on all ethical questions; but it must be utility in the largest sense, grounded on the permanent interests of man as a progressive being. Those interests, I contend, authorize the subjection of individual spontaneity to external control only in respect to those actions of each which concern the interest of other people. If anyone does an act hurtful to others, there is a *prima facie* case for punishing him by law or, where legal penalties are not safely applicable, by general disapprobation. There are also many positive acts for the benefit of others which he may rightfully be compelled to perform, such as to give evidence in a court of justice, to bear his fair share in the common defense or in any other joint work necessary to the interest of the society of which he enjoys the protection, and to perform certain acts of individual beneficence, such as saving a fellow creature's life or interposing to protect the defenseless against ill usage—things which whenever it is obviously a man's duty to do he may rightfully be made responsible to society for not doing. A person may cause evil to others not only by his actions but by his inaction, and in either case he is justly accountable to them for the injury. The latter case, it is true, requires a much more cautious exercise of compulsion than the former. To make anyone answerable for doing evil to others is the rule; to make him answerable for not preventing evil is, comparatively speaking, the exception. Yet there are many cases clear enough and grave enough to justify that exception. In all things which regard the external relations of the individual, he is *de jure* amenable to those whose interests are concerned, and, if need be, to society as their protector. There are often good reasons for not holding him to the responsibility; but these reasons must arise from the special expediencies of the case; either because it is a kind of case in which he is on the whole likely to act better when left to his own discretion than when controlled in any way in which society have it in their power to control him; or because the attempt to exercise control would produce other evils, greater than those which it would prevent. When such reasons as these preclude the enforcement of responsibility, the conscience of the agent himself should step into the vacant judgment seat and protect those interests of others which have no external protection; judging himself all the more rigidly, because the case does not admit of his being made accountable to the judgment of his fellow creatures.

But there is a sphere of action in which society, as distinguished from the individual, has, if any, only an indirect interest: comprehending all that portion of a person's life and conduct which affects only himself or, if it also affects others, only with their free, voluntary, and undeceived consent and participation. When I say only himself, I mean directly and in the first instance; for whatever affects himself may affect others through himself: and the objection which may be grounded on this contingency will receive consideration in the sequel. This, then, is the appropriate region of human liberty. It comprises, first, the inward domain of consciousness, demanding liberty of conscience in the most comprehensive sense, liberty of thought and feeling, absolute freedom of opinion and sentiment on all subjects, practical or speculative, scientific, moral, or theological. The liberty of expressing and publishing opinions may seem to fall under a different principle, since it belongs to that part of the conduct of an individual which concerns other people, but, being almost of as much importance as the liberty of thought itself and resting in great part on the same reasons, is practically inseparable from it. Secondly, the principle requires liberty of tastes and pursuits, of framing the plan of our life to suit our own character, of doing as we like, subject to such consequences as may follow, without impediment from our fellow creatures, so long as what we do does not harm them, even though they should think our conduct foolish, perverse, or wrong. Thirdly, from this liberty of each individual follows the liberty, within the same limits, of combination among individuals; freedom to unite for any purpose not involving harm to others: the persons combining being supposed to be of full age and not forced or deceived.

No society in which these liberties are not, on the whole, respected is free, whatever may be its form of government; and none is completely free in which they do not exist absolute and unqualified. The only freedom which deserves the name is that of pursuing our own good in our own way, so long as we do not attempt to deprive others of theirs or impede their efforts to obtain it. Each is the proper guardian of his own health, whether bodily *or* mental and spiritual. Mankind are greater gainers by suffering each other to live as seems good to themselves than by compelling each to live as seems good to the rest.

Though this doctrine is anything but new and, to some persons, may have the air of truism, there is no doctrine which stands more directly opposed to the general tendency of existing opinion and practice. Society has expended fully as much effort in the attempt (according to its lights) to compel people to conform to its notions of personal as of social excellence. The ancient commonwealths thought themselves entitled to practice, and the ancient philosophers countenanced, the regulation of every part of private conduct by public authority, on the ground that the State had a deep interest in the whole bodily and mental discipline of every one of its citizens—a mode of thinking which may have been admissible in small republics surrounded by powerful enemies, in constant peril of being subverted by foreign attack or internal commotion, and to which even a short interval of relaxed energy and self-command might so easily be fatal that they could not afford to wait for the salutary permanent effects of freedom. In the modern world, the greater size of political communities and, above all, the separation between spiritual and temporal authority (which placed the direction of men's consciences in other hands than those which controlled their worldly affairs) prevented so great an interference by law in the details of private life; but the engines of moral repression have been wielded more strenuously against divergence from the reigning opinion in self-regarding than even in social matters; religion, the most powerful of the elements which have entered into the formation of moral feeling, having almost always been governed either by the ambition of a hierarchy seeking control over every department of human conduct, or by the spirit of Puritanism. And some of those modern reformers who have placed themselves in strongest opposition to the religions of the past have been noway behind either churches or sects in their assertion of the right of spiritual domination: M. Comte, in particular, whose social system, as unfolded in his *Système de Politique Positive*, aims at establishing (though by moral more than by legal appliances) a despotism of society over the individual surpassing anything contemplated in the political ideal of the most rigid disciplinarian among the ancient philosophers.

Apart from the peculiar tenets of individual thinkers, there is also in the world at large an increasing inclination to stretch unduly the powers of society over the individual both by force of opinion and even by that of legislation; and as the tendency of all the changes taking place in the world is to strengthen society and diminish the power of the individual, this encroachment is not one of the evils which tend spontaneously to disappear, but, on the contrary, to grow more and more formidable. The disposition of mankind, whether as rulers or as fellow citizens, to impose their own opinions and inclinations as a rule of conduct on others is so energetically supported by some of the best and by some of the worst feelings incident to human nature that it is hardly ever kept under restraint by anything but want of power; and as the power is not declining, but growing, unless a strong barrier of moral conviction can be raised against the mischief, we must expect, in the present circumstances of the world, to see it increase.

It will be convenient for the argument if, instead of at once entering upon the general thesis, we confine ourselves in the first instance to a single branch of it on which the principle here stated is, if not fully, yet to a certain point, recognized by the current opinions. This one branch is the Liberty of Thought, from which it is impossible to separate the cognate liberty of speaking and of writing. Although these liberties, to some considerable amount, form part of the political morality of all countries which profess religious toleration and free institutions, the grounds, both philosophical and practical, on which they rest are perhaps not so familiar to the general mind, nor so thoroughly appreciated by many, even of the leaders of opinion, as might have been expected. Those grounds, when rightly understood, are of much wider application than to only one division of the subject, and a thorough consideration of this part of the question will be found the best introduction to the remainder. Those to whom nothing which I am about to say will be new may therefore, I hope, excuse me if on a subject which for now three centuries has been so often discussed I venture on one discussion more.

Of the Liberty of Thought and Discussion

. . . If all mankind minus one were of one opinion, mankind would be no more justified in silencing that one person than he, if he had the power, would be justified in silencing mankind. Were an opinion a personal possession of no value except to the owner, if to be obstructed in the enjoyment of it were simply a private injury, it would make some difference whether the injury was inflicted only on a few persons or on many. But the peculiar evil of silencing the expression of an opinion is that it is robbing the human race, posterity as well as the existing generation—those who dissent from the opinion, still more than those who hold it. If the opinion is right, they are deprived of the opportunity of exchanging error for truth; if wrong, they lose, what is almost as great a benefit, the clearer perception and livelier impression of truth produced by its collision with error.

It is necessary to consider separately these two hypotheses, each of which has a distinct branch of the argument corresponding to it. We can never be sure that the opinion we are endeavoring to stifle is a false opinion; and if we were sure, stifling it would be an evil still.

First, the opinion which it is attempted to suppress by authority may possibly be true. Those who desire to suppress it, of course, deny its truth; but they are not infallible. They have no authority to decide the question for all mankind and exclude every other person from the means of judging. To refuse a hearing to an opinion because they are sure that it is false is to assume that *their* certainty is the same thing as *absolute* certainty. All silencing of discussion is an assumption of infallibility. Its condemnation may be allowed to rest on this common argument, not the worse for being common. . . .

The objection likely to be made to this argument would probably take some such form as the following. There is no greater assumption of infallibility in forbidding the propagation of error than in any other thing which is done by public authority on its own judgment and responsibility. Judgment is given to men that they may use it. Because it may be used erroneously, are men to be told that they ought not to use it at all? To prohibit what they think pernicious is not claiming exemption from error, but fulfilling the duty incumbent on them, although fallible, of acting on their conscientious conviction. If we were never to act on our opinions, because those opinions may be wrong, we should leave all our interests uncared for, and all our duties unperformed. An objection which applies to all conduct can be no valid objection to any conduct in particular. It is the duty of governments, and of individuals, to form the truest opinions they can; to form them carefully, and never impose them upon others unless they are quite sure of being right. But when they are sure (such reasoners may say), it is not conscientiousness but cowardice to shrink from acting on their opinions and allow doctrines which they honestly think dangerous to the welfare of mankind, either in this life or in another, to be scattered abroad without restraint, because other people, in less enlightened times, have persecuted opinions now believed to be true. Let us take care, it may be said, not to make the same mistake; but governments and nations have made mistakes in other things which are not denied to be fit subjects for the exercise of authority: they have laid on bad taxes, made unjust wars. Ought we therefore to lay on no taxes and, under whatever provocation, make no wars? Men and governments must act to the best of their ability. There is no such thing as absolute certainty, but there is assurance sufficient for the purposes of human life. We may, and must, assume our opinion to be true for the guidance of our own conduct; and it is assuming no more when we forbid bad men to pervert society by the propagation of opinions which we regard as false and pernicious.

I answer, that it is assuming very much more. There is the greatest difference between presuming an opinion to be true because, with every opportunity for contesting it, it has not been refuted, and assuming its truth for the purpose of not permitting its refutation. Complete liberty of contradicting and disproving our opinion is the very condition which justifies us in assuming its truth for purposes of action; and on no other terms can a being with human faculties have any rational assurance of being right.

When we consider either the history of opinion or the ordinary conduct of human life, to what is it to be ascribed that the one and the other are no worse than they are? Not certainly to the inherent force of the human understanding, for on any matter not self-evident there are ninety-nine persons totally incapable of judging of it for one who is capable; and the capacity of the hundredth person is only comparative, for the majority of the eminent men of every past generation held many opinions now known to be erroneous, and did or approved numerous things which no one will now justify. Why is it, then, that there is on the whole a preponderance among mankind of rational opinions and rational conduct? If there really is this preponderance—which there must be unless human affairs are, and have always been, in an almost desperate state—it is owing to a quality of the human mind, the source of everything respectable in man either as an intellectual or as a moral being, namely, that his errors are corrigible. He is capable of rectifying his mistakes by discussion and experience. Not by experience alone. There must be discussion to show how experience is to be interpreted. Wrong opinions and practices gradually yield to fact and argument; but facts and arguments, to produce any effect on the mind, must be brought before it. Very few facts are able to tell their own story, without comments to bring out their meaning. The whole strength and value, then, of human judgment depending on the one property, that it can be set right when it is wrong, reliance can be placed on it only when the means of setting it right are kept constantly at hand. . . .

In order more fully to illustrate the mischief of denying a hearing to opinions because we, in our own judgment, have condemned them, it will be desirable to fix down the discussion to a concrete case; and I choose, by preference, the cases which are least favorable to me—in which the argument against freedom of opinion, both on the score of truth and on that of utility, is considered the strongest. Let the opinions impugned be the belief in a God and in a future state, or any of the commonly received doctrines of morality. To fight the battle on such ground gives a great advantage to an unfair antagonist, since he will be sure to say (and many who have no desire to be unfair will say it internally), are these the doctrines which you do not deem sufficiently certain to be taken under the protection of law? Is the belief in a God one of the opinions to feel sure of which you hold to be assuming infallibility? But I must be permitted to observe that it is not the feeling sure of a doctrine (be it what it may) which I call an assumption of infallibility. It is the undertaking to decide that question *for others*, without allowing them to hear what can be said on the contrary side. And I denounce and reprobate this pretension not the less if put forth on the side of my most solemn convictions. However positive anyone's persuasion may be, not only of the falsity but of the pernicious consequences—not only of the pernicious consequences, but (to adopt expressions which I altogether condemn) the immorality and impiety of an opinion—yet if, in pursuance of that private judgment, though backed by the public judgment of his country or his contemporaries, he prevents the opinion from being heard in its defense, he assumes infallibility. And so far from the assumption being less objectionable or less dangerous because the opinion is called immoral or impious, this is the case of all others in which it is most fatal. These are exactly the occasions on which the men of one generation commit those dreadful mistakes which excite the astonishment and horror of posterity. It is among such that we find the instances memorable in history, when the arm of the law has been employed to root out the best men and the noblest doctrines; with deplorable success as to the men, though some of the doctrines have survived to be (as if in mockery) invoked in defense of similar conduct toward those who dissent from *them*, or from their received interpretation. . . .

It will be said that we do not now put to death the introducers of new opinions; we are not like our fathers who slew the prophets; we even build sepulchers to them. It is true we no longer put heretics to death; and the amount of penal infliction which modern feeling would probably tolerate, even against the most obnoxious opinions, is not sufficient to extirpate them. . . . But unhappily there is no security in the state of the public mind that the suspension of worse forms of legal persecution, which has lasted for about the space of a generation, will continue. In this age the quiet surface of routine is as often ruffled by attempts to resuscitate past evils as to introduce new benefits. What is boasted of at the present time as the revival of religion is always, in narrow and uncultivated minds, at least as much the revival of bigotry; and where there is the strong permanent leaven of intolerance in the feelings of a people, which at all times abides in the middle classes of this country, it needs but little to provoke them into actively persecuting those whom they have never ceased to think proper objects of persecution. . . . For it is this—it is the opinions men entertain, and the feelings they cherish, respecting those who disown the beliefs they deem important which makes this country not a place of mental freedom. For a long time past, the chief mischief of the legal penalties is that they strengthen the social stigma. It is that stigma which is really effective, and so effective is it that the profession of opinions which are under the ban of society is much less common in England than is, in many other countries, the avowal of those which incur risk of judicial punishment. In respect to all persons but those whose pecuniary circumstances make them independent of the good will of other people, opinion, on this subject, is as efficacious as law; men might as well be imprisoned as excluded from the means of earning their bread. . . . And thus is kept up a state of things very satisfactory to some minds, because, without the unpleasant process of fining or imprisoning anybody, it maintains all prevailing opinions outwardly undisturbed, while it does not absolutely interdict the exercise of reason by dissentients afflicted with the malady of thought. A convenient plan for having peace in the intellectual world, and keeping all things going on therein very much as they do already. But the price paid for this sort of intellectual pacification is the sacrifice of the entire moral courage of the human mind. A state of things in which a large portion of the most active and inquiring intellects find it advisable to keep the general principles and grounds of their convictions within their own breasts, and attempt, in what they address to the public, to fit as much as they can of their own conclusions to premises which they have internally renounced, cannot send forth the open, fearless characters and logical, consistent intellects who once adorned the thinking world. The sort of men who can be looked for under it are either mere conformers to commonplace, or timeservers for truth, whose arguments on all great subjects are meant for their hearers, and are not those which have convinced themselves. Those who avoid this alternative do so by narrowing their thoughts and interest to things which can be spoken of without venturing within the region of principles, that is, to small practical matters which would come right of themselves, if but the minds of mankind were strengthened and enlarged, and which will never be made effectually right until then, while that which would strengthen and enlarge men's minds—free and daring speculation on the highest subjects—is abandoned.

Those in whose eyes this reticence on the part of heretics is no evil should consider, in the first place, that in consequence of it there is never any fair and thorough discussion of heretical opinions; and that such of them as could not stand such a discussion, though they may be prevented from spreading, do not disappear. But it is not the minds of heretics that are deteriorated most by the ban placed on all inquiry which does not end in the orthodox conclusions. The greatest harm done is to those who are not heretics, and whose whole mental development is cramped and their reason cowed by the fear of heresy. Who can compute what the world loses in the multitude of promising intellects combined with timid characters, who dare not follow out any bold, vigorous, independent train of thought, lest it should land them in something which would admit of being considered irreligious or immoral? Among them we may occasionally see some man of deep conscientiousness and subtle and refined understanding, who spends a life in sophisticating with an intellect which he cannot silence, and exhausts the resources of ingenuity in attempting to reconcile the promptings of his conscience and reason with orthodoxy, which yet he does not, perhaps, to the end succeed in doing. No one can be a great thinker who does not recognize that as a thinker it is his first duty to follow his intellect to whatever conclusions it may lead. Truth gains more even by the errors of one who, with due study and preparation, thinks for himself than by the true opinions of those who only hold them because they do not suffer themselves to think. Not that it is solely, or chiefly, to form great thinkers that freedom of thinking is required. On the contrary, it is as much and even more indispensable to enable average human beings to attain the mental stature which they are capable of. There have been, and may again be, great individual thinkers in a general atmosphere of mental slavery. But there never has been, nor ever will be, in that atmosphere an intellectually active people. Where any people has made a temporary approach to such a character, it has been because the dread of heterodox speculation was for a time suspended. Where there is a tacit convention that principles are not to be disputed, where the discussion of the greatest questions which can occupy humanity is considered to be closed, we cannot hope to find that generally high scale of mental activity which has made some periods of history so remarkable. Never when controversy avoided the subjects which are large and important enough to kindle enthusiasm was the mind of a people stirred up from its foundations, and the impulse given which raised even persons of the most ordinary intellect to something of the dignity of thinking beings. . . .

Let us now pass to the second division of the argument, and dismissing the supposition that any of the received opinions may be false, let us assume them to be true and examine into the worth of the manner in which they are likely to be held when their truth is not freely and openly canvassed. However unwillingly a person who has a strong opinion may admit the possibility that his opinion may be false, he ought to be moved by the consideration that, however true it may be, if it is not fully, frequently, and fearlessly discussed, it will be held as a dead dogma, not a living truth.

There is a class of persons (happily not quite so numerous as formerly) who think it enough if a person assents undoubtingly to what they think true, though he has no knowledge whatever of the grounds of the opinion and could not make a tenable defense of it against the most superficial objections. Such persons, if they can once get their creed taught from authority, naturally think that no good, and some harm, comes of its being allowed to be questioned. Where their influence prevails, they make it nearly impossible for the received opinion to be rejected wisely and considerately, though it may still be rejected rashly and ignorantly; for to shut out discussion entirely is seldom possible, and when it once gets in, beliefs not grounded on conviction are apt to give way before the slightest semblance of an argument. Waiving, however, this possibility—assuming that the true opinion abides in the mind, but abides as a prejudice, a belief independent of, and proof against, argument—this is not the way in which truth ought to be held by a rational being. This is not knowing the truth. Truth, thus held, is but one superstition the more, accidentally clinging to the words which enunciate a truth. . . . He who knows only his own side of the case knows little of that. His reasons may be good, and no one may have been able to refute them. But if he is equally unable to refute the reasons on the opposite side, if he does not so much as know what they are, he has no ground for preferring either opinion. The rational position for him would be suspension of judgment, and unless he contents himself with that, he is either led by authority or adopts, like the generality of the world, the side to which he feels most inclination. Nor is it enough that he should hear the arguments of adversaries from his own teachers, presented as they state them, and accompanied by what they offer as refutations. That is not the way to do justice to the arguments or bring them into real contact with his own mind. He must be able to hear them from persons who actually believe them, who defend them in earnest and do their very utmost for them. He must know them in their most plausible and persuasive form; he must feel the whole force of the difficulty which the true view of the subject has to encounter and dispose of, else he will never really possess himself of the portion of truth which meets and removes that difficulty. Ninety-nine in a hundred of what are called educated men are in this condition, even of those who can argue fluently for their opinions. Their conclusion may be true, but it might be false for anything they know; they have never thrown themselves into the mental position of those who think differently from them, and considered what such persons may have to say; and, consequently, they do not, in any proper sense of the word, know the doctrine which they themselves profess. They do not know those parts of it which explain and justify the remainder—the considerations which show that a fact which seemingly conflicts with another is reconcilable with it, or that, of two apparently strong reasons, one and not the other ought to be preferred. All that part of the truth which turns the scale and decides the judgment of a completely informed mind, they are strangers to; nor is it ever really known but to those who have attended equally and impartially to both sides and endeavored to see the reasons of both in the strongest light. So essential is this discipline to a real understanding of moral and human subjects that, if opponents of all-important truths do not exist, it is indispensable to imagine them and supply them with the strongest arguments which the most skillful devil's advocate can conjure up.

To abate the force of these considerations, an enemy of free discussion may be supposed to say that there is no necessity for mankind in general to know and understand all that can be said against or for their opinions by philosophers and theologians. That it is not needful for common men to be able to expose all the misstatements or fallacies of an ingenious opponent. That it is enough if there is always somebody capable of answering them, so that nothing likely to mislead uninstructed persons remains unrefuted. That simple minds, having been taught the obvious grounds of the truths inculcated in them, may trust to authority for the rest and, being aware that they have neither knowledge nor talent to resolve every difficulty which can be raised, may repose in the assurance that all those which have been raised have been or can be answered by those who are specially trained to the task.

Conceding to this view of the subject the utmost that can be claimed for it by those most easily satisfied with the amount of understanding of truth which ought to accompany the belief of it, even so, the argument for free discussion is noway weakened. For even this doctrine acknowledges that mankind ought to have a rational assurance that all objections have been satisfactorily answered; and how are they to be answered if that which requires to be answered is not spoken? Or how can the answer be known to be satisfactory if the objectors have no opportunity of showing that it is unsatisfactory? If not the public, at least the philosophers and theologians who are to resolve the difficulties must make themselves familiar with those difficulties in their most puzzling form; and this cannot be accomplished unless they are freely stated and placed in the most advantageous light which they admit of. . . . If the teachers of mankind are to be cognizant of all that they ought to know, everything must be free to be written and published without restraint. . . .

But what! (it may be asked), Is the absence of unanimity an indispensable condition of true knowledge? Is it necessary that some part of mankind should persist in error to enable any to realize the truth? Does a belief cease to be real and vital as soon as it is generally received—and is a proposition never thoroughly understood and felt unless some doubt of it remains? As soon as mankind have unanimously accepted a truth, does the truth perish within them? The highest aim and best result of improved intelligence, it has hitherto been thought, is to unite mankind more and more in the acknowledgment of all important truths; and does the intelligence only last as long as it has not achieved its object? Do the fruits of conquest perish by the very completeness of the victory?

I affirm no such thing. As mankind improve, the number of doctrines which are no longer disputed or doubted will be constantly on the increase; and the well-being of mankind may almost be measured by the number and gravity of the truths which have reached the point of being uncontested. The cessation, on one question after another, of serious controversy is one of the necessary incidents of the consolidation of opinion—a consolidation as salutary in the case of true opinions as it is dangerous and noxious when the opinions are erroneous. But though this gradual narrowing of the bounds of diversity of opinion is necessary in both senses of the term, being at once inevitable and indispensable, we are not therefore obliged to conclude that all its consequences must be beneficial. The loss of so important an aid to the intelligent and living apprehension of a truth as is afforded by the necessity of explaining it to, or defending it against, opponents, though not sufficient to outweigh, is no trifling drawback from the benefit of its universal recognition. Where this advantage can no longer be had, I confess I should like to see the teachers of mankind endeavoring to provide a substitute for it—some contrivance for making the difficulties of the question as present to the learner's consciousness as if they were pressed upon him by a dissentient champion, eager for his conversion. . . .

It still remains to speak of one of the principal causes which make diversity of opinion advantageous, and will continue to do so until mankind shall have entered a stage of intellectual advancement which at present seems at an incalculable distance. We have hitherto considered only two possibilities; that the received opinion may be false, and some other opinion, consequently, true; or that, the received opinion being true, a conflict with the opposite error is essential to a clear apprehension and deep feeling of its truth. But there is a commoner case than either of these: when the conflicting doctrines, instead of being one true and the other false, share the truth between them, and the nonconforming opinion is needed to supply the remainder of the truth of which the received doctrine embodies only a part. Popular opinions, on subjects not palpable to sense, are often true, but seldom or never the whole truth. They are a part of the truth, sometimes a greater, sometimes a smaller part, but exaggerated, distorted, and disjointed from the truths by which they ought to be accompanied and limited. Heretical opinions, on the other hand, are generally some of these suppressed and neglected truths, bursting the bonds which kept them down, and either seeking reconciliation with the truth contained in the common opinion, or fronting it as enemies, and setting themselves up, with similar exclusiveness, as the whole truth. The latter case is hitherto the most frequent, as, in the human mind, one-sidedness has always been the rule, and many-sidedness the exception. Hence, even in revolutions of opinion, one part of the truth usually sets while another rises. Even progress, which ought to superadd, for the most part only substitutes one partial and incomplete truth for another; improvement consisting chiefly in this, that the new fragment of truth is more wanted, more adapted to the needs of the time than that which it displaces. Such being the partial character of prevailing opinions, even when resting on a true foundation, every opinion which embodies somewhat of the portion of truth which the common opinion omits ought to be considered precious, with whatever amount of error and confusion that truth may be blended. No sober judge of human affairs will feel bound to be indignant because those who force on our notice truths which we should otherwise have overlooked, overlook some of those which we see. Rather, he will think that so long as popular truth is one-sided, it is more desirable than otherwise that unpopular truth should have one-sided assertors, too, such being usually the most energetic and the most likely to compel reluctant attention to the fragment of wisdom which they proclaim as if it were the whole. . . .

In politics, again, it is almost a commonplace that a party of order or stability and a party of progress or reform are both necessary elements of a healthy state of political life, until the one or the other shall have so enlarged its mental grasp as to be a party equally of order and of progress, knowing and distinguishing what is fit to be preserved from what ought to be swept away. Each of these modes of thinking derives its utility from the deficiencies of the other; but it is in a great measure the opposition of the other that keeps each within the limits of reason and sanity. Unless opinions favorable to democracy and to aristocracy, to property and to equality, to co-operation and to competition, to luxury and to abstinence, to sociality and individuality, to liberty and discipline, and all the other standing antagonisms of practical life, are expressed with equal freedom and enforced and defended with equal talent and energy, there is no chance of both elements obtaining their due; one scale is sure to go up, and the other down. Truth, in the great practical concerns of life, is so much a question of the reconciling and combining of opposites that very few have minds sufficiently capacious and impartial to make the adjustment with an approach to correctness, and it has to be made by the rough process of a struggle between combatants fighting under hostile banners. On any of the great open questions just enumerated, if either of the two opinions has a better claim than the other, not merely to be tolerated, but to be encouraged and countenanced, it is the one which happens at the particular time and place to be in a minority. That is the opinion which, for the time being, represents the neglected interests, the side of human well-being which is in danger of obtaining less than its share. I am aware that there is not, in this country, any intolerance of differences of opinion on most of these topics. They are adduced to show, by admitted and multiplied examples, the universality of the fact that only through diversity of opinion is there, in the existing state of human intellect, a chance of fair play to all sides of the truth. When there are persons to be found who form an exception to the apparent unanimity of the world on any subject, even if the world is in the right, it is always probable that dissentients have something worth hearing to say for themselves, and that truth would lose something by their silence. . . .

We have now recognized the necessity to the mental well-being of mankind (on which all their other well-being depends) of freedom of opinion, and freedom of the expression of opinion, on four distinct grounds, which we will now briefly recapitulate:

First, if any opinion is compelled to silence, that opinion may, for aught we can certainly know, be true. To deny this is to assume our own infallibility.

Secondly, though the silenced opinion be an error, it may, and very commonly does, contain a portion of truth; and since the general or prevailing opinion on any subject is rarely or never the whole truth, it is only by the collision of adverse opinions that the remainder of the truth has any chance of being supplied.

Thirdly, even if the received opinion be not only true, but the whole truth; unless it is suffered to be, and actually is, vigorously and earnestly contested, it will, by most of those who receive it, be held in the manner of a prejudice, with little comprehension or feeling of its rational grounds. And not only this, but, fourthly, the meaning of the doctrine itself will be in danger of being lost or enfeebled, and deprived of its vital effect on the character and conduct: the dogma becoming a mere formal profession, inefficacious for good, but cumbering the ground and preventing the growth of any real and heartfelt conviction from reason or personal experience. . . .

Of Individuality, As One of the Elements of Well-Being

Such being the reasons which make it imperative that human beings should be free to form opinions and to express their opinions without reserve; and such the baneful consequences to the intellectual, and through that to the moral nature of man, unless this liberty is either conceded or asserted in spite of prohibition; let us next examine whether the same reasons do not require that men should be free to act upon their opinions—to carry these out in their lives without hindrance, either physical or moral, from their fellow men, so long as it is at their own risk and peril. This last proviso is of course indispensable. No one pretends that actions should be as free as opinions. On the contrary, even opinions lose their immunity when the circumstances in which they are expressed are such as to constitute their expression a positive instigation to some mischievous act. An opinion that corn dealers are starvers of the poor, or that private property is robbery, ought to be unmolested when simply circulated through the press, but may justly incur punishment when delivered orally to an excited mob assembled before the house of a corn dealer, or when handed about among the same mob in the form of a placard. Acts, of whatever kind, which without justifiable cause do harm to others may be, and in the more important cases absolutely require to be, controlled by the unfavorable sentiments, and, when needful, by the active interference of mankind. The liberty of the individual must be thus far limited; he must not make himself a nuisance to other people. But if he refrains from molesting others in what concerns them, and merely acts according to his own inclination and judgment in things which concern himself, the same reasons which show that opinion should be free prove also that he should be allowed, without molestation, to carry his opinions into practice at his own cost. That mankind are not infallible; that their truths, for the most part, are only half-truths; that unity of opinion, unless resulting from the fullest and freest comparison of opposite opinions, is not desirable, and diversity not an evil, but a good, until mankind are much more capable than at present of recognizing all sides of the truth, are principles applicable to men's modes of action not less than to their opinions. As it is useful that while mankind are imperfect there should be different opinions, so it is that there should be different experiments of living; that free scope should be given to varieties of character, short of injury to others; and that the worth of different modes of life should be proved practically, when anyone thinks fit to try them. It is desirable, in short, that in things which do not primarily concern others individuality should assert itself. Where not the person's own character but the traditions or customs of other people are the rule of conduct, there is wanting one of the principal ingredients of human happiness, and quite the chief ingredient of individual and social progress.

In maintaining this principle, the greatest difficulty to be encountered does not lie in the appreciation of means toward an acknowledged end, but in the indifference of persons in general to the end itself. If it were felt that the free development of individuality is one of the leading essentials of well-being; that it is not only a co-ordinate element with all that is designated by the terms civilization, instruction, education, culture, but is itself a necessary part and condition of all those things, there would be no danger that liberty should be undervalued, and the adjustment of the boundaries between it and social control would present no extraordinary difficulty. But the evil is that individual spontaneity is hardly recognized by the common modes of thinking as having any intrinsic worth, or deserving any regard on its own account.

The majority, being satisfied with the ways of mankind as they now are (for it is they who make them what they are), cannot comprehend why those ways should not be good enough for everybody; and what is more, spontaneity forms no part of the ideal of the majority of moral and social reformers, but is rather looked on with jealousy, as a troublesome and perhaps rebellious obstruction to the general acceptance of what these reformers, in their own judgment, think would be best for mankind. . . . It would be absurd to pretend that people ought to live as if nothing whatever had been known in the world before they came into it; as if experience had as yet done nothing toward showing that one mode of existence, or of conduct, is preferable to another. Nobody denies that people should be so taught and trained in youth as to know and benefit by the ascertained results of human experience. But it is the privilege and proper condition of a human being, arrived at the maturity of his faculties, to use and interpret experience in his own way. It is for him to find out what part of recorded experience is properly applicable to his own circumstances and character. The traditions and customs of other people are, to a certain extent, evidence of what their experience has taught *them*—presumptive evidence, and as such, have a claim to his deference: but, in the first place, their experience may be too narrow, or they may have not interpreted it rightly. Secondly, their interpretation of experience may be correct, but unsuitable to him. Customs are made for customary circumstances and customary characters; and his circumstances or his character may be uncustomary. Thirdly, though the customs be both good as customs and suitable to him, yet to conform to custom merely *as* custom does not educate or develop in him any of the qualities which are the distinctive endowment of a human being. The human faculties of perception, judgment, discriminative feeling, mental activity, and even moral preference are exercised only in making a choice. He who does anything because it is the custom makes no choice. He gains no practice either in discerning or in desiring what is best. The mental and moral, like the muscular, powers are improved only by being used. The faculties are called into no exercise by doing a thing merely because others do it, no more than by believing a thing only because others believe it. If the grounds of an opinion are not conclusive to the person's own reason, his reason cannot be strengthened, but is likely to be weakened, by his adopting it: and if the inducements to an act are not such as are consentaneous to his own feelings and character (where affection, or the rights of others, are not concerned), it is so much done toward rendering his feelings and character inert and torpid instead of active and energetic. . . .

It will probably be conceded that it is desirable people should exercise their understandings, and that an intelligent following of custom, or even occasionally an intelligent deviation from custom, is better than a blind and simply mechanical adhesion to it. To a certain extent it is admitted that our understanding should be our own; but there is not the same willingness to admit that our desires and impulses should be our own likewise, or that to possess impulses of our own, and of any strength, is anything but a peril and a snare. Yet desires and impulses are as much a part of a perfect human being as beliefs and restraints; and strong impulses are only perilous when not properly balanced, when one set of aims and inclinations is developed into strength, while others, which ought to coexist with them, remain weak and inactive. It is not because men's desires are strong that they act ill; it is because their consciences are weak. There is no natural connection between strong impulses and a weak conscience. The natural connection is the other way. To say that one person's desires and feelings are stronger and more various than those of another is merely to say that he has more of the raw material of human nature and is therefore capable, perhaps of more evil, but certainly of more good. Strong impulses are but another name for energy. Energy may be turned to bad uses; but more good may always be made of an energetic nature than of an indolent and impassive one. Those who have most natural feeling are always those whose cultivated feelings may be made the strongest. The same strong susceptibilities which make the personal impulses vivid and powerful are also the source from whence are generated the most passionate love of virtue and the sternest self-control. It is through the cultivation of these that society both does its duty and protects its interests, not by rejecting the stuff of which heroes are made, because it knows not how to make them. A person whose desires and impulses are his own—are the expression of his own nature, as it has been developed and modified by his own culture—is said to have a character. One whose desires and impulses are not his own has no character, no more than a steam engine has a character. If, in addition to being his own, his impulses are strong and are under the government of a strong will, he has an energetic character. Whoever thinks that individuality of desires and impulses should not be encouraged to unfold itself must maintain that society has no need of strong natures—is not the better for containing many persons who have much character—and that a high general average of energy is not desirable. . . .

It is not by wearing down into uniformity all that is individual in themselves, but by cultivating it and calling it forth, within the limits imposed by the rights and interests of others, that human beings become a noble and beautiful object of contemplation; and as the works partake the character of those who do them, by the same process human life also becomes rich, diversified, and animating, furnishing more abundant aliment to high thoughts and elevating feelings, and strengthening the tie which binds every individual to the race, by making the race infinitely better worth belonging to. In proportion to the development of his individuality, each person becomes more valuable to himself, and is, therefore, capable of being more valuable to others. There is a greater fullness of life about his own existence, and when there is more life in the units there is more in the mass which is composed of them. As much compression as is necessary to prevent the stronger specimens of human nature from encroaching on the rights of others cannot be dispensed with; but for this there is ample compensation even in the point of view of human development. The means of development which the individual loses by being prevented from gratifying his inclinations to the injury of others are chiefly obtained at the expense of the development of other people. And even to himself there is a full equivalent in the better development of the social part of his nature, rendered possible by the restraint put upon the selfish part. To be held to rigid rules of justice for the sake of others develops the feelings and capacities which have the good of others for their object. But to be restrained in things not affecting their good, by their mere displeasure, develops nothing valuable except such force of character as may unfold itself in resisting the restraint. If acquiesced in, it dulls and blunts the whole nature. To give any fair play to the nature of each, it is essential that different persons should be allowed to lead different lives. In proportion as this latitude has been exercised in any age has that age been noteworthy to posterity. Even despotism does not produce its worst effects so long as individuality exists under it; and whatever crushes individuality is despotism, by whatever name it may be called and whether it professes to be enforcing the will of God or the injunctions of men.

Having said that the individuality is the same thing with development, and that it is only the cultivation of individuality which produces, or can produce, well-developed human beings, I might here close the argument; for what more or better can be said of any condition of human affairs than that it brings human beings themselves nearer to the best thing they can be? Or what worse can be said of any obstruction to good than that it prevents this? Doubtless, however, these considerations will not suffice to convince those who most need convincing; and it is necessary further to show that these developed human beings are of some use to the undeveloped—to point out to those who do not desire liberty, and would not avail themselves of it, that they may be in some intelligible manner rewarded for allowing other people to make use of it without hindrance.

In the first place, then, I would suggest that they might possibly learn something from them. It will not be denied by anybody that originality is a valuable element in human affairs. There is always need of persons not only to discover new truths and point out when what were once truths are true no longer, but also to commence new practices and set the example of more enlightened conduct and better taste and sense in human life. This cannot well be gainsaid by anybody who does not believe that the world has already attained perfection in all its ways and practices. It is true that this benefit is not capable of being rendered by everybody alike; there are but few persons, in comparison with the whole of mankind, whose experiments, if adopted by others, would be likely to be any improvement on established practice. But these few are the salt of the earth; without them, human life would become a stagnant pool. Not only is it they who introduce good things which did not before exist; it is they who keep the life in those which already exist. . . .

I insist thus emphatically on the importance of genius and the necessity of allowing it to unfold itself freely both in thought and in practice, being well aware that no one will deny the position in theory, but knowing also that almost everyone, in reality, is totally indifferent to it. People think a genius a fine thing if it enables a man to write an exciting poem or paint a picture. But in its true sense, that of originality in thought and action, though no one says that it is not a thing to be admired, nearly all, at heart, think that they can do very well without it. Unhappily this is too natural to be wondered at. Originality is the one thing which unoriginal minds cannot feel the use of. They cannot see what it is to do for them: how should they? If they could see what it would do for them, it would not be originality. The first service which originality has to render them is that of opening their eyes: which being once fully done, they would have a chance of being themselves original. Meanwhile, recollecting that nothing was ever done which someone was not the first to do, and that all good things which exist are the fruits of originality, let them be modest enough to believe that there is something still left for it to accomplish, and assure themselves that they are more in need of originality, the less they are conscious of the want.

In sober truth, whatever homage may be professed, or even paid, to real or supposed mental superiority, the general tendency of things throughout the world is to render mediocrity the ascendant power among mankind. In ancient history, in the Middle Ages, and in a diminishing degree through the long transition from feudality to the present time, the individual was a power in himself; and if he had either great talents or a high social position, he was a considerable power. At present individuals are lost in the crowd. In politics it is almost a triviality to say that public opinion now rules the world. The only power deserving the name is that of masses, and of governments while they make themselves the organ of the tendencies and instincts of masses. . . . It is in these circumstances most especially that exceptional individuals, instead of being deterred, should be encouraged in acting differently from the mass. In other times there was no advantage in their doing so, unless they acted not only differently but better. In this age, the mere example of nonconformity, the mere refusal to bend the knee to custom, is itself a service. Precisely because the tyranny of opinion is such as to make eccentricity a reproach, it is desirable, in order to break through that tyranny, that people should be eccentric. Eccentricity has always abounded when and where strength of character has abounded; and the amount of eccentricity in a society has generally been proportional to the amount of genius, mental vigor, and moral courage it contained. That so few now dare to be eccentric marks the chief danger of the time.

I have said that it is important to give the freest scope possible to uncustomary things, in order that it may in time appear which of these are fit to be converted into customs. But independence of action and disregard of custom are not solely deserving of encouragement for the chance they afford that better modes of action, and customs more worthy of general adoption, may be struck out; nor is it only persons of decided mental superiority who have a just claim to carry on their lives in their own way. There is no reason that all human existence should be constructed on some one or some small number of patterns. If a person possesses any tolerable amount of common sense and experience, his own mode of laying out his existence is the best, not because it is the best in itself, but because it is his own mode. Human beings are not like sheep; and even sheep are not undistinguishably alike. A man cannot get a coat or a pair of boots to fit him unless they are either made to his measure or he has a whole warehouseful to choose from; and is it easier to fit him with a life than with a coat, or are human beings more like one another in their whole physical and spiritual conformation than in the shape of their feet? If it were only that people have diversities of taste, that is reason enough for not attempting to shape them all after one model. But different persons also require different conditions for their spiritual development; and can no more exist healthily in the same moral than all the variety of plants can in the same physical, atmosphere and climate. The same things which are helps to one person toward the cultivation of his higher nature are hindrances to another. The same mode of life is a healthy excitement to one, keeping all his faculties of action and enjoyment in their best order, while to another it is a distracting burden which suspends or crushes all internal life. Such are the differences among human beings in their sources of pleasure, their susceptibilities of pain, and the operation on them of different physical and moral agencies that, unless there is a corresponding diversity in their modes of life, they neither obtain their fair share of happiness, nor grow up to the mental, moral, and aesthetic stature of which their nature is capable. Why then should tolerance, as far as the public sentiment is concerned, extend only to tastes and modes of life which extort acquiescence by the multitude of their adherents? Nowhere (except in some monastic institutions) is diversity of taste entirely unrecognized; a person may, without blame, either like or dislike rowing, or smoking, or music, or athletic exercises, or chess, or cards, or study, because both those who like each of these things and those who dislike them are too numerous to be put down. But the man, and still more the woman, who can be accused either of doing "what nobody does," or of not doing "what everybody does," is the subject of as much depreciatory remark as if he or she had committed some grave moral delinquency. . . .

The despotism of custom is everywhere the standing hindrance to human advancement, being in unceasing antagonism to that disposition to aim at something better than customary, which is called, according to circumstances, the spirit of liberty, or that of progress or improvement. The spirit of improvement is not always a spirit of liberty, for it may aim at forcing improvements on an unwilling people; and the spirit of liberty, in so far as it resists such attempts, may ally itself locally and temporarily with the opponents of improvement; but the only unfailing and permanent source of improvement is liberty, since by it there are as many possible independent centers of improvement as there are individuals. The progressive principle, however, in either shape, whether as the love of liberty or of improvement, is antagonistic to the sway of custom, involving at least emancipation from that yoke; and the contest between the two constitutes the chief interest of the history of mankind. . . .

Of the Limits To The Authority of Society Over The Individual

What, then, is the rightful limit to the sovereignty of the individual over himself? Where does the authority of society begin? How much of human life should be assigned to individuality, and how much to society?

Each will receive its proper share if each has that which more particularly concerns it. To individuality should belong the part of life in which it is chiefly the individual that is interested; to society, the part which chiefly interests society.

Though society is not founded on a contract, and though no good purpose is answered by inventing a contract in order to deduce social obligations from it, everyone who receives the protection of society owes a return for the benefit, and the fact of living in society renders it indispensable that each should be bound to observe a certain line of conduct toward the rest. This conduct consists, first, in not injuring the interests of one another, or rather certain interests which, either by express legal provision or by tacit understanding, ought to be considered as rights; and secondly, in each person's bearing his share (to be fixed on some equitable principle) of the labors and sacrifices incurred for defending the society or its members from injury and molestation. These conditions society is justified in enforcing at all costs to those who endeavor to withhold fulfillment. Nor is this all that society may do. The acts of an individual may be hurtful to others or wanting in due consideration for their welfare, without going to the length of violating any of their constituted rights. The offender may then be justly punished by opinion, though not by law. As soon as any part of a person's conduct affects prejudicially the interests of others, society has jurisdiction over it, and the question whether the general welfare will or will not be promoted by interfering with it becomes open to discussion. But there is no room for entertaining any such question when a person's conduct affects the interests of no persons besides himself, or needs not affect them unless they like (all the persons concerned being of full age and the ordinary amount of understanding). In all such cases, there should be perfect freedom, legal and social, to do the action and stand the consequences.

It would be a great misunderstanding of this doctrine to suppose that it is one of selfish indifference which pretends that human beings have no business with each other's conduct in life, and that they should not concern themselves about the well-doing or well-being of one another, unless their own interest is involved. Instead of any diminution, there is need of a great increase of disinterested exertion to promote the good of others. But disinterested benevolence can find other instruments to persuade people to their good than whips and scourges, either of the literal or the metaphorical sort. I am the last person to undervalue the self-regarding virtues; they are only second in importance, if even second, to the social. It is equally the business of education to cultivate both. But even education works by conviction and persuasion as well as by compulsion, and it is by the former only that, when the period of education is passed, the self-regarding virtues should be inculcated. Human beings owe to each other help to distinguish the better from the worse, and encouragement to choose the former and avoid the latter. They should be forever stimulating each other to increased exercise of their higher faculties and increased direction of their feelings and aims toward wise instead of foolish, elevating instead of degrading, objects and contemplations. But neither one person, nor any number of persons, is warranted in saying to another human creature of ripe years that he shall not do with his life for his own benefit what he chooses to do with it. He is the person most interested in his own well-being: the interest which any other person, except in cases of strong personal attachment, can have in it is trifling compared with that which he himself has; the interest which society has in him individually (except as to his conduct to others) is fractional and altogether indirect, while with respect to his own feelings and circumstances the most ordinary man or woman has means of knowledge immeasurably surpassing those that can be possessed by anyone else. The interference of society to overrule his judgment and purposes in what only regards himself must be grounded on general presumptions which may be altogether wrong and, even if right, are as likely as not to be misapplied to individual cases, by persons no better acquainted with the circumstances of such cases than those are who look at them merely from without. In this department, therefore, of human affairs, individuality has its proper field of action. In the conduct of human beings toward one another it is necessary that general rules should for the most part be observed in order that people may know what they have to except; but in each person's own concerns his individual spontaneity is entitled to free exercise. Considerations to aid his judgment, exhortations to strengthen his will may be offered to him, even obtruded on him, by others; but he himself is the final judge. All errors which he is likely to commit against advice and warning are far outweighed by the evil of allowing others to constrain him to what they deem his good.

I do not mean that the feelings with which a person is regarded by others ought not to be in any way affected by his self-regarding qualities or deficiencies. This is neither possible nor desirable. If he is eminent in any of the qualities which conduce to his own good, he is, so far, a proper object of admiration. He is so much the nearer to the ideal perfection of human nature. If he is grossly deficient in those qualities, a sentiment the opposite of admiration will follow. There is a degree of folly, and a degree of what may be called (though the phrase is not unobjectionable) lowness or depravation of taste, which, though it cannot justify doing harm to the person who manifests it, renders him necessarily and properly a subject of distaste, or, in extreme cases, even of contempt: a person could not have the opposite qualities in due strength without entertaining these feelings. Though doing no wrong to anyone, a person may so act as to compel us to judge him, and feel to him, as a fool or as a being of an inferior order; and since this judgment and feeling are a fact which he would prefer to avoid, it is doing him a service to warn him of it beforehand, as of any other disagreeable consequence to which he exposes himself. It would be well, indeed, if this good office were much more freely rendered than the common notions of politeness at present permit, and if one person could honestly point out to another that he thinks him in fault, without being considered unmannerly or presuming. We have a right, also, in various ways, to act upon our unfavorable opinion of anyone, not to the oppression of his individuality, but in the exercise of ours. We are not bound, for example, to seek his society; we have a right also, to avoid it (though not to parade the avoidance), for we have a right to choose the society most acceptable to us. We have a right, and it may be our duty, to caution others against him if we think his example or conversation likely to have a pernicious effect on those with whom he associates. We may give others a preference over him in optional good offices, except those which tend to his improvement. In these various modes a person may suffer very severe penalties at the hands of others for faults which directly concern only himself; but he suffers these penalties only in so far as they are the natural and, as it were, the spontaneous consequences of the faults themselves, not because they are purposely inflicted on him for the sake of punishment. A person who shows rashness, obstinacy, self-conceit—who cannot live within moderate means; who cannot restrain himself from hurtful indulgence; who pursues animal pleasures at the expense of those of feeling and intellect—must expect to be lowered in the opinion of others, and to have a less share of their favorable sentiments; but of this he has no right to complain unless he has merited their favor by special excellence in his social relations and has thus established a title to their good offices, which is not affected by his demerits toward himself.

What I contend for is that the inconveniences which are strictly inseparable from the unfavorable judgment of others are the only ones to which a person should ever be subjected for that portion of his conduct and character which concerns his own good, but which does not affect the interest of others in their relations with him. Acts injurious to others require a totally different treatment. Encroachment on their rights; infliction on them of any loss or damage not justified by his own rights; falsehood or duplicity in dealing with them; unfair or ungenerous use of advantages over them; even selfish abstinence from defending them against injury—these are fit objects of moral reprobation and, in grave ones, of moral retribution and punishment. And not only these acts, but the dispositions which lead to them, are properly immoral and fit subjects of disapprobation which may rise to abhorrence. Cruelty of disposition; malice and ill-nature; that most antisocial and odious of all passions, envy; dissimulation and insincerity, irascibility on insufficient cause, and resentment disproportioned to the provocation; the love of domineering over others; the desire to engross more than one's share of advantages (the *pleonexia* of the Greeks); the pride which derives gratification from the abasement of others; the egotism which thinks self and its concerns more important than everything else, and decides all doubtful questions in its own favor—these are moral vices and constitute a bad and odious moral character; unlike the self-regarding faults previously mentioned, which are not properly immoralities and, to whatever pitch they may be carried, do not constitute wickedness. They may be proofs of any amount of folly or want of personal dignity and self-respect, but they are only a subject of moral reprobation when they involve a breach of duty to others, for whose sake the individual is bound to have care for himself. What are called duties to ourselves are not socially obligatory unless circumstances render them at the same time duties to others. The term duty to onself, when it means anything more than prudence, means self-respect or self-development, and for none of these is anyone accountable to his fellow creatures, because for none of them is it for the good of mankind that he be held accountable to them.

The distinction between the loss of consideration which a person may rightly incur by defect of prudence or of personal dignity, and the reprobation which is due to him for an offense against the rights of others, is not a merely nominal distinction. It makes a vast difference both in our feelings and in our conduct toward him whether he displeases us in things in which we think we have a right to control him or in things in which we know that we have not. If he displeases us, we may express our distaste, and we may stand aloof from a person as well as from a thing that displeases us; but we shall not therefore feel called on to make his life uncomfortable. We shall reflect that he already bears, or will bear, the whole penalty of his error; if he spoils his life by mismanagement, we shall not, for that reason, desire to spoil it still further; instead of wishing to punish him, we shall rather endeavor to alleviate his punishment by showing him how he may avoid or cure the evils his conduct tends to bring upon him. He may be to us an object of pity, perhaps of dislike, but not of anger or resentment; we shall not treat him like an enemy of society; the worst we shall think ourselves justified in doing is leaving him to himself, if we do not interfere benevolently by showing interest or concern for him. It is far otherwise if he has infringed the rules necessary for the protection of his fellow creatures, individually or collectively. The evil consequences of his acts do not then fall on himself, but on others; and society, as the protector of all its members, must retaliate on him, must inflict pain on him for the express purpose of punishment, and must take care that it be sufficiently severe. In the one case, he is an offender at our bar, and we are called on not only to sit in judgment on him, but, in one shape or another, to execute our own sentence; in the other case, it is not our part to inflict any suffering on him, except what may incidentally follow from our using the same liberty in the regulation of our own affairs which we allow to him in his.

The distinction here pointed out between the part of a person's life which concerns only himself and that which concerns others, many persons will refuse to admit. How (it may be asked) can any part of the conduct of a member of society be a matter of indifference to the other members? No person is an entirely isolated being; it is impossible for a person to do anything seriously or permanently hurtful to himself without mischief reaching at least to his near connections, and often far beyond them. If he injures his property, he does harm to those who directly or indirectly derived support from it, and usually diminishes, by a greater or less amount, the general resources of the community. If he deteriorates his bodily or mental faculties, he not only brings evil upon all who depended upon him for any portion of their happiness, but disqualifies himself for rendering the services which he owes to his fellow creatures generally, perhaps becomes a burden on their affection or benevolence; and if such conduct were very frequent hardly any offense that is committed would detract more from the general sum of good. Finally, if by his vices or follies a person does no direct harm to others, he is nevertheless (it may be said) injurious by his example, and ought to be compelled to control himself for the sake of those whom the sight or knowledge of his conduct might corrupt or mislead.

And even (it will be added) if the consequences of misconduct could be confined to the vicious or thoughtless individual, ought society to abandon to their own guidance those who are manifestly unfit for it? If protection against themselves is confessedly due to children and persons under age, is not society equally bound to afford it to persons of mature years who are equally incapable of self-government? If gambling, or drunkenness, or incontinence, or idleness, or uncleanliness are as injurious to happiness, and as great a hindrance to improvement, as many or most of the acts prohibited by law, why (it may be asked) should not law, so far as is consistent with practicability and social convenience, endeavor to repress these also? And as a supplement to the unavoidable imperfections of law, ought not opinion at least to organize a powerful police against these vices and visit rigidly with social penalties those who are known to practice them? There is no question here (it may be said) about restricting individuality, or impeding the trial of new and original experiments in living. The only things it is sought to prevent are things which have been tried and condemned from the beginning of the world until now—things which experience has shown not to be useful or suitable to any person's individuality. There must be some length of time and amount of experience after which a moral or prudential truth may be regarded as established; and it is merely desired to prevent generation after generation from falling over the same precipice which has been fatal to their predecessors.

I fully admit that the mischief which a person does to himself may seriously affect, both through their sympathies and their interests, those nearly connected with him and, in a minor degree, society at large. When, by conduct of this sort, a person is led to violate a distinct and assignable obligation to any other person or persons, the case is taken out of the self-regarding class and becomes amenable to moral disapprobation in the proper sense of the term. If, for example, a man, through intemperance or extravagance, becomes unable to pay his debts, or, having undertaken the moral responsibility of a family, becomes from the same cause incapable of supporting or educating them, he is deservedly reprobated and might be justly punished; but it is for the breach of duty to his family or creditors, not for the extravagance. If the resources which ought to have been devoted to them had been diverted from them for the most prudent investment, the moral culpability would have been the same. George Barnwell murdered his uncle to get money for his mistress, but if he had done it to set himself up in business, he would equally have been hanged. Again, in the frequent case of a man who causes grief to his family by addiction to bad habits, he deserves reproach for his unkindness or ingratitude; but so he may for cultivating habits not in themselves vicious, if they are painful to those with whom he passes his life, or who from personal ties are dependent on him for their comfort. Whoever fails in the consideration generally due to the interests and feelings of others, not being compelled by some more imperative duty, or justified by allowable self-preference, is a subject of moral disapprobation for that failure, but not for the cause of it, nor for the errors, merely personal to himself, which may have remotely led to it. In like manner, when a person disables himself, by conduct purely self-regarding, from the performance of some definite duty incumbent on him to the public, he is guilty of a social offense. No person ought to be punished simply for being drunk; but a soldier or policeman should be punished for being drunk on duty. Whenever, in short, there is a definite damage, or a definite risk of damage, either to an individual or to the public, the case is taken out of the province of liberty and placed in that of morality or law.

But with regard to the merely contingent or, as it may be called, constructive injury which a person causes to society by conduct which neither violates any specific duty to the public, nor occasions perceptible hurt to any assignable individual except himself, the inconvenience is one which society can afford to bear, for the sake of the greater good of human freedom. If grown persons are to be punished for not taking proper care of themselves, I would rather it were for their own sake than under pretense of preventing them from impairing their capacity or rendering to society benefits which society does not pretend it has a right to exact. But I cannot consent to argue the point as if society had no means of bringing its weaker members up to its ordinary standard of rational conduct, except waiting till they do something irrational, and then punishing them, legally or morally, for it. Society has had absolute power over them during all the early portion of their existence; it has had the whole period of childhood and nonage in which to try whether it could make them capable of rational conduct in life. The existing generation is master both of the training and the entire circumstances of the generation to come; it cannot indeed make them perfectly wise and good, because it is itself so lamentably deficient in goodness and wisdom; and its best efforts are not always, in individual cases, its most successful ones; but it is perfectly well able to make the rising generation, as a whole, as good as, and a little better than, itself. If society lets any considerable number of its members grow up mere children, incapable of being acted on by rational consideration of distant motives, society has itself to blame for the consequences. Armed not only with all the powers of education, but with the ascendency which the authority of a received opinion always exercises over the minds who are least fitted to judge for themselves, and aided by the *natural* penalties which cannot be prevented from falling on those who incur the distaste or the contempt of those who know them—let not society pretend that it needs, besides all this, the power to issue commands and enforce obedience in the personal concerns of individuals in which, on all principles of justice and policy, the decision ought to rest with those who are to abide the consequences. Nor is there anything which tends more to discredit and frustrate the better means of influencing conduct than a resort to the worse. If there be among those whom it is attempted to coerce into prudence or temperance any of the material of which vigorous and independent characters are made, they will infallibly rebel against the yoke. No such person will ever feel that others have a right to control him in his concerns, such as they have to prevent him from injuring them in theirs; and it easily comes to be considered a mark of spirit and courage to fly in the face of such usurped authority and do with ostentation the exact opposite of what it enjoins, as in the fashion of grossness which succeeded, in the time of Charles II, to the fanatical moral intolerance of the Puritans. With respect to what is said of the necessity of protecting society from the bad example set to others by the vicious or the self-indulgent, it is true that bad example may have a pernicious effect, especially the example of doing wrong to others with impunity to the wrongdoer. But we are now speaking of conduct which, while it does not wrong to others, is supposed to do great harm to the agent himself; and I do not see how those who believe this can think otherwise than that the example, on the whole, must be more salutary than hurtful, since, if it displays the misconduct, it displays also the painful or degrading consequences which, if the conduct is justly censured, must be supposed to be in all or most cases attendant on it.

But the strongest of all the arguments against the interference of the public with purely personal conduct is that, when it does interfere, the odds are that it interferes wrongly and in the wrong place. On questions of social morality, of duty to others, the opinion of the public, that is, of an overruling majority, though often wrong, is likely to be still oftener right, because on such questions they are only required to judge of their own interests, of the manner in which some mode of conduct, if allowed to be practiced, would affect themselves. But the opinion of a similar majority, imposed as a law on the minority, on questions of self-regarding conduct is quite as likely to be wrong as right, for in these cases public opinion means, at the best, some people's opinion of what is good or bad for other people, while very often it does not even mean that—the public, with the most perfect indifference, passing over the pleasure or convenience of those whose conduct they censure and considering only their own preference. There are many who consider as an injury to themselves any conduct which they have a distaste for, and resent it as an outrage to their feelings; as a religious bigot, when charged with disregarding the religious feelings of others, has been known to retort that they disregard his feelings by persisting in their abominable worship or creed. But there is no parity between the feeling of a person for his own opinion and the feeling of another who is offended at his holding it, no more than between the desire of a thief to take a purse and the desire of the right owner to keep it. And a person's taste is as much his own peculiar concern as his opinion or his purse. . . .

Aristotle

Ethica Nicomachea

(Nicomachean Ethics)

Book I

[Happiness: The Supreme Good]*

1. Every art and every inquiry, and similarly every action and pursuit, is thought to aim at some good; and for this reason the good has rightly been declared to be that at which all things aim. But a certain difference is found among ends; some are activities, others are products apart from the activities that produce them. Where there are ends apart from the actions, it is the nature of the products to be better than the activities. Now, as there are many actions, arts, and sciences, their ends also are many; the end of the medical art is health, that of shipbuilding a vessel, that of strategy victory, that of economics wealth. But where such arts fall under a single capacity—as bridle-making and the other arts concerned with the equipment of horses fall under the art of riding, and this and every military action under strategy, in the same way other arts fall under yet others—in all of these the ends of the master arts are to be preferred to all the subordinate ends; for it is for the sake of the former that the latter are pursued. It makes no difference whether the activities themselves are the ends of the actions, or something else apart from the activities, as in the case of the sciences just mentioned.

[Political Science: The Science of the Good]

2. If, then, there is some end of the things we do, which we desire for its own sake (everything else being desired for the sake of this), and if we do not choose everything for the sake of something else (for at that rate the process would go on to infinity, so that our desire would be empty and vain), clearly this must be the good and the chief good. Will not the knowledge of it, then, have a great influence on life? Shall we not, like archers who have a mark to aim at, be more likely to hit upon what is right? If so, we must try, in outline at least to determine what it is, and of which of the sciences or capacities it is the object. It would seem to belong to the most authoritative art and that which is most truly

* Headings enclosed in square brackets have been added to the text by the Editors.

the master art. And politics appears to be of this nature; for it is this that ordains which of the sciences should be studied in a state, and which each class of citizens should learn and up to what point they should learn them; and we see even the most highly esteemed of capacities to fall under this, e.g. strategy, economics, rhetoric; now, since politics uses the rest of the sciences, and since, again, it legislates as to what we are to do and what we are to abstain from, the end of this science must include those of the others, so that this end must be the good for man. For even if the end is the same for a single man and for a state, that of the state seems at all events something greater and more complete whether to attain or to preserve; though it is worth while to attain the end merely for one man, it is finer and more godlike to attain it for a nation or for city-states. These, then, are the ends at which our inquiry aims, since it is political science, in one sense of that term.

[The Investigation of Political Science]

3. Our discussion will be adequate if it has as much clearness as the subject-matter admits of, for precision is not to be sought for alike in all discussions, any more than in all the products of the crafts. Now fine and just actions, which political science investigates, admit of much variety and fluctuation of opinion, so that they may be thought to exist only by convention, and not by nature. And goods also give rise to a similar fluctuation because they bring harm to many people; for before now men have been undone by reason of their wealth, and others by reason of their courage. We must be content, then, in speaking of such subjects and with such premisses to indicate the truth roughly and in outline, and in speaking about things which are only for the most part true and with premisses of the same kind to reach conclusions that are no better. In the same spirit, therefore, should each type of statement be *received*; for it is the mark of an educated man to look for precision in each class of things just so far as the nature of the subject admits; it is evidently equally foolish to accept probable reasoning from a mathematician and to demand from a rhetorician scientific proofs.

Now each man judges well the things he knows, and of these he is a good judge. And so the man who has been educated in a subject is a good judge of that subject, and the man who has received an all-round education is a good judge in general. Hence a young man is not a proper hearer of lectures on political science; for he is inexperienced in the actions that occur in life, but its discussions start from these and are about these; and, further, since he tends to follow his passions, his study will be vain and unprofitable, because the end aimed at is not knowledge but action. And it makes no difference whether he is young in years or youthful in character; the defect does not depend on time, but on his living, and pursuing each successive object, as passion directs. For to such persons, as to the incontinent, knowledge brings no profit; but to those who desire and act in accordance with a rational principle knowledge about such matters will be of great benefit.

These remarks about the student, the sort of treatment to be expected, and the purpose of the inquiry, may be taken as our preface.

[Three Prominent Types of Life]

5. Let us, however, resume our discussion from the point at which we digressed. To judge from the lives that men lead, most men, and men of the most vulgar type, seem (not without some ground) to identify the good, or happiness, with pleasure; which is the reason why they love the life of enjoyment. For there are, we may say, three prominent types of life—that just mentioned, the political, and thirdly the contemplative life. Now the mass of mankind are evidently quite slavish in their tastes, preferring a life suitable to beasts, but they get some ground for their view from the fact that many of those in high places share the tastes of Sardanapallus. A consideration of the prominent types of life shows that people of superior refinement and of active disposition identify happiness with honour; for this is, roughly speaking, the end of the political life. But it seems too superficial to be what we are looking for, since it is thought to depend on those who bestow honour rather than on him who receives it, but the good we divine to be something proper to a man and not easily taken from him. Further, men seem to pursue honour in order that they may be assured of their goodness; at least it is by men of practical wisdom that they seek to be honoured, and among those who know them, and on the ground of their virtue; clearly, then, according to them, at any rate, virtue is better. And perhaps one might even suppose this to be, rather than honour, the end of the political life. But even this appears somewhat incomplete; for possession of virtue seems actually compatible with being asleep, or with lifelong inactivity, and, further, with the greatest sufferings and misfortunes; but a man who was living so no one would call happy; unless he were maintaining a thesis at all costs. But enough of this; for the subject has been sufficiently treated even in the current discussions. Third comes the contemplative life, which we shall consider later.

The life of money-making is one undertaken under compulsion, and wealth is evidently not the good we are seeking; for it is merely useful and for the sake of something else. And so one might rather take the aforenamed objects to be ends; for they are loved for themselves. But it is evident that not even these are ends; yet many arguments have been thrown away in support of them. Let us leave this subject, then.

[The Chief and Final Good: Happiness]

7. Let us again return to the good we are seeking, and ask what it can be. It seems different in different actions and arts; it is different in medicine, in strategy, and in the other arts likewise. What then is the good of each? Surely that for whose sake everything else is done. In medicine this is health, in strategy victory, in architecture a house, in any other sphere something else, and in every action and pursuit the end; for it is for the sake of this that all men do whatever else they do. Therefore, if there is an end for all that we do, this will be the good achievable by action, and if there are more than one, these will be the goods achievable by action.

So the argument has by a different course reached the same point; but we must try to state this even more clearly. Since there are evidently more than one end, and we choose some of these (e.g. wealth, flutes, and in general instruments) for the sake of something else, clearly not all ends are final ends; but the chief good is evidently something final. Therefore, if there is only one final end, this will be what we are seeking, and if there are more than one, the most final of these will be what we are seeking. Now we call that which is in itself worthy of pursuit more final than that which is worthy of pursuit for the sake of something else, and that which is never desirable for the sake of something else more final than the things that are desirable both in themselves and for the sake of that other thing, and therefore we call final without qualification that which is always desirable in itself and never for the sake of something else.

Now such a thing happiness, above all else, is held to be; for this we choose always for itself and never for the sake of something else, but honour, pleasure, reason, and every virtue we choose indeed for themselves (for if nothing resulted from them we should still choose each of them), but we choose them also for the sake of happiness, judging that by means of them we shall be happy. Happiness, on the other hand, no one chooses for the sake of these, nor, in general, for anything other than itself.

From the point of view of self-sufficiency the same result seems to follow; for the final good is thought to be self-sufficient. Now by self-sufficient we do not mean that which is sufficient for a man by himself, for one who lives a solitary life, but also for parents, children, wife, and in general for his friends and fellow citizens, since man is born for citizenship. But some limit must be set to this; for if we extend our requirement to ancestors and descendants and friends' friends we are in for an infinite series. Let us examine this question, however, on another occasion; the self-sufficient we now define as that which when isolated makes life desirable and lacking in nothing; and such we think happiness to be; and further we think it most desirable of all things, without being counted as one good thing among others—if it were so counted it would clearly be made more desirable by the addition of even the least of goods; for that which is added becomes an excess of goods, and of goods the greater is always more desirable. Happiness, then, is something final and self-sufficient, and is the end of action.

Presumably, however, to say that happiness is the chief good seems a platitude, and a clearer account of what it is is still desired. This might perhaps be given, if we could first ascertain the function of man. For just as for a flute-player, a sculptor, or any artist, and, in general, for all things that have a function or activity, the good and the well is thought to reside in the function, so would it seem to be for man, if he has a function. Have the carpenter, then, and the tanner certain functions or activities, and has man none? Is he born without a function? Or as eye, hand, foot, and in general each of the parts evidently has a function, may one lay it down that man similarly has a function apart from all these? What then can this be? Life seems to be common even to plants, but we are seeking what is peculiar to man. Let us exclude, therefore, the life of nutrition and growth. Next there would be a life of perception, but *it* also seems to be common even to the horse, the ox, and every animal. There remains, then, an active life of the element that has a rational principle; of this, one part has such a principle in the sense of being obedient to one, the other in the sense of possessing one and exercising thought. And, as "life of the rational element" also has two meanings, we must state that life in the sense of activity is what we mean; for this seems to be the more proper sense of the term. Now if the function of man is an activity of soul which follows or implies a rational principle, and if we say "a so-and-so" and "a good so-and-so" have a function which is the same in kind, e.g. a lyre-player and a good lyre-player, and so without qualification in all cases, eminence in respect of goodness being added to the name of the function (for the function of a lyre-player is to play the lyre, and that of a good lyre-player is to do so well): if this is the case, [and we state the function of man to be a certain kind of life, and this to be an activity or actions of the soul implying a rational principle, and the function of a good man to be the good and noble performance of these, and if any action is well performed when it is performed in accordance with the appropriate excellence: if this is the case,] human good turns out to be activity of soul in accordance with virtue, and if there are more than one virtue, in accordance with the best and most complete.

But we must add "in a complete life". For one swallow does not make a summer, nor does one day; and so too one day, or a short time, does not make a man blessed and happy. . . .

[The Nature of Happiness]

8. We must consider it, however, in the light not only of our conclusion and our premisses, but also of what is commonly said about it; for with a true view all the data harmonize, but with a false one the facts soon clash. Now goods have been divided into three classes, and some are described as external, others as relating to soul or to body; we call those that relate to soul most properly and truly goods, and psychical actions and activities we class as relating to soul. Therefore our account must be sound, at least according to this view, which is an old one and agreed on by philosophers. It is correct also in that we identify the end with certain actions and activities; for thus it falls among goods of the soul and not among external goods. Another belief which harmonizes with our account is that the happy man lives well and does well; for we have practically defined happiness as a sort of good life and good action. The characteristics that are looked for in happiness seem also, all of them, to belong to what we have defined happiness as being. For some identify happiness with virtue, some with practical wisdom, others with a kind of philosophic wisdom, others with these, or one of these, accompanied by pleasure or not without pleasure; while others include also external prosperity. Now some of these views have been held by many men and men of old, others by a few eminent persons; and it is not probable that either of these should be entirely mistaken, but rather that they should be right in at least some one respect or even in most respects.

With those who identify happiness with virtue or some one virtue our account is in harmony; for to virtue belongs virtuous activity. But it makes, perhaps, no small difference whether we place the chief good in possession or in use, in state of mind or in activity. For the state of mind may exist without producing any good result, as in a man who is asleep or in some other way quite inactive, but the activity cannot; for one who has the activity will of necessity be acting, and acting well. And as in the Olympic Games it is not the most beautiful and the strongest that are crowned but those who compete (for it is some of these that are victorious), so those who act win, and rightly win, the noble and good things in life.

Their life is also in itself pleasant. For pleasure is a state of *soul*, and to each man that which he is said to be a lover of is pleasant; e.g. not only is a horse pleasant to the lover of horses, and a spectacle to the lover of sights, but also in the same way just acts are pleasant to the lover of justice and in general virtuous acts to the lover of virtue. Now for most men their pleasures are in conflict with one another because these are not by nature pleasant, but the lovers of what is noble find pleasant the things that are by nature pleasant; and virtuous actions are such, so that these are pleasant for such men as well as in their own nature. Their life, therefore, has no further need of pleasure as a sort of adventitious charm, but has its pleasure in itself. For, besides what we have said, the man who does not rejoice in noble actions is not even good; since no one would call a man just who did not enjoy acting justly, nor any man liberal who did not enjoy liberal actions; and similarly in all other cases. If this is so, virtuous actions must be in themselves pleasant. But they are also *good* and *noble*, and have each of these attributes in the highest degree, since the good man judges well about these attributes; his judgement is such as we have described. Happiness then is the best, noblest, and most pleasant thing in the world, and these attributes are not severed as in the inscription at Delos—

> Most noble is that which is justest, and best is health;
> But pleasantest is it to win what we love.

For all these properties belong to the best activities; and these, or one—the best—of these, we identify with happiness.

Yet evidently, as we said, it needs the external goods as well; for it is impossible, or not easy, to do noble acts without the proper equipment. In many actions we use friends and riches and political power as instruments; and there are some things the lack of which takes the lustre from happiness, as good birth, goodly children, beauty; for the man who is very ugly in appearance or ill-born or solitary and childless is not very likely to be happy, and perhaps a man would be still less likely if he had thoroughly bad children or friends or had lost good children or friends by death. As we said, then, happiness seems to need this sort of prosperity in addition; for which reason some identify happiness with good fortune, though others identify it with virtue.

9. For this reason also the question is asked, whether happiness is to be acquired by learning or by habituation or some other sort of training,

or comes in virtue of some divine providence or again by chance. Now if there is *any* gift of the gods to men, it is reasonable that happiness should be god-given, and most surely god-given of all human things inasmuch as it is the best. But this question would perhaps be more appropriate to another inquiry; happiness seems, however, even if it is not god-sent but comes as a result of virtue and some process of learning or training, to be among the most godlike things; for that which is the prize and end of virtue seems to be the best thing in the world, and something godlike and blessed.

It will also on this view be very generally shared; for all who are not maimed as regards their potentiality for virtue may win it by a certain kind of study and care. But if it is better to be happy thus than by chance, it is reasonable that the facts should be so, since everything that depends on the action of nature is by nature as good as it can be, and similarly everything that depends on art or any rational cause, and especially if it depends on the best of all causes. To entrust to chance what is greatest and most noble would be a very defective arrangement.

The answer to the question we are asking is plain also from the definition of happiness; for it has been said to be a virtuous activity of soul, of a certain kind. Of the remaining goods, some must necessarily pre-exist as conditions of happiness, and others are naturally co-operative and useful as instruments. And this will be found to agree with what we said at the outset; for we stated the end of political science to be the best end, and political science spends most of its pains on making the citizens to be of a certain character, viz. good and capable of noble acts.

It is natural, then, that we call neither ox nor horse nor any other of the animals happy; for none of them is capable of sharing in such activity. For this reason also a boy is not happy; for he is not yet capable of such acts, owing to his age; and boys who are called happy are being congratulated by reason of the hopes we have for them. For there is required, as we said, not only complete virtue but also a complete life, since many changes occur in life, and all manner of chances, and the most prosperous may fall into great misfortunes in old age, as is told of Priam in the Trojan Cycle; and one who has experienced such chances and has ended wretchedly no one calls happy.

10. Must no one at all, then, be called happy while he lives; must we, as Solon says, see the end? Even if we are to lay down this doctrine, is it also the case that a man *is* happy when he is *dead*? Or is not this quite absurd, especially for us who say that happiness is an activity?. . . Now if we must see the end and only then call a man happy, not as being

happy but as having been so before, surely this is a paradox, that when he is happy the attribute that belongs to him is not to be truly predicated of him because we do not wish to call living men happy, on account of the changes that may befall them, and because we have assumed happiness to be something permanent and by no means easily changed, while a single man may suffer many turns of fortune's wheel. For clearly if we were to keep pace with his fortunes, we should often call the same man happy and again wretched, making the happy man out to be a 'chameleon and insecurely based'. Or is this keeping pace with his fortunes quite wrong? Success or failure in life does not depend on these, but human life, as we said, needs these as mere additions, while virtuous activities or their opposites are what constitute happiness or the reverse.

The question we have now discussed confirms our definition. For no function of man has so much permanence as virtuous activities (these are thought to be more durable even than knowledge of the sciences), and of these themselves the most valuable are more durable because those who are happy spend their life most readily and most continuously in these; for this seems to be the reason why we do not forget them. The attribute in question, then, will belong to the happy man, and he will be happy throughout his life; for always, or by preference to everything else, he will be engaged in virtuous action and contemplation, and he will bear the chances of life most nobly and altogether decorously, if he is 'truly good' and 'foursquare beyond reproach'.

Now many events happen by chance, and events differing in importance; small pieces of good fortune or of its opposite clearly do not weigh down the scales of life one way or the other, but a multitude of great events if they turn out well will make life happier (for not only are they themselves such as to add beauty to life, but the way a man deals with them may be noble and good), while if they turn out ill they crush and maim happiness; for they both bring pain with them and hinder many activities. Yet even in these nobility shines through, when a man bears with resignation many great misfortunes, not through insensibility to pain but through nobility and greatness of soul.

If activities are, as we said, what gives life its character, no happy man can become miserable; for he will never do the acts that are hateful and mean. For the man who is truly good and wise, we think, bears all the chances of life becomingly and always makes the best of circumstances, as a good general makes the best military use of the army at his command and a good shoemaker makes the best shoes out of the hides that are given him; and so with all other craftsmen. And if this is the case, the happy man can never become miserable—though he will not reach *blessedness*, if he meet with fortunes like those of Priam.

Nor, again, is he many-coloured and changeable; for neither will he be moved from his happy state easily or by any ordinary misadventures, but only by many great ones, nor, if he has had many great misadventures, will he recover his happiness in a short time, but if at all, only in a long and complete one in which he has attained many splendid successes.

Why then should we not say that he is happy who is active in accordance with complete virtue and is sufficiently equipped with external goods, not for some chance period but throughout a complete life? Or must we add 'and who is destined to live thus and die as befits his life'? Certainly the future is obscure to us, while happiness, we claim, is an end and something in every way final. If so, we shall call happy those among living men in whom these conditions are, and are to be, fulfilled—but happy *men*. So much for these questions.

[Virtue and the Elements of the Soul]

13. Since happiness is an activity of soul in accordance with perfect virtue, we must consider the nature of virtue; for perhaps we shall thus see better the nature of happiness. The true student of politics, too, is thought to have studied virtue above all things; for he wishes to make his fellow citizens good and obedient to the laws. As an example of this we have the lawgivers of the Cretans and the Spartans, and any others of the kind that there may have been. And if this inquiry belongs to political science, clearly the pursuit of it will be in accordance with our original plan. But clearly the virtue we must study is human virtue; for the good we were seeking was human good and the happiness human happiness. By human virtue we mean not that of the body but that of the soul; and happiness also we call an activity of soul. But if this is so, clearly the student of politics must know somehow the facts about soul, as the man who is to heal the eyes or the body as a whole must know about the eyes or the body; and all the more since politics is more prized and better than medicine; but even among doctors the best educated spend much labour on acquiring knowledge of the body. The student of politics, then, must study the soul, and must study it with these objects in view, and do so just to the extent which is sufficient for the questions we are discussing; for further precision is perhaps something more laborious than our purposes require.

Some things are said about it, adequately enough, even in the discussions outside our school, and we must use these, e.g. that one element in the soul is irrational and one has a rational principle. Whether these are separated as the parts of the body or of anything divisible are, or are distinct by definition but by nature inseparable, like convex and concave in the circumference of a circle, does not affect the present question.

Of the irrational element one division seems to be widely distributed, and vegetative in its nature, I mean that which causes nutrition and growth; for it is this kind of power of the soul that one must assign to all nurslings and to embryos, and this same power to full-grown creatures; this is more reasonable than to assign some different power to them. Now the excellence of this seems to be common to all species and not specifically human; for this part or faculty seems to function most in sleep, while goodness and badness are least manifest in sleep (whence comes the saying that the happy are no better off than the wretched for half their lives; and this happens naturally enough, since sleep is an inactivity of the soul in that respect in which it is called good or bad), unless perhaps to a small extent some of the movements actually penetrate to the soul, and in this respect the dreams of good men are better than those of ordinary people. Enough of this subject, however; let us leave the nutritive faculty alone, since it has by its nature no share in human excellence.

There seems to be also another irrational element in the soul—one which in a sense, however, shares in a rational principle. For we praise the rational principle of the continent man and of the incontinent, and the part of their soul that has such a principle, since it urges them aright and towards the best objects; but there is found in them also another element naturally opposed to the rational principle, which fights against and resists that principle. For exactly as paralyzed limbs when we intend to move them to the right turn on the contrary to the left, so is it with the soul; the impulses of incontinent people move in contrary directions. But while in the body we see that which moves astray, in the soul we do not. No doubt, however, we must none the less suppose that in the soul too there is something contrary to the rational principle, resisting and opposing it. In what sense it is distinct from the other elements does not concern us. Now even this seems to have a share in a rational principle, as we said; at any rate in the continent man it obeys the rational principle—and presumably in the temperate and brave man it is still more obedient; for in him it speaks, on all matters, with the same voice as the rational principle.

Therefore the irrational element also appears to be twofold. For the vegetative element in no way shares in a rational principle, but the appetitive, and in general the desiring element in a sense shares in it, in so far as it listens to and obeys it; this is the sense in which we speak of 'taking account' of one's father or one's friends, not that in which we speak of 'accounting' for a mathematical property. That the irrational element is in some sense persuaded by a rational principle is indicated also by the giving of advice and by all reproof and exhortation. And if this element also must be said to have a rational principle, that which has a rational principle (as well as that which has not) will be twofold, one subdivision having it in the strict sense and in itself, and the other having a tendency to obey as one does one's father.

Virtue too is distinguished into kinds in accordance with this difference; for we say that some of the virtues are intellectual and others moral, philosophic wisdom and understanding and practical wisdom being intellectual, liberality and temperance moral. For in speaking about a man's character we do not say that he is wise or has understanding but that he is good-tempered or temperate; yet we praise the wise man also with respect to his state of mind; and of states of mind we call those which merit praise virtues.

Book II

[Acquiring Moral Virtue: Habituation]

1. Virtue, then, being of two kinds, intellectual and moral, intellectual virtue in the main owes both its birth and its growth to teaching (for which reason it requires experience and time), while moral virtue comes about as a result of habit, whence also its name *ethike* is one that is formed by a slight variation from the word *ethos* (habit). From this it is also plain that none of the moral virtues arises in us by nature. For instance the stone which by nature moves downwards cannot be habituated to move upwards, not even if one tries to train it by throwing it up ten thousand times; nor can fire be habituated to move downwards, nor can anything else that by nature behaves in one way be trained to behave in another. Neither by nature, then, nor contrary to nature do the virtues arise in us; rather we are adapted by nature to receive them, and are made perfect by habit.

Again, of all things that come to us by nature we first acquire the potentiality and later exhibit the activity (this is plain in the case of the senses; for it was not by often seeing or often hearing that we got these senses, but on the contrary we had them before we used them, and did not come to have them by using them); but the virtues we get by first exercising them, as also happens in the case of the arts as well. For the things we have to learn before we can do them, we learn by doing them, e.g. men become builders by building and lyre-players by playing the lyre; so too we become just by doing just acts, temperate by doing temperate acts, brave by doing brave acts.

This is confirmed by what happens in states; for legislators make the citizens good by forming habits in them, and this is the wish of every legislator, and those who do not effect it miss their mark, and it is in this that a good constitution differs from a bad one.

Again, it is from the same causes and by the same means that every virtue is both produced and destroyed, and similarly every art; for it is from playing the lyre that both good and bad lyre-players are produced. And the corresponding statement is true of builders and of all the rest; men will be good or bad builders as a result of building well or badly. For if this were not so, there would have been no need of a teacher, but all men would have been born good or bad at their craft. This, then, is the case with the virtues also: by doing the acts that we do in our transactions with other men we become just or unjust, and by doing the acts that we do in the presence of danger, and being habituated to feel fear or confidence, we become brave or cowardly. The same is true of appetites and feelings of anger; some men become temperate and good-tempered, others self-indulgent and irascible, by behaving in one way or the other in the appropriate circumstances. Thus, in one word, states of character arise out of like activities. This is why the activities we exhibit must be of a certain kind; it is because the states of character correspond to the differences between these. It makes no small difference, then, whether we form habits of one kind or of another from our very youth; it makes a very great difference, or rather *all* the difference.

[Avoiding Excess and Deficit in Conduct]

2. Since, then, the present inquiry does not aim at theoretical knowledge like the others (for we are inquiring not in order to know what virtue is, but in order to become good, since otherwise our inquiry would have been of no use), we must examine the nature of actions, namely how we ought to do them; for these determine also the nature of the states of character that are produced, as we have said. Now, that we must act according to the right rule is a common principle and must be assumed—it will be discussed later, i.e. both what the right rule is, and how it is related to the other virtues. But this must be agreed upon beforehand, that the whole account of matters of conduct must be given in outline and not precisely, as we said as the very beginning that the accounts we demand must be in accordance with the subject-matter;

matters concerned with conduct and questions of what is good for us have no fixity, any more than matters of health. The general account being of this nature, the account of particular cases is yet more lacking in exactness; for they do not fall under any art or precept but the agents themselves must in each case consider what is appropriate to the occasion, as happens also in the art of medicine or of navigation.

But though our present account is of this nature we must give what help we can. First, then, let us consider this, that it is the nature of such things to be destroyed by defect and excess, as we see in the case of strength and of health (for to gain light on things imperceptible we must use the evidence of sensible things); both excessive and defective exercise destroy the strength, and similarly drink or food which is above or below a certain amount destroys the health, while that which is proportionate both produces and increases and preserves it. So too is it, then, in the case of temperance and courage and the other virtues. For the man who flies from and fears everything and does not stand his ground against anything becomes a coward, and the man who fears nothing at all but goes to meet every danger becomes rash; and similarly the man who indulges in every pleasure and abstains from none becomes self-indulgent, while the man who shuns every pleasure, as boors do, becomes in a way insensible; temperance and courage, then, are destroyed by excess and defect, and preserved by the mean.

But not only are the sources and causes of their origination and growth the same as those of their destruction, but also the sphere of their actualization will be the same; for this is also true of the things which are more evident to sense, e.g. of strength; it is produced by taking much food and undergoing much exertion, and it is the strong man that will be most able to do these things. So too is it with the virtues; by abstaining from pleasures we become temperate, and it is when we have become so that we are most able to abstain from them; and similarly too in the case of courage; for by being habituated to despise things that are terrible and to stand our ground against them we become brave, and it is when we have become so that we shall be most able to stand our ground against them.

[Becoming a Just Man]

4. The question might be asked, what we mean by saying that we must become just by doing just acts, and temperate by doing temperate acts; for if men do just and temperate acts, they are already just and temperate, exactly as, if they do what is in accordance with the laws of grammar and of music, they are grammarians and musicians.

Or is this not true even of the arts? It is possible to do something that is in accordance with the laws of grammar, either by chance or at the suggestion of another. A man will be a grammarian, then, only when he has both done something grammatical and done it grammatically; and this means doing it in accordance with the grammatical knowledge in himself.

Again, the case of the arts and that of the virtues are not similar; for the products of the arts have their goodness in themselves, so that it is enough that they should have a certain character, but if the acts that are in accordance with the virtues have themselves a certain character it does not follow that they are done justly or temperately. The agent also must be in a certain condition when he does them; in the first place he must have knowledge, secondly he must choose the acts, and choose them for their own sakes, and thirdly his action must proceed from a firm and unchangeable character. These are not reckoned in as conditions of the possession of the arts, except the bare knowledge; but as a condition of the possession of the virtues knowledge has little or no weight, while the other conditions count not for a little but for everything, i.e. the very conditions which result from often doing just and temperate acts.

Actions, then, are called just and temperate when they are such as the just or the temperate man would do; but it is not the man who does these that is just and temperate, but the man who also does them *as* just and temperate men do them. It is well said, then, that it is by doing just acts that the just man is produced, and by doing temperate acts the temperate man; without doing these no one would have even a prospect of becoming good.

But most people do not do these, but take refuge in theory and think they are being philosophers and will become good in this way, behaving somewhat like patients who listen attentively to their doctors, but do none of the things they are ordered to do. As the latter will not be made well in body by such a course of treatment, the former will not be made well in soul by such a course of philosophy.

[Virtues: States of Character]

5. Next we must consider what virtue is. Since things that are found in the soul are of three kinds—passions, faculties, states of character, virtue must be one of these. By passions I mean appetite, anger, fear, confidence, envy, joy, friendly feeling, hatred, longing, emulation, pity, and in general the feelings that are accompanied by pleasure or pain; by faculties the things in virtue of which we are said to be capable of feeling

these, e.g. of becoming angry or being pained or feeling pity; by states of character the things in virtue of which we stand well or badly with reference to the passions, e.g. with reference to anger we stand badly if we feel it violently or too weakly, and well if we feel it moderately; and similarly with reference to the other passions.

Now neither the virtues nor the vices are *passions*, because we are not called good or bad on the ground of our passions, but are so called on the ground of our virtues and our vices, and because we are neither praised nor blamed for our passions (for the man who feels fear or anger is not praised, nor is the man who simply feels anger blamed, but the man who feels it in a certain way), but for our virtues and our vices we *are* praised or blamed.

Again, we feel anger and fear without choice, but the virtues are modes of choice or involve choice. Further, in respect of the passions we are said to be moved, but in respect of the virtues and the vices we are said not to be moved but to be disposed in a particular way.

For these reasons also they are not *faculties*; for we are neither called good nor bad, nor praised nor blamed, for the simple capacity of feeling the passions; again, we have the faculties by nature, but we are not made good or bad by nature; we have spoken of this before.

If, then, the virtues are neither passions nor faculties, all that remains is that they should be *states of character*.

Thus we have sated what virtue is in respect of its genus.

[The Doctrine of the Mean in Actions]

6. We must, however, not only describe virtue as a state of character, but also say what sort of state it is. We may remark, then, that every virtue or excellence both brings into good condition the thing of which it is the excellence and makes the work of that thing be done well; e.g. the excellence of the eye makes both the eye and its work good; for it is the excellence of the eye that we see well. Similarly the excellence of the horse makes a horse both good in itself and good at running and at carrying its rider and at awaiting the attack of the enemy. Therefore, if this is true in every case, the virtue of man also will be the state of character which makes a man good and which makes him do his own work well.

How this is to happen we have stated already, but it will be made plain also by the following consideration of the specific nature of virtue. In everything that is continuous and divisible it is possible to take more, less, or an equal amount, and that either in terms of the thing itself or relatively to us; and the equal is an intermediate between excess and defect. By the intermediate in the object I mean that which is equidistant from each of the extremes, which is one and the same for all men; by the intermediate relatively to us that which is neither too much nor too little—and this is not one, nor the same for all. For instance, if ten is many and two is few, six is the intermediate, taken in terms of the object; for it exceeds and is exceeded by an equal amount; this is intermediate according to arithmetical proportion. But the intermediate relatively to us is not to be taken so; if ten pounds are too much for a particular person to eat and two too little, it does not follow that the trainer will order six pounds; for this also is perhaps too much for the person who is to take it, or too little—too little for Milo, too much for the beginner in athletic exercises. The same is true of running and wrestling. Thus a master of any art avoids excess and defect, but seeks the intermediate and chooses this—the intermediate not in the object but relatively to us.

If it is thus, then, that every art does its work well—by looking to the intermediate and judging its works by this standard (so that we often say of good works of art that it is not possible either to take away or to add anything, implying that excess and defect destroy the goodness of works of art, while the mean preserves it; and good artists, as we say, look to this in their work), and if, further, virtue is more exact and better than any art, as nature also is, then virtue must have the quality of aiming at the intermediate. I mean moral virtue; for it is this that is concerned with passions and actions, and in these there is excess, defect, and the intermediate. For instance, both fear and confidence and appetite and anger and pity and in general pleasure and pain may be felt both too much and too little, and in both cases not well; but to feel them at the right times, with reference to the right objects, towards the right people, with the right motive, and in the right way, is what is both intermediate and best, and this is characteristic of virtue. Similarly with regard to actions also there is excess, defect, and the intermediate. Now virtue is concerned with passions and actions, in which excess is a form of failure, and so is defect, while the intermediate is praised and is a form of success; and being praised and being successful are both characteristics of virtue. Therefore virtue is a kind of mean, since, as we have seen, it aims at what is intermediate.

Again, it is possible to fail in many ways (for evil belongs to the class of the unlimited, as the Pythagoreans conjectured, and good to that of the limited), while to succeed is possible only in one way (for which reason also one is easy and the other difficult—to miss the mark easy, to hit it difficult); for these reasons also, then, excess and defect are characteristic of vice, and the mean of virtue;

For men are good in but one way, but bad in many.

Virtue, then, is a state of character concerned with choice, lying in a mean, i.e. the mean relative to us, this being determined by a rational principle, and by that principle by which the man of practical wisdom would determine it. Now it is a mean between two vices, that which depends on excess and that which depends on defect; and again it is a mean because the vices respectively fall short of or exceed what is right in both passions and actions, while virtue both finds and chooses that which is intermediate. Hence in respect of its substance and the definition which states its essence virtue is a mean, with regard to what is best and right an extreme.

But not every action nor every passion admits of a mean; for some have names that already imply badness, e.g. spite, shamelessness, envy, and in the case of actions adultery, theft, murder; for all of these and suchlike things imply by their names that they are themselves bad, and not the excesses or deficiencies of them. It is not possible, then, ever to be right with regard to them; one must always be wrong. Nor does goodness or badness with regard to such things depend on committing adultery with the right woman, at the right time, and in the right way, but simply to do any of them is to go wrong. It would be equally absurd, then, to expect that in unjust, cowardly, and voluptuous action there should be a mean, an excess, and a deficiency; for at that rate there would be a mean of excess and of deficiency, an excess of excess, and a deficiency of deficiency. But as there is no excess and deficiency of temperature and courage because what is intermediate is in a sense an extreme, so too of the actions we have mentioned there is no mean nor any excess and deficiency, but however they are done they are wrong; for in general there is neither a mean of excess and deficiency, nor excess and deficiency of a mean.

[Character Traits and the Mean]

7. We must, however, not only make this general statement, but also apply it to the individual facts. For among statements about conduct those which are general apply more widely, but those which are particular are more genuine, since conduct has to do with individual cases, and our statements must harmonize with the facts in these cases. We may take these cases from our table. With regard to feelings of fear

and confidence courage is the mean; of the people who exceed, he who exceeds in fearlessness has no name (many of the states have no name), while the man who exceeds in confidence is rash, and he who exceeds in fear and falls short in confidence is a coward. With regard to pleasures and pains—not all of them, and not so much with regard to the pains—the mean is temperance, the excess self-indulgence. Persons deficient with regard to the pleasures are not often found; hence such persons also have received no name. But let us call them 'insensible'.

With regard to giving and taking of money the mean is liberality, the excess and the defect prodigality and meanness. In these actions people exceed and fall short in contrary ways; the prodigal exceeds in spending and falls short in taking, while the mean man exceeds in taking and falls short in spending. (At present we are giving a mere outline or summary, and are satisfied with this; later these states will be more exactly determined.) With regard to money there are also other dispositions—a mean, magnificence (for the magnificent man differs from the liberal man; the former deals with large sums, the latter with small ones), an excess, tastelessness and vulgarity, and a deficiency, niggardliness; these differ from the states opposed to liberality, and the mode of their difference will be stated later. . . .

[Achieving the Mean]

9. That moral virtue is a mean, then, and in what sense it is so, and that it is a mean between two vices, the one involving excess, the other deficiency, and that it is such because its character is to aim at what is intermediate in passions and in actions, has been sufficiently stated. Hence also it is no easy task to be good. For in everything it is no easy task to find the middle, e.g. to find the middle of a circle is not for every one but for him who knows; so, too, any one can get angry—that is easy—or give or spend money; but to do this to the right person, to the right extent, at the right time, with the right motive, and in the right way, *that* is not for every one, nor is it easy; wherefore goodness is both rare and laudable and noble.

Hence he who aims at the intermediate must first depart from what is the more contrary to it, as Calypso advises—

> Hold the ship out beyond that surf and spray.

For of the extremes one is more erroneous, one less so; therefore, since to hit the mean is hard in the extreme, we must as a second best, as people say, take the least of the evils; and this will be done best in the way we describe.

But we must consider the things towards which we ourselves also are easily carried away; for some of us tend to one thing, some to another; and this will be recognizable from the pleasure and the pain we feel. We must drag ourselves away to the contrary extreme; for we shall get into the intermediate state by drawing well away from error, as people do in straightening sticks that are bent.

Now in everything the pleasant or pleasure is most to be guarded against; for we do not judge it impartially. We ought, then, to feel towards pleasure as the elders of the people felt towards Helen, and in all circumstances repeat their saying; for if we dismiss pleasure thus we are less likely to go astray. it is by doing this, then (to sum the matter up) that we shall best be able to hit the mean.

But this is no doubt difficult, and especially in individual cases; for it is not easy to determine both how and with whom and on what provocation and how long one should be angry; for we too sometimes praise those who fall short and call them good-tempered, but sometimes we praise those who get angry and call them manly. The man, however, who deviates little from goodness is not blamed, whether he do so in the direction of the more or of the less, but only the man who deviates more widely; for *he* does not fail to be noticed. But up to what point and to what extent a man must deviate before he becomes blameworthy it is not easy to determine by reasoning, any more than anything else that is perceived by the senses; such things depend on particular facts, and the decision rests with perception. So much, then, is plain, that the intermediate state is in all things to be praised, but that we must incline sometimes towards the excess, sometimes towards the deficiency; for so shall we most easily hit the mean and what is right.

Book III

[Virtue and Volition]

1. Since virtue is concerned with passions and actions, and on voluntary passions and actions praise and blame are bestowed, on those that are involuntary pardon, and sometimes also pity, to distinguish the voluntary and the involuntary is presumably necessary for those who are studying the nature of virtue, and useful also for legislators with a view to the assigning both of honours and of punishments.

Those things, then, are thought involuntary, which take place under compulsion or owing to ignorance; and that is compulsory of which the moving principle is outside, being a principle in which nothing is contributed by the person who is acting or is feeling the passion, e.g. if he were to be carried somewhere by a wind, or by men who had him in their power.

But with regard to the things that are done from fear of greater evils or for some noble object (e.g. if a tyrant were to order one to do something base, having one's parents and children in his power, and if one did the action they were to be saved, but otherwise would be put to death), it may be debated whether such actions are involuntary or voluntary. Something of the sort happens also with regard to the throwing of goods overboard in a storm; for in the abstract no one throws goods away voluntarily, but on condition of its securing the safety of himself and his crew any sensible man does so. Such actions, then, are mixed, but are more like voluntary actions; for they are worthy of choice at the time when they are done, and the end of an action is relative to the occasion. Both the terms, then, 'voluntary' and 'involuntary', must be used with reference to the moment of action. Now the man acts voluntarily; for the principle that moves the instrumental parts of the body in such actions is in him, and the things of which the moving principle is in a man himself are in his power to do or not to do. Such actions, therefore, are voluntary, but in the abstract perhaps involuntary, for no one would choose any such act in itself.

For such actions men are sometimes even praised, when they endure something base or painful in return for great and noble objects gained; in the opposite case they are blamed, since to endure the greatest indignities for no noble end or for a trifling end is the mark of an inferior person. On some actions praise indeed is not bestowed, but pardon is, when one does what he ought not under pressure which overstrains human nature and which no one could withstand. But some acts, perhaps, we cannot be forced to do, but ought rather to face death after the most fearful sufferings; for the things that 'forced' Euripides' Alcmaeon to slay his mother seem absurd. It is difficult sometimes to determine what should be chosen at what cost, and what should be endured in return for what gain, and yet more difficult to abide by our decisions; for as a rule what is expected is painful, and what we are forced to do is base, whence praise and blame are bestowed on those who have been compelled or have not.

What sort of acts, then, should be called compulsory? We answer that without qualification actions are so when the cause is in the external circumstances and the agent contributes nothing. But the things that in themselves are involuntary, but now and in return for these gains are worthy of choice, and whose moving principle is in the agent, are in themselves involuntary, but now and in return for these gains voluntary. They are more like voluntary acts; for actions are in the class of particulars, and the particular acts here are voluntary. What sort of things are to be chosen, and in return for what, it is not easy to state; for there are many differences in the particular cases.

But if some one were to say that pleasant and noble objects have a compelling power, forcing us from without, all acts would be for him compulsory; for it is for these objects that all men do everything they do. And those who act under compulsion and unwillingly act with pain, but those who do acts for their pleasantness and nobility do them with pleasure; it is absurd to make external circumstances responsible, and not oneself, as being easily caught by such attractions and to make oneself responsible for noble acts but the pleasant objects responsible for base acts. The compulsory, then, seems to be that whose moving principle is outside, the person compelled contributing nothing.

Everything that is done by reason of ignorance is *not* voluntary; it is only what produces pain and repentance that is *in*voluntary. For the man who has done something owing to ignorance, and feels not the least vexation at his action, has not acted voluntarily, since he did not know what he was doing, nor yet involuntarily, since he is not pained. Of people, then, who act by reason of ignorance he who repents is thought an involuntary agent, and the man who does not repent may, since he is different, be called a not voluntary agent; for, since he differs from the other, it is better that he should have a name of his own.

Acting by reason of ignorance seems also to be different from acting *in* ignorance; for the man who is drunk or in a rage is thought to act as a result not of ignorance but of one of the causes mentioned, yet not knowingly but in ignorance.

Now every wicked man is ignorant of what he ought to do and what he ought to abstain from, and it is by reason of error of this kind that men become unjust and in general bad; but the term 'involuntary' tends to be used not if a man is ignorant of what is to his advantage—for it is not mistaken purpose that causes involuntary action (it leads rather to wickedness), nor ignorance of the universal (for *that* men are *blamed*), but ignorance of particulars, i.e. of the circumstances of the action and the objects with which it is concerned. For it is on these that both pity and pardon depend, since the person who is ignorant of any of these acts involuntarily.

Perhaps it is just as well, therefore, to determine their nature and number. A man may be ignorant, then, of who he is, what he is doing, what or whom he is acting on, and sometimes also what (e.g. what instrument) he is doing it with, and to what end (e.g. he may think his act will conduce to some one's safety), and how he is doing it (e.g. whether gently or violently). Now of all of these no one could be ignorant unless he were mad, and evidently also he could not be ignorant of the agent; for how could he not know himself? But of what he is doing a man might be ignorant, as for instance people say 'it slipped out of their mouths as they were speaking', of 'they did not know it was a secret', as Aeschylus said of the mysteries, or a man might say he 'let it go off when he merely wanted to show its working', as the man did with the catapult. Again, one might think one's son was an enemy, as Merope did, or that a pointed spear had a button on it, or that a stone was pumice-stone; or one might want to touch a man, as people do in sparring, and really wound him. The ignorance may relate, then, to any of these things, i.e. of the circumstances of the action, and the man who was ignorant of any of these is thought to have acted involuntarily, and especially if he was ignorant on the most important points; and these are thought to be the circumstances of the action and its end. Further, the doing of an act that is called involuntary in virtue of ignorance of this sort must be painful and involve repentance.

Since that which is done under compulsion or by reason of ignorance is involuntary, the voluntary would seem to be that of which the moving principle is in the agent himself, he being aware of the particular circumstances of the action. Presumably acts done by reason of anger or appetite are not rightly called involuntary. For in the first place, on that showing none of the other animals will act voluntarily, nor will children; and secondly, is it meant that we do not do voluntarily *any* of the acts that are due to appetite or anger, or that we do the noble acts voluntarily and the base acts involuntarily? Is not this absurd, when one and the same thing is the cause? But it would surely be odd to describe as involuntary the things one ought to desire; and we ought both to be angry at certain things and to have an appetite for certain things, e.g. for health and for learning. Also what is involuntary is thought to be painful, but what is in accordance with appetite is thought to be pleasant. Again, what is the difference in respect of involuntariness between errors committed upon calculation and those committed in anger? Both are to be avoided, but the irrational passions are thought not less human than reason is, and therefore also the actions which proceed from anger or appetite are the man's actions. It would be odd, then, to treat them as involuntary.

[The Nature of Choice]

2. Both the voluntary and the involuntary having been delimited, we must next discuss choice; for it is thought to be most closely bound up with virtue and to discriminate characters better than actions do.

Choice, then, seems to be voluntary, but not the same thing as the voluntary; the latter extends more widely. For both children and the lower animals share in voluntary action, but not in choice, and acts done on the spur of the moment we describe as voluntary, but not as chosen.

Those who say it is appetite or anger or wish or a kind of opinion do not seem to be right. For choice is not common to irrational creatures as well, but appetite and anger are. Again, the incontinent man acts with appetite, but not with choice; while the continent man on the contrary acts with choice, but not with appetite. Again, appetite is contrary to choice, but not appetite to appetite. Again, appetite relates to the pleasant and the painful, choice neither to the painful nor to the pleasant.

Still less is it anger; for acts due to anger are thought to be less than any others objects of choice.

But neither is it wish, though it seems near to it; for choice cannot relate to impossibles, and if any one said he chose them he would be thought silly; but there may be a wish even for impossibles, e.g. for immortality. And wish may relate to things that could in no way be brought about by one's own efforts, e.g. that a particular actor or athlete should win in a competition; but no one chooses such things, but only the things that he thinks could be brought about by his own efforts. Again, wish relates rather to the end, choice to the means; for instance, we wish to be healthy, but we choose the acts which will make us healthy, and we wish to be happy and say we do, but we cannot well say we choose to be so; for, in general, choice seems to relate to the things that are in our own power.

For this reason, too, it cannot be opinion; for opinion is thought to relate to all kinds of things, no less to eternal things and impossible things than to things in our own power; and it is distinguished by its falsity or truth, not by its badness or goodness, while choice is distinguished rather by these.

Now with opinion in general perhaps no one even says it is identical. But it is not identical even with any kind of opinion; for by choosing what is good or bad we are men of a certain character, which we are not by holding certain opinions. And we choose to get or avoid something good or bad, but we have opinion about what a thing is or whom it is good for or how it is good for him; we can hardly be said to opine to get or avoid anything. And choice is praised for being related to the right object rather than for being rightly related to it, opinion for being truly related to this object. And we choose what we best know to be good, but we opine what we do not quite know; and it is not the same people that are thought to make the best choices and to have the best opinions, but some are thought to have fairly good opinions, but by reason of vice to choose what they should not. If opinion precedes choice or accompanies it, that makes no difference; for it is not this that we are considering, but whether it is *identical* with some kind of opinion.

What, then, or what kind of thing is it, since it is none of the things we have mentioned? It seems to be voluntary, but not all that is voluntary . . . [is] an object of choice. Is it, then, what has been decided on by previous deliberation? At any rate choice involves a rational principle and thought. Even the name seems to suggest that it is what is chosen before other things.

[The Method of Deliberation]

3. Do we deliberate about everything, and is everything a possible subject of deliberation, or is deliberation impossible about some things? We ought presumably to call not what a fool or a madman would deliberate about, but what a sensible man would deliberate about, a subject of deliberation. Now about eternal things no one deliberates, e.g. about the material universe or the incommensurability of the diagonal and the side of a square. But no more do we deliberate about the things that involve movement but always happen in the same way, whether of necessity or by nature or from any other cause, e.g. the solstices and the risings of the stars; nor about things that happen now in one way, now in another, e.g. droughts and rains; nor about chance events, like the finding of treasure. But we do not deliberate even about all human affairs; for instance, no Spartan deliberates about the best constitution for the Scythinas. For none of these things can be brought about by our own efforts.

We deliberate about things that are in our power and can be done; and these are in fact what is left. For nature, necessity, and chance are thought to be causes, and also reason and everything that depends on man. Now every class of men deliberates about the things that can be done by their own efforts. And in the case of exact and self-contained sciences there is no deliberation, e.g. about the letters of the alphabet (for we have no doubt how they should be written); but the things that are brought about by our own efforts, but not always in the same way, are the things about which we deliberate, e.g. questions of medical treatment or of money-making. And we do so more in the case of the art of navigation than in that of gymnastics, inasmuch as it has been less exactly worked out, and again about other things in the same ratio, and more also in the case of the arts than in that of the sciences; for we have more doubt about the former. Deliberation is concerned with things that happen in a certain way for the most part, but in which the event is obscure, and with things in which it is indeterminate. We call in others to aid us in deliberation on important questions, distrusting ourselves as not being equal to deciding.

We deliberate not about ends but about means. For a doctor does not deliberate whether he shall heal, nor an orator whether he shall persuade, nor a statesman whether he shall produce law and order, nor does any one else deliberate about his end. They assume the end and consider how and by what means it is to be attained; and if it seems to be produced by several means they consider by which it is most easily and best produced, while if it is achieved by one only they consider how it will be achieved by this and by what means *this* will be achieved, till they come to the first cause, which in the order of discovery is last. For the person who deliberates seems to investigate and analyse in the way described as though he were analysing a geometrical construction (not all investigation appears to be deliberation—for instance mathematical investigations—but all deliberation is investigation), and what is last in the order of analysis seems to be first in the order of becoming. And if we come on an impossibility, we give up the search, e.g. if we need money and this cannot be got; but if a thing appears possible we try to do it. By 'possible' things I mean things that might be brought about by our own efforts; and these in a sense include things that can be brought about by the efforts of our friends, since the moving principle is in ourselves. The subject of investigation is sometimes the instruments, sometimes the use of them; and similarly in the other cases—sometimes the means, sometimes the mode of using it or the means of bringing it about. It seems, then, as has been said, that man is a moving principle of actions; now deliberation is about the things to be done by the agent himself, and actions are for the sake of things other than themselves. For the end cannot be a subject of deliberation, but only the means; nor indeed can the particular facts be a subject of it, as whether this is bread or has been baked as it should; for these are matters of perception. If we are to be always deliberating, we shall have to go on to infinity.

The same thing is deliberated upon and is chosen, except that the object of choice is already determinate, since it is that which has been decided upon as a result of deliberation that is the object of choice. For every one ceases to inquire how he is to act when he has brought the moving principle back to himself and to the ruling part of himself; for this is what chooses. This is plain also from the ancient constitutions, which Homer represented; for the kings announced their choices to the people. The object of choice being one of the things in our own power which is desired after deliberation, choice will be deliberate desire of things in our own power; for when we have decided as a result of deliberation, we desire in accordance with our deliberation.

We may take it, then, that we have described choice in outline, and stated the nature of its object and the fact that it is concerned with means.

[The Good is the Object of Choice]

4. That *wish* is for the end has already been stated; some think it is for the good, others for the apparent good. Now those who say that the good is the object of wish must admit in consequences that that which the man who does not choose aright wishes for is not an object of wish (for if it is to be so, it must also be good; but it was, if it so happened, bad); while those who say the apparent good is the object of wish must admit that there is no natural object of wish, but only what seems good to each man. Now different things appear good to different people, and, if it so happens, even contrary things.

If these consequences are unpleasing, are we to say that absolutely and in truth the good is the object of wish, but for each person the apparent good; that that which is in truth an object of wish is an object of wish to the good man, while any chance thing may be so to the bad man, as in the case of bodies also the things that are in truth wholesome are wholesome for bodies which are in good condition, while for those that are diseased other things are wholesome—or bitter or sweet or hot or heavy, and so on; since the good man judges each class of things rightly, and in each the truth appears to him? For each state of character has its own ideas of the noble and the pleasant, and in each class of things, being as it were the norm and measure of them. In most things the error seems to be due to pleasure; for it appears a good when it is not. We therefore choose the pleasant as a good, and avoid pain as an evil.

[Virtue and Vice Are Voluntary]

5. The end, then, being what we wish for, the means what we deliberate about and choose, actions concerning means must be accord-

ing to choice and voluntary. Now the exercise of the virtues is concerned with means. Therefore virtue also is in our own power, and so too vice. For where it is in our power to act it is also in our power not to act, and *vice versa*; so that, if to act, where this is noble, is in our power, not to act, which will be base, will also be in our power, and if not to act, where this is noble, is in our power, to act, which will be base, will also be in our power. Now if it is in our power to do noble or base acts, and likewise in our power not to do them, and this was what being good or bad meant, then it is in our power to be virtuous or vicious.

The saying that 'no one is voluntarily wicked nor involuntarily happy' seems to be partly false and partly true; for no one is involuntarily happy, but wickedness *is* voluntary. Or else we shall have to dispute what has just been said, at any rate, and deny that man is a moving principle or begetter of his actions as of children. But if these facts are evident and we cannot refer actions to moving principles other than those in ourselves, the acts whose moving principles are in us must themselves also be in our power and voluntary.

Witness seems to be borne to this both by individuals in their private capacity and by legislators themselves; for these punish and take vengeance on those who do wicked acts (unless they have acted under compulsion or as a result of ignorance for which they are not themselves responsible), while they honour those who do noble acts, as though they meant to encourage the latter and deter the former. But no one is encouraged to do the things that are neither in our power nor voluntary; it is assumed that there is no gain in being persuaded not to be hot or in pain or hungry or the like, since we shall experience these feelings none the less. Indeed, we punish a man for his very ignorance, if he is thought responsible for the ignorance, as when penalties are doubled in the case of drunkenness; for the moving principle is in the man himself, since he had the power of not getting drunk and his getting drunk was the cause of his ignorance. And we punish those who are ignorant of anything in the laws that they ought to know and that is not difficult, and so too in the case of anything else that they are thought to be ignorant of through carelessness; we assume that it is in their power not to be ignorant, since they have the power of taking care.

But perhaps a man is the kind of man not to take care. Still they are themselves by their slack lives responsible for becoming men of that kind, and men make themselves responsible for being unjust or self-indulgent, in the one case by cheating and in the other by spending their time in drinking bouts and the like; for it is activities exercised on particular objects that make the corresponding character. This is plain from the case of people training for any contest or action; they practise the activity the whole time. Now not to know that it is from the exercise of activities on particular objects that states of character are produced is the mark of a thoroughly senseless person. Again, it is irrational to suppose that a man who acts unjustly does not wish to be unjust or a man who acts self-indulgently to be self-indulgent. But if *without* being ignorant a man does the things which will make him unjust, he will be unjust voluntarily. Yet it does not follow that if he wishes he will cease to be unjust and will be just. For neither does the man who is ill become well on those terms. We may suppose a case in which he is ill voluntarily, through living incontinently and disobeying his doctors. In that case it was *then* open to him not to be ill, but not now, when he has thrown away his chance, just as when you have let a stone go it is too late to recover it; but yet it was in your power to throw it, since the moving principle was in you. So, too, to the unjust and to the self-indulgent man it was open at the beginning not to become men of this kind, and so they are unjust and self-indulgent voluntarily; but now that they have become so it is not possible for them not to be so.

But not only are the vices of the soul voluntary, but those of the body also for some men, whom we accordingly blame; while no one blames those who are ugly by nature, we blame those who are so owing to want of exercise and care. So it is, too, with respect to weakness and infirmity; no one would reproach a man blind from birth or by disease or from a blow, but rather pity him, while every one would blame a man who was blind from drunkenness or some other form of self-indulgence. Of vices of the body, then, those in our own power are blamed, those not in our power are not. And it this be so, in the other cases also the vices that are blamed must be in our own power.

Now some one may say that all men desire the apparent good, but have no control over the appearance, but the end appears to each man in a form answering to his character. We reply that if each man is somehow responsible for his state of mind, he will also be himself somehow responsible for the appearance; but if not, no one is responsible for his own evildoing, but every one does evil acts through ignorance of the end, thinking that by these he will get what is best, and the aiming at the end is not self-chosen but one must be born with an eye, as it were, by which to judge rightly and choose what is truly good, and he is well endowed by nature who is well endowed with this. For it is what is greatest and most noble, and what we cannot get or learn from another, but must have just such as it was when given us at birth, and to be well and nobly endowed with this will be perfect and true excellence of natural endowment. If this is true, then, how will virtue be more voluntary than vice? To both men alike, the good and the bad, the end appears and is fixed by nature or however it may be, and it is by referring everything else to this that men do whatever they do.

Whether, then, it is not by nature that the end appears to each man such as it does appear, but something also depends on him, or the end is natural but because the good man adopts the means voluntarily virtue is voluntary, vice also will be none the less voluntary; for in the case of the bad man there is equally present that which depends on himself in his actions even if not in his end. If, then, as is asserted, the virtues are voluntary (for we are ourselves somehow partly responsible for our states of character, and it is by being persons of a certain kind that we assume the end to be so and so), the vices also will be voluntary; for the same is true of them.

With regard to the virtues in *general* we have stated their genus in outline, viz. that they are means and that they are states of character, and that they tend, and by their own nature, to the doing of the acts by which they are produced, and that they are in our power and voluntary, and act as the right rule prescribes. But actions and states of character are not voluntary in the same way; for we are masters of our actions from the beginning right to the end, if we know the particular facts, but though we control the beginning of our states of character the gradual progress is not obvious, any more than it is in illnesses; because it was in our power, however, to act in this way or not in this way, therefore the states are voluntary.

Let us take up the several virtues, however, and say which they are and what sort of things they are concerned with and how they are concerned with them; at the same time it will become plain how many they are. And first let us speak of courage.

[Courage]

6. That it is a mean with regard to feelings of fear and confidence has already been made evident; and plainly the things we fear are terrible things, and these are, to speak without qualification, evils; for which reason people even define fear as expectation of evil. Now we fear all evils, e.g. disgrace, poverty, disease, friendlessness, death, but the brave man is not thought to be concerned with all; for to fear some things is even right and noble, and it is base not to fear them—e.g.disgrace; he who fears this is good and modest, and he who does not is shameless. He is, however, by some people called brave, by a transference of the word to a new meaning; for he has in him something

which is like the brave man, since the brave man also is a fearless person. Poverty and disease we perhaps ought not to fear, nor in general the things that do not proceed from vice and are not due to a man himself. But not even the man who is fearless of these is brave. Yet we apply the word to him also in virtue of a similarity; for some who in the dangers of war are cowards are liberal and are confident in face of the loss of money. Nor is a man a coward if he fears insult to his wife and children or envy or anything of the kind; nor brave if he is confident when he is about to be flogged. With what sort of terrible things, then, is the brave man concerned? Surely with the greatest, for no one is more likely than he to stand his ground against what is awe-inspiring. Now death is the most terrible of all things; for it is the end, and nothing is thought to be any longer either good or bad for the dead. But the brave man would not seem to be concerned even with death in *all* circumstances, e.g. at sea or in disease. In what circumstances, then? Surely in the noblest. Now such deaths are those in battle; for these take place in the greatest and noblest danger. And these are correspondingly honoured in city-states and at the courts of monarchs. Properly, then, he will be called brave who is fearless in face of a noble death, and of all emergencies that involve death; and the emergencies of war are in the highest degree of this kind. yet at sea also, and in disease; the brave man is fearless, but not in the same way as the seamen; for he has given up hope of safety, and is disliking the thought of death in this shape, while they are hopeful because of their experience. At the same time, we show courage in situations where there is the opportunity of showing prowess or where death is noble; but in these forms of death neither of these conditions is fulfilled.

7. What is terrible is not the same for all men; but we say there are things terrible even beyond human strength. These, then, are terrible to every one—at least to every sensible man; but the terrible things that are *not* beyond human strength differ in magnitude and degree, and so too do the things that inspire confidence. Now the brave man is as dauntless as man may be. Therefore, while he will fear even the things that are not beyond human strength, he will face them as he ought and as the rule directs, for honour's sake; for this is the end of virtue. But it is possible to fear these more, or less, and again to fear things that are not terrible as if they were. Of the faults that are committed one consists in fearing what one should not, another in fearing as we should not, another in fearing when we should not, and so on; and so too with respect to the things that inspire confidence. The man, then, who faces and who fears the right things and from the right motive, in the right way and at the

right time, and who feels confidence under the corresponding conditions, is brave; for the brave man feels and acts according to the merits of the case and in whatever way the rule directs. Now the end of every activity is conformity to the corresponding state of character. This is true, therefore, of the brave man as well as of others. But courage is noble. Therefore the end also is noble; for each thing is defined by its end. Therefore it is for a noble end that the brave man endures and acts as courage directs.

Of those who go to excess he who exceeds in fearlessness has no name (we have said previously that many states of character have no names), but he would be a sort of madman or insensible person if he feared nothing, neither earthquakes nor the waves, as they say the Celts do not; while the man who exceeds in confidence about what really is terrible is rash. The rash man, however, is also thought to be boastful and only a pretender to courage; at all events, as the brave man *is* with regard to what is terrible, so the rash man wishes to *appear*; and so he imitates him in situations where he can. Hence also most of them are a mixture of rashness and cowardice; for, while in these situations they display confidence, they do not hold their ground against what is really terrible. The man who exceeds in fear is a coward; for he fears both what he ought not and as he ought not, and all the similar characterizations attach to him. He is lacking also in confidence; but he is more conspicuous for his excess of fear in painful situations. The coward, then, is a despairing sort of person; for he fears everything. The brave man, on the other hand, has the opposite disposition; for confidence is the mark of a hopeful disposition. The coward, the rash man, and the brave man, then, are concerned with the same objects but are differently disposed towards them; for the first two exceed and fall short, while the third holds the middle, which is the right, position; and rash men are precipitate, and wish for dangers beforehand but draw back when they are in them, while brave men are keen in the moment of action, but quiet beforehand.

As we have said, then, courage is a mean with respect to things that inspire confidence or fear, in the circumstances that have been stated; and it chooses or endures things because it is noble to do so, or because it is base not to do so. But to die to escape from poverty or love anything painful is not the mark of a brave man, but rather of a coward; for it is softness to fly from what is troublesome, and such a man endures death not because it is noble but to fly from evil.

9. We have, then, described the character both of brave men and of those who are thought to be brave.

Though courage is concerned with feelings of confidence and of fear, it is not concerned with both alike, but more with the things that inspire fear; for he who is undisturbed in face of these and bears himself as he should towards these is more truly brave than the man who does so towards the things that inspire confidence. It is for facing what is painful, then, as has been said, that men are called brave. Hence also courage involves pain, and is justly praised; for it is harder to face what is painful than to abstain from what is pleasant. yet the end which courage sets before it would seem to be pleasant, but to be concealed by the attending circumstances, as happens also in athletic contests; for the end at which boxers aim is pleasant—the crown and the honours—but the blows they take are distressing to flesh and blood, and painful, and so is their whole exertion; and because the blows and the exertions are many the end, which is but small, appears to have nothing pleasant in it. And so, if the case of courage is similar, death and wounds will be painful to the brave man and against his will, but he will face them because it is noble to do so or because it is base not to do so. And the more he is possessed of virtue in its entirety and the happier he is, the more he will be pained at the thought of death; for life is best worth living for such a man, and he is knowingly losing the greatest goods, and this is painful. But he is none the less brave, and perhaps all the more so, because he chooses noble deeds of war at that cost. It is not the case, then, with all the virtues that the exercise of them is pleasant, except in so far as it reaches its end. But it is quite possible that the best soldiers may be not men of this sort but those who are less brave but have no other good; for these are ready to face danger, and they sell their life for trifling gains.

So much, then, for courage; it is not difficult to grasp its nature in outline, at any rate, from what has been said.

After courage let us speak of temperance; for these seem to be the virtues of the irrational parts.

[Temperance]

10. We have said that temperance is a mean with regard to pleasures (for it is less, and not in the same way, concerned with pains); self-indulgence also is manifested in the same sphere. Now, therefore, let us determine with what sort of pleasures they are concerned. We may assume the distinction between bodily pleasures and those of the soul, such as love of honour and love of learning; for the lover of each of these delights in that of which he is a lover, the body being in no way affected, but rather the mind; but men who are concerned with such

pleasures are called neither temperate nor self-indulgent. Nor, again, are those who are concerned with the other pleasures that are not bodily; for those who are fond of hearing and telling stories and who spend their days on anything that turns up are called gossips, but not self-indulgent, nor are those who are pained at the loss of money or of friends.

Temperance must be concerned with bodily pleasures, but not all even of these; for those who delight in objects of vision, such as colours and shapes and painting, are called neither temperate nor self-indulgent; yet it would seem possible to delight even in these either as one should or to excess or to a deficient degree.

And so too is it with objects of hearing; no one calls those who delight extravagantly in music or acting self-indulgent, nor those who do so as they ought temperate.

Nor do we apply these names to those who delight in odour, unless it be incidentally; we do not call those self-indulgent who delight in the odour of apples or roses or incense; but rather those who delight in the odour of unguents or of dainty dishes; for self-indulgent people delight in these because these remind them of the objects of their appetite. And one may see even other people, when they are hungry, delighting in the smell of food; but to delight in this kind of thing is the mark of the self-indulgent man; for these are objects of appetite to him. . . .

11. Of the appetites some seem to be common, others to be peculiar to individuals and acquired; e.g. the appetite for food is natural, since every one who is without it craves for food or drink, and sometimes for both, and for love also (as Homer says) if he is young and lusty; but not every one craves for this or that kind of nourishment or love, nor for the same things. Hence such craving appears to be our very own. Yet it has of course something natural about it; for different things are pleasant to different kinds of people, and some things are more pleasant to every one than chance objects. Now in the natural appetites few go wrong, and only in one direction, that of excess; for to eat or drink whatever offers itself till one is surfeited is to exceed the natural amount, since natural appetite is the replenishment of one's deficiency. Hence these people are called belly-gods, this implying that they fill their belly beyond what is right. It is people of entirely slavish character that become like this. But with regard to the pleasures peculiar to individuals many people go wrong and in many ways. For while the people who are 'fond of so and so' are so called because they delight either in the wrong things, or more than most people do, or in the wrong way, the self-indulgent exceed in all three ways; they both delight in some things

that they ought not to delight in (since they are hateful), and if one ought to delight in some of the things they delight in, they do so more than one ought and than most men do.

Plainly, then, excess with regard to pleasures is self-indulgence and is culpable; with regard to pains one is not, as in the case of courage, called temperate for facing them or self-indulgent for not doing so, but the self-indulgent man is so called because he is pained more than he ought at not getting pleasant things (even his pain being caused by pleasure), and the temperate man is so called because he is not pained at the absence of what is pleasant and at his abstinence from it.

The self-indulgent man, then, craves for all pleasant things or those that are most pleasant, and is led by his appetite to choose these at the cost of everything else; hence he is pained both when he fails to get them and when he is merely craving for them (for appetite involves pain); but it seems absurd to be pained for the sake of pleasure. People who fall short with regard to pleasures and delight in them less than they should are hardly found; for such insensibility is not human. Even the other animals distinguish different kinds of food and enjoy some and not others; and if there is any one who finds nothing pleasant and nothing more attractive than anything else, he must be something quite different from a man; this sort of person has not received a name because he hardly occurs. The temperate man occupies a middle position with regard to these objects. For he neither enjoys the things that the self-indulgent man enjoys most—but rather dislikes them—nor in general the things that he should not, nor anything of this sort to excess, nor does he feel pain or craving when they are absent, or does so only to a moderate degree, and not more than he should, nor when he should not, and so on; but the things that, being pleasant, make for health or for good condition, he will desire moderately and as he should, and also other pleasant things if they are not hindrances to these ends, or contrary to what is noble, or beyond his means. For he who neglects these conditions loves such pleasures more than they are worth, but the temperate man is not that sort of person, but the sort of person that the right rule prescribes.

12. Self-indulgence is more like a voluntary state than cowardice. For the former is actuated by pleasure, the latter by pain, of which the one is to be chosen and the other to be avoided; and pain upsets and destroys the nature of the person who feels it, while pleasure does nothing of the sort. Therefore self-indulgence is more voluntary. Hence also it is more a matter of reproach; for it is easier to become accustomed to its objects, since there are many things of this sort in life, and the

process of habituation to them is free from danger, while with terrible objects the reverse is the case. But cowardice would seem to be voluntary in a different degree from its particular manifestations; for it is itself painless, but in these we are upset by pain, so that we even throw down our arms and disgrace ourselves in other ways; hence our acts are even thought to be done under compulsion. For the self-indulgent man, on the other hand, the particular acts are voluntary (for he does them with craving and desire), but the whole state is less so; for no one craves to be self-indulgent.

The name self-indulgence is applied also to childish faults; for they bear a certain resemblance to what we have been considering. Which is called after which, makes no difference to our present purpose; plainly, however, the later is called after the earlier. The transference of the name seems not a bad one; for that which desires what is base and which develops quickly ought to be kept in a chastened condition, and these characteristics belong above all to appetite and to the child, since children in fact live at the beck and call of appetite, and it is in them that the desire for what is pleasant is strongest. If, then, it is not going to be obedient and subject to the ruling principle, it will go to great lengths; for in an irrational being the desire for pleasure is insatiable even if it tries every source of gratification, and the exercise of appetite increases its innate force, and if appetites are strong and violent they even expel the power of calculation. Hence they should be moderate and few, and should in no way oppose the rational principle—and this is what we call an obedient and chastened state—and as the child should live according to the direction of his tutor, so the appetitive element should live according to rational principle. Hence the appetitive element in a temperate man should harmonize with the rational principle; for the noble is the mark at which both aim, and the temperate man craves for the things he ought, as he ought, and when he ought; and this is what rational principle directs.

Here we conclude our account of temperance.

Book V

[Justice]

1. With regard to justice and injustice we must consider (1) what kind of actions they are concerned with, (2) what sort of mean justice is, and (3) between what extremes the just act is intermediate. Our investigation shall follow the same course as the preceding discussions . . . . Let us take as a starting-point, then, the various meanings of 'an unjust man'.

Both the lawless man and the grasping and unfair man are thought to be unjust, so that evidently both the law-abiding and the fair man will be just. The just, then, is the lawful and the fair, the unjust the unlawful and the unfair.

Since the unjust man is grasping, he must be concerned with goods—not all goods, but those with which prosperity and adversity have to do, which taken absolutely are always good, but for a particular person are not always good. Now men pray for and pursue these things; but they should not, but should pray that the things that are good absolutely may also be good for them, and should choose the things that *are* good for them. The unjust man does not always choose the greater, but also the less—in the case of things bad absolutely; but because the lesser evil is itself thought to be in a sense good, and graspingness is directed at the good, therefore he is thought to be grasping. And he is unfair; for this contains and is common to both.

Since the lawless man was seen to be unjust and the law-abiding man just, evidently all lawful acts are in a sense just acts; for the acts laid down by the legislative art are lawful, and each of these, we say, is just. Now the laws in their enactments on all subjects aim at the common advantage either of all or of the best or of those who hold power, or something of the sort; so that in one sense we call those acts just that tend to produce and preserve happiness and its components for the political society. And the law bids us do both the acts of a brave man (e.g. not to desert our post nor take to flight nor throw away our arms), and those of a temperate man (e.g. not to commit adultery nor to gratify one's lust), and those of a good-tempered man (e.g. not to strike another nor to speak evil), and similarly with regard to the other virtues and forms of wickedness, commanding some acts and forbidding others; and the rightly-framed law does this rightly, and the hastily conceived one less well.

This form of justice, then, is complete virtue, but not absolutely but in relation to our neighbour. And therefore justice is often thought to be the greatest of virtues, and 'neither evening nor morning star' is so wonderful; and proverbially 'in justice is every virtue comprehended'. And it is complete virtue in its fullest sense, because it is the actual exercise of complete virtue. It is complete because he who possesses it can exercise his virtue not only in himself but towards his neighbour also; for many men can exercise virtue in their own affairs, but not in their relations to their neighbour. This is why the saying of Bias is thought to be true, that 'rule will show the man'; for a ruler is necessarily in relation to other men and a member of a society. For this same reason justice, alone of the virtues, is thought to be 'another's good', because it is related to our neighbour; for it does what is advantageous to another, either a ruler or a copartner. Now the worst man is he who exercises his wickedness both towards himself and towards his friends, and the best man is not he who exercises his virtue towards himself but he who exercises it towards another; for this is a difficult task. Justice in this sense, then, is not part of virtue but virtue entire, nor is the contrary injustice a part of vice but vice entire. What the difference is between virtue and justice in this sense is plain from what we have said; they are the same but their essence is not the same; what, as a relation to one's neighbour, is justice, as a certain kind of state without qualification, virtue.

[Justice as a Part of Virtue]

2. But at all events what we are investigating is the justice which is a *part* of virtue; for there is a justice of this kind, as we maintain. Similarly, it is with injustice in the particular sense that we are concerned.

That there is such a thing is indicated by the fact that while the man who exhibits in action the other forms of wickedness acts wrongly indeed, but not graspingly (e.g. the man who throws away his shield through cowardice or speaks harshly through bad temper or fails to help a friend with money through meanness), when a man acts graspingly he often exhibits none of these vices—no, nor all together, but certainly wickedness of some kind (for we blame him) and injustice. There is, then, another kind of injustice which is a part of injustice in the wide sense, and a use of the word 'unjust' which answers to a part of what is unjust in the wide sense of 'contrary to the law'. Again, if one man commits adultery for the sake of gain and makes money by it, while another does so at the bidding of appetite though he loses money and is penalized for it, the latter would be held to be self-indulgent rather than grasping, but the former is unjust, but not self-indulgent; evidently, therefore, he is unjust by reason of his making gain by his act. Again, all other unjust acts are ascribed invariably to some particular kind of wickedness, e.g. adultery to self-indulgence, the desertion of a comrade in battle to cowardice, physical violence to anger; but if a man makes gain, his action is ascribed to no form of wickedness but injustice. Evidently, therefore, there is apart from injustice in the wide sense another, 'particular', injustice which shares the name and nature of the first, because its definition falls within the same genus; for the significance of both consists in a relation to one's neighbour, but the one is concerned with honour or money or safety—or that which includes all these, if we had a single name for it—and its motive is the pleasure that arises from gain; while the other is concerned with all the objects with which the good man is concerned.

It is clear, then, that there is more than one kind of justice, and that there is one which is distinct from virtue entire; we must try to grasp its genus and differentia.

The unjust has been divided into the unlawful and the unfair, and the just into the lawful and the fair. To the unlawful answers the aforementioned sense of injustice. But since the unfair and the unlawful are not the same, but are different as a part is from its whole (for all that is unfair is unlawful, but not all that is unlawful is unfair), the unjust and injustice in the sense of the unfair are not the same as but different from the former kind, as part from whole; for injustice in this sense is a part of injustice in the wide sense, and similarly justice in the one sense of justice in the other. Therefore we must speak also about particular justice and particular injustice, and similarly about the just and the unjust. The justice, then, which answers to the whole of virtue, and the corresponding injustice, one being the exercise of virtue as a whole, and the other that of vice as a whole, towards one's neighbour, we may leave on one side. And how the meanings of 'just' and 'unjust' which answer to these are to be distinguished is evident; for practically the majority of the acts commanded by the law are a whole; for the law bids us practise every virtue and forbids us to practise any vice. And the things that tend to produce virtue taken as a whole are those of the acts prescribed by the law which have been prescribed with a view to education for the common good. But with regard to the education of the individual as such, which makes him without qualification a good *man*, we must determine later whether this is the function of the political art or of another; for perhaps it is not the same to be a good man and a good citizen of any state taken at random.

Of particular justice and that which is just in the corresponding sense, (A) one kind is that which is manifested in distributions of honour or money or the other things that fall to be divided among those who have a share in the constitution (for in these it is possible for one man to have a share either unequal or equal to that of another), and (B) one is that which plays a rectifying part in transactions between man and man. Of this there are two divisions; of transactions (1) some are voluntary and (2) others involuntary—voluntary such transactions as sale, purchase, loan for consumption, pledging, loan for use, depositing, letting (they are called voluntary because the origin of these transactions is voluntary), while of the involuntary (*a*) some are clandestine, such as theft, adultery, poisoning, procuring, enticement of slaves, assassination, false witness, and (*b*) others are violent, such as assault, imprisonment, murder, robbery with violence, mutilation, abuse, insult.

[Justice in Distribution]

3. (A) We have shown that both the unjust man and the unjust act are unfair or unequal; now it is clear that there is also an intermediate between the two unequals involved in either case. And this is the equal; for in any kind of action in which there is a more and a less there is also what is equal. If, then, the unjust is unequal, the just is equal, as all men suppose it to be, even apart from argument. And since the equal is intermediate, the just will be intermediate. Now equality implies at least two things. The just, then, must be both intermediate and equal and relative (i.e. for certain persons). And *qua* intermediate it must be between certain things (which are respectively greater and less); *qua* equal, it involves *two* things; *qua* just, it is for certain people. The just, therefore, involves at least four terms; for the persons for whom it is in fact just are two, and the things in which it is manifested, the objects distributed, are two. And the same equality will exist between the persons and between the things concerned; for as the latter—the things concerned—are related, so are the former; if they are not equal, they will not have what is equal, but this is the origin of quarrels and complaints—when either equals have and are awarded unequal shares, or unequals equal shares. Further, this is plain from the fact that awards should be 'according to merit'; for all men agree that what is just in distribution must be according to merit in some sense, though they do not all specify the same sort of merit, but democrats identify it with the status of freeman, supporters of oligarchy with wealth (or with noble birth), and supporters of aristocracy with excellence. . . .

This, then, is what the just is—the proportional; the unjust is what violates the proportion. Hence one term becomes too great, the other too small, as indeed happens in practice; for the man who acts unjustly has too much, and the man who is unjustly treated too little, of what is good. In the case of evil the reverse is true; for the lesser evil is reckoned a good in comparison with the greater evil, since the lesser evil is rather to be chosen than the greater, and what is worthy of choice is good, and what is worthier of choice a greater good.

This, then, is one species of the just.

[Justice in Rectification]

4. (B) The remaining one is the rectificatory, which arises in connexion with transactions both voluntary and involuntary. This form of the just has a different specific character from the former. For the justice which distributes common possessions is always in accordance with the kind of proportion mentioned above (for in the case also in which the distribution is made from the common funds of a partnership it will be according to the same ratio which the funds put into the business by the partners bear to one another); and the injustice opposed to this kind of justice is that which violates the proportion. But the justice in transactions between man and man is a sort of equality indeed, and the injustice a sort of inequality; not according to that kind or proportion, however, but according to arithmetical proportion. For it makes no difference whether a good man has defrauded a bad man or a bad man a good one, nor whether it is a good or a bad man that has committed adultery; the law looks only to the distinctive character of the injury, and treats the parties as equal, if one is in the wrong and the other is being wronged, and if one inflicted injury and the other has received it. Therefore, this kind of injustice being an inequality, the judge tries to equalize it; for in the case also in which one has received and the other has inflicted a wound, or one has slain and the other been slain, the suffering and the action have been unequally distributed; but the judge tries to equalize things by means of the penalty, taking away from the gain of the assailant. For the term 'gain' is applied generally to such cases, even if it be not a term appropriate to certain cases, e.g. to the person who inflicts a wound—and 'loss' to the sufferer; at all events when the suffering has been estimated, the one is called loss and the other gain. Therefore the equal is intermediate between the greater and the less, but the gain and the loss are respectively greater and less in contrary ways; more of the good and less of the evil are gain, and the contrary is loss; intermediate between them is, as we saw, the equal, which we say is just; therefore corrective justice will be the intermediate between loss and gain. This is why, when people dispute, they take refuge in the judge; and to go to the judge is to go to justice; for the nature of the judge is to be a sort of animate justice; and they seek the judge as an intermediate, and in some states they call judges mediators, on the assumption that if they get what is intermediate they will get what is just. The just, then, is an intermediate, since the judge is so. . . .

Therefore the just is intermediate between a sort of gain and a sort of loss, viz. those which are involuntary; it consists in having an equal amount before and after the transaction.

[Justice and Reciprocity]

5. Some think that *reciprocity* is without qualification just, as the Pythagoreans said; for they defined justice without qualification as reciprocity. Now 'reciprocity' fits neither distributive nor rectificatory justice—yet people *want* even the justice of Rhadamanthus to mean this:

> Should a man suffer what he did, right justice would be done

—for in many cases reciprocity and rectificatory justice are not in accord, e.g. (1) if an official has inflicted a wound, he should not be wounded in return, and if some one has wounded an official, he ought not to be wounded only but punished in addition. Further (2) there is a great difference between a voluntary and an involuntary act. But in associations for exchange this sort of justice does hold men together—reciprocity in accordance with a proportion and not on the basis of precisely equal return. For it is by proportionate requital that the city holds together. Men seek to return either evil for evil—and if they cannot do so, think their position mere slavery—or good for good—and if they cannot do so there is no exchange, but it is by exchange that they hold together. This is why they give a prominent place to the temple of the Graces—to promote the requital of services; for this is characteristic of grace—we should serve in return one who has shown grace to us, and should another time take the initiative in showing it. . . .

[Justice and the Mean]

We have now defined the unjust and the just. These having been marked off from each other, it is plain that just action is intermediate between acting unjustly and being unjustly treated; for the one is to have too much and the other to have too little. Justice is a kind of mean, but not in the same way as the other virtues, but because it relates to an intermediate amount, while injustice relates to the extremes. And justice is that in virtue of which the just man is said to be a doer, by choice, of that which is just, and one who will distribute either between himself and another or between two others not so as to give more of what is desirable to himself and less to his neighbour (and conversely with what is harmful), but so as to give what is equal in accordance with proportion; and similarly in distributing between two other persons. Injustice on the other hand is similarly related to the unjust, which is excess and defect, contrary to proportion, of the useful or hurtful. For which reason injustice is excess and defect, viz. because it is productive of excess and defect—in one's own case excess of what is in its own nature useful and defect of what is hurtful, while in the case of others it is as a whole like what it is in one's own case, but proportion may be violated in either direction. In the unjust act to have too little is to be unjustly treated; to have too much is to act unjustly.

Let this be taken as our account of the nature of justice and injustice, and similarly of the just and the unjust in general.

[Political Justice]

6. Since acting unjustly does not necessarily imply being unjust, we must ask what sort of unjust acts imply that the doer is unjust with respect to each type of injustice, e.g. a thief, an adulterer, or a brigand. Surely the answer does not turn on the difference between these types. For a man might even lie with a woman knowing who she was, but the origin of his act might be not deliberate choice but passion. He acts unjustly, then, but is not unjust; e.g. a man is not a thief, yet he stole, nor an adulterer, yet he committed adultery; and similarly in all other cases.

Now we have previously stated how the reciprocal is related to the just; but we must not forget that what we are looking for is not only what is just without qualification but also political justice. This is found among men who share their life with a view to self-sufficiency, men who are free and either proportionately or arithmetically equal, so that between those who do not fulfil this condition there is no political justice but justice in a special sense and by analogy. For justice exists only between men whose mutual relations are governed by law; and law exists for men between whom there is injustice; for legal justice is the discrimination of the just and the unjust. And between men between whom there is injustice there is also unjust action (though there is not injustice between all between whom there is unjust action), and this is assigning too much to oneself of things good in themselves and too little of things evil in themselves. This is why we do not allow a *man* to rule, but *rational principle*, because a man behaves thus in his own interests and becomes a tyrant. The magistrate on the other hand is the guardian of justice, and, if of justice, then of equality also. And since he is assumed to have no more than his share, if he is just (for he does not assign to himself more of what is good in itself, unless such a share is proportional to his merits—so that it is for others that he labours, and it is for this reason that men, as we stated previously, say that justice is 'another's good'), therefore a reward must be given him, and this is honour and privilege; but those for whom such things are not enough become tyrants.

The justice of a master and that of a father are not the same as the justice of citizens, though they are like it; for there can be no injustice in the unqualified sense towards things that are one's own, but a man's chattel, and his child until it reaches a certain age and sets up for itself, are as it were part of himself, and no one chooses to hurt himself (for which reason there can be no injustice towards oneself). Therefore the justice or injustice of citizens is not manifested in these relations; for it was as we saw according to law, and between people naturally subject to law, and these as we saw are people who have an equal share in ruling and being ruled. Hence justice can more truly be manifested towards a wife than towards children and chattels, for the former is household justice; but even this is different from political justice.

[Justice in Nature and Justice Under Law]

7. Of political justice part is natural, part legal—natural, that which everywhere has the same force and does not exist by people's thinking this or that; legal, that which is originally indifferent, but when it has been laid down is not indifferent, e.g. that a prisoner's ransom shall be a mina, or that a goat and not two sheep shall be sacrificed, and again all the laws that are passed for particular cases, e.g. that sacrifice shall be made in honour of Brasidas, and the provisions of decrees. Now some think that all justice is of this sort, because that which is by nature is unchangeable and has everywhere the same force (as fire burns both here and in Persia), while they see change in the things recognized as just. This, however, is not true in this unqualified way, but is true in a sense; or rather, with the gods it is perhaps not true at all, while with us there is something that is just even by nature, yet all of it is changeable; but still some is by nature, some not by nature. It is evident which sort of thing, among things capable of being otherwise, is by nature; and which is not but is legal and conventional, assuming that both are equally changeable. And in all other things the same distinction will apply; by nature the right hand is stronger, yet it is possible that all men should come to be ambidextrous. The things which are just by virtue of convention end expediency are like measures; for wine and corn measures are not everywhere equal, but larger in wholesale and smaller in retail markets. Similarly, the things which are just not by nature but by human enactment are not everywhere the same, since constitutions

also are not the same, though there is but one which is everywhere by nature the best.

Of things just and lawful each is related as the universal to its particulars; for the things that are done are many, but of *them* each is one, since it is universal.

There is a difference between the act of injustice and what in unjust, and between the act of justice and what is just; for a thing is unjust by nature or by enactment; and this very thing, when it has been done, is an act of injustice, but before it is done is not yet that but is unjust. So, too, with an act of justice (though the general term is rather 'just action', and 'act of justice' is applied to the correction of the act of injustice).

Each of these must later be examined separately with regard to the nature and number of its species and the nature of the things with which it is concerned.

[Acting Justly]

8. Acts just and unjust being as we have described them, a man acts unjustly or justly whenever he does such acts voluntarily; when involuntarily, he acts neither unjustly nor justly except in an incidental way; for he does things which happen to be just or unjust. Whether an act is or is not one of injustice (or of justice) is determined by its voluntariness or involuntariness; for when it is voluntary it is blamed, and at the same time is then an act of injustice; so that there will be things that are unjust but not yet acts of injustice, if voluntariness be not present as well. By the voluntary I mean, as has been said before, any of the things in a man's own power which he does with knowledge, i.e. not in ignorance either of the person acted on or of the instrument used or of the end that will be attained (e.g. whom he is striking, with what, and to what end), each such act being done not incidentally nor under compulsion (e.g. if A takes B's hand and therewith strikes C, B does not act voluntarily; for the act was not in his own power). The person struck may be the striker's father, and the striker may know that it is a man or one of the persons present, but not know that it is his father; a similar distinction may be made in the case of the end, and with regard to the whole action. Therefore that which is done in ignorance, or though not done in ignorance is not in the agent's power, or is done under compulsion, is involuntary (for many natural processes, even, we knowingly both perform and experience, none of which is either voluntary or involuntary; e.g. growing old or dying). But in the case of unjust and just acts alike the injustice or justice may be only incidental; for a man might return a deposit unwillingly and from fear, and then he

must not be said either to do what is just or to act justly, except in an incidental way. Similarly the man who under compulsion and unwillingly fails to return the deposit must be said to act unjustly, and to do what is unjust, only incidentally. Of voluntary acts we do some by choice, others not by choice; by choice those which we do after deliberation, not by choice those which we do without previous deliberation. Thus there are three kinds of injury in transactions between man and man; those done in ignorance are *mistakes* when the person acted on, the act, the instrument, or the end that will be attained is other than the agent supposed; the agent thought either that he was not hitting any one or that he was not hitting with this missile or not hitting this person or to this end, but a result followed other than that which he thought likely (e.g. he threw not with intent to wound but only to prick), or the person hit or the missile was other than he supposed. Now when (1) the injury takes place contrary to reasonable expectation, it is a *misadventure*. When (2) it is not contrary to reasonable expectation, but does not imply vice, it is a *mistake* (for a man makes a mistake when the fault originates in him, but is the victim of accident when the origin lies outside him). When (3) he acts with knowledge but not after deliberation, it is an *act of injustice*—e.g. the acts due to anger or to other passions necessary or natural to man; for when men do such harmful and mistaken acts they act unjustly, and the acts are acts of injustice, but this does not imply that the doers are unjust or wicked; for the injury is not due to vice. But when (4) a man acts from choice, he is an *unjust man* and a vicious man.

Hence acts proceeding from anger are rightly judged not to be done of malice aforethought; for it is not the man who acts in anger but he who enraged him that starts the mischief. Again, the matter in dispute is not whether the thing happened or not, but its justice; for it is apparent injustice that occasions rage. For they do not dispute about the occurrence of the act—as in commercial transactions where one of the two parties *must* be vicious—unless they do so owing to forgetfulness; but, agreeing about the fact, they dispute on which side justice lies (whereas a man who has deliberately injured another cannot help knowing that he has done so), so that the one thinks he is being treated unjustly and the other disagrees.

But if a man harms another by choice, he acts unjustly; and *these* are the acts of injustice which imply that the doer is an unjust man, provided that the act violates proportion or equality. Similarly, a man *is just* when he acts justly by choice; but he *acts justly* if he merely acts voluntarily.

Of voluntary acts some are excusable, others not. For the mistakes which men make not only in ignorance but also from ignorance are excusable, while those which men do not from ignorance but (though they do them *in* ignorance) owing to a passion which is neither natural nor such as man is liable to, are not excusable.

Book VI

[Virtues of the Intellect]

1. Since we have previously said that one ought to choose that which is intermediate, not the excess nor the defect, and that the intermediate is determined by the dictates of the right rule, let us discuss the nature of these dictates. In all the states of character we have mentioned, as in all other matters, there is a mark to which the man who has the rule looks, and heightens or relaxes his activity accordingly, and there is a standard which determines the mean states which we say are intermediate between excess and defect, being in accordance with the right rule. But such a statement, though true, is by no means clear; for not only here in all other pursuits which are objects of knowledge it is indeed true to say that we must not exert ourselves nor relax our efforts too much nor too little, but to an intermediate extent and as the right rule dictates; but if a man had only this knowledge he would be none the wiser—e.g. we should not know what sort of medicines to apply to our body if some one were to say 'all those which the medical art prescribes, and which agree with the practice of one who possesses the art.' Hence it is necessary with regard to the states of the soul also not only that this true statement should be made, but also that is should be determined what is the right rule and what is the standard that fixes it.

We divided the virtues of the soul and said that some are virtues of character and others of intellect. Now we have discussed in detail the moral virtues; with regard to the others let us express our view as follows, beginning with some remarks about the soul. We said before that there are two parts of the soul—that which grasps a rule or rational principle, and the irrational; let us now draw a similar distinction within the part which grasps a rational principle. And let it be assumed that there are two parts which grasp a rational principle—one by which we contemplate the kind of things whose originative causes are invariable, and one by which we contemplate variable things; for where objects differ in kind the part of the soul answering to each of the two is different in kind, since it is in virtue of a certain likeness and kinship with their objects that they have the knowledge they have. Let one of these parts be called the scientific and the other the calculative; for to deliberate and to calculate are the same thing, but no one deliberates about the invariable. Therefore the calculative is one part of the faculty which grasps a rational principle. We must, then, learn what is the best state of each of these two parts; for this is the virtue of each.

[Intellectual Virtue: Practice and Contemplation]

2. The virtue of a thing is relative to its proper work. Now there are three things in the soul which control action and truth—sensation, reason, desire.

Of these sensation originates no action; this is plain from the fact that the lower animals have sensation but no share in action.

What affirmation and negation are in thinking, pursuit and avoidance are in desire; so that since moral virtue is a state of character concerned with choice, and choice is deliberate desire, therefore both the reasoning must be true and the desire right, if the choice is to be good, and the latter must pursue just what the former asserts. Now this kind of intellect and of truth is practical; of the intellect which is contemplative, not practical nor productive, the good and the bad state are truth and falsity respectively (for this is the work of everything intellectual); while of the part which is practical and intellectual the good state is truth in agreement with right desire.

The origin of action—its efficient, not its final cause—is choice, and that of choice is desire and reasoning with a view to an end. This is why choice cannot exist either without reason and intellect or without a moral state; for good action and its opposite cannot exist without a combination of intellect and character. Intellect itself, however, moves nothing, but only the intellect which aims at an end and is practical; for this rules the productive intellect as well, since every one who makes makes for an end, and that which is made is not an end in the unqualified sense (but only an end in a particular relation, and the end of a particular operation)—only that which is *done* is that; for good action is an end, and desire aims at this. Hence choice is either desiderative reason or ratiocinative desire, and such an origin of action is a man. (It is to be noted that nothing that is past is an object of choice, e.g. no one chooses to have sacked Troy; for no one *deliberates* about the past, but about what is future and capable of being otherwise, while what is past is not capable of not having taken place; hence Agathon is right in saying

> For this alone is lacking even to God,
> To make undone things that have once been done.)

The work of both the intellectual parts, then, is truth. Therefore the states that are most strictly those in respect of which each of these parts will reach truth are the virtues of the two parts.

[Practical Wisdom]

5. Regarding *practical wisdom* we shall get at the truth by considering who are the persons we credit with it. Now it is thought to be the mark of a man of practical wisdom to be able to deliberate well about what is good and expedient for himself, not in some particular respect, e.g. about what sorts of thing conduce to health or to strength, but about what sorts of thing conduce to the good life in general. This is shown by the fact that we credit men with practical wisdom in some particular respect when they have calculated well with a view to some good end which is one of those that are not the object of any art. It follows that in the general sense also the man who is capable of deliberating has practical wisdom. Now no one deliberates about things that are invariable, nor about things that it is impossible for him to do. Therefore, since scientific knowledge involves demonstration, but there is no demonstration of things whose first principles are variable (for all such things might actually be otherwise), and since it is impossible to deliberate about things that are of necessity, practical wisdom cannot be scientific knowledge nor art; not science because that which can be done is capable of being otherwise, not art because action and making are different kinds of thing. The remaining alternative, then, is that it is a true and reasoned state of capacity to act with regard to the things that are good or bad for man. For while making has an end other than itself, action cannot; for good action itself is its end. It is for this reason that we think Pericles and men like him have practical wisdom, viz. because they can see what is good for themselves and what is good for men in general; we consider that those can do this who are good at managing households or states. (This is why we call temperance (*sophrosyne*) by this name; we imply that it preserves one's practical wisdom (*sodsousa ten phronesin*). Now what it preserves is a judgement of the kind we have described. For it is not any and every judgement that pleasant and painful objects destroy and pervert, e.g. the judgement that the triangle has or has not its angles equal to two right angles, but only judgements about what is to be done. For the originating causes of the things that are done consist in the end at which they are aimed; but the man who has

been ruined by pleasure or pain forthwith fails to see any such originating cause—to see that for the sake of this or because of this he ought to choose and do whatever he chooses and does; for vice is destructive of the originating cause of action.

Practical wisdom, then, must be a reasoned and true state of capacity to act with regard to human goods. But further, while there is such a thing as excellence in art, there is no such thing as excellence in practical wisdom; and in art he who errs willingly is preferable, but in practical wisdom, as in the virtues, he is the reverse. Plainly, then practical wisdom is a virtue and not an art. There being two parts of the soul that can follow a course of reasoning, it must be the virtue of one of the two, i.e. of that part which forms opinions; for opinion is about the variable and so is practical wisdom. But yet it is not only a reasoned state; this is shown by the fact that a state of that sort may be forgotten but practical wisdom cannot.

[Philosophic Wisdom]

7. *Wisdom* (1) in the arts we ascribe to their most finished exponents, e.g. to Phidias as a sculptor and to Polyclitus as a maker of portrait-statues, and here we mean nothing by wisdom except excellence in art; but (2) we think that some people are wise in general, not in some particular field or in any other limited respect, as Homer says in the *Margites*,

> Him did the gods make neither a digger nor yet a ploughman
> Nor wise in anything else.

Therefore wisdom must plainly be the most finished of the forms of knowledge. It follows that the wise man must not only know what follows from the first principles, but must also possess truth about the first principles. Therefore wisdom must be intuitive reason combined with scientific knowledge—scientific knowledge of the highest objects which has received as it were its proper completion.

Of the highest objects, we say; for it would be strange to think that the art of politics, or practical wisdom, is the best knowledge, since man is not the best thing in the world. Now if what is healthy or good is different for men and for fishes, but what is white or straight is always the same, any one would say that what is wise is the same but what is practically wise is different; for it is to that which observes well the various matters concerning itself that one ascribes practical wisdom, and it is to this that one will entrust such matters. This is why we say that some even of the lower animals have practical wisdom, viz. those which are found to have a power of foresight with regard to their own life. It is evident also that philosophic wisdom and the art of politics cannot be the same; for if the state of mind concerned with a man's own interests is to be called philosophic wisdom, there will be many philosophic wisdoms; there will not be one concerned with the good of all animals (any more than there is one art of medicine for all existing things), but a different philosophic wisdom about the good of each species.

But if the argument be that man is the best of the animals, this makes no difference; for there are other things much more divine in their nature even than man, e.g., most conspicuously, the bodies of which the heavens are framed. From what has been said it is plain, then, that philosophic wisdom is scientific knowledge, combined with intuitive reason, of the things that are highest by nature. This is why we say Anaxagoras, Thales, and men like them have philosophic but not practical wisdom, when we see them ignorant of what is to their own advantage, and why we say that they know things that are remarkable, admirable, difficult, and divine, but useless; viz. because it is not human goods that they seek.

Practical wisdom on the other hand is concerned with things human and things about which it is possible to deliberate; for we say this is above all the work of the man of practical wisdom, to deliberate well, but no one deliberates about things invariable, nor about things which have not an end, and that a good that can be brought about by action. The man who is without qualification good at deliberating is the man who is capable of aiming in accordance with calculation at the best for man of things attainable by actions. Nor is practical wisdom concerned with universals only—it must also recognize the particulars; for it is practical, and practice is concerned with particulars. This is why some who do not know, and especially those who have experience, are more practical than others who know; for if a man knew that light meats are digestible and wholesome, but did not know which sorts of meat are light, he would not produce health, but the man who knows that chicken is wholesome is more likely to produce health.

Now practical wisdom is concerned with action; therefore one should have both forms of it, or the latter in preference to the former. But of practical as of philosophic wisdom there must be a controlling kind.

[Excellence in Deliberation]

9. There is a difference between inquiry and deliberation; for deliberation is inquiry into a particular kind of thing. We must grasp the nature

of excellence in deliberation as well—whether it is a form of scientific knowledge, or opinion, or skill in conjecture, or some other kind of thing. *Scientific knowledge* it is not; for men do not inquire about the things they know about, but good deliberation is a kind of deliberation, and he who deliberates inquires and calculates. Nor is it *skill in conjecture*; for this both involves no reasoning and is something that is quick in its operation, while men deliberate a long time, and they say that one should carry out quickly the conclusions of one's deliberation, but should deliberate slowly. Again, *readiness of mind* is different from excellence in deliberation; it is a sort of skill in conjecture. Nor again is excellence in deliberation *opinion* of any sort. But since the man who deliberates badly makes a mistake, while he who deliberates well does so correctly, excellence in deliberation is clearly a kind of correctness, but neither of knowledge nor of opinion; for there is no such thing as correctness of knowledge (since there is no such thing as error of knowledge), and correctness of opinion is truth; and at the same time everything that is an object of opinion is already determined. But again excellence in deliberation involves reasoning. The remaining alternative, then, is that it is *correctness of thinking*; for this is not yet assertion, since, while even opinion is not inquiry but has reached the stage of assertion, the man who is deliberating, whether he does so well or ill, is searching for something and calculating.

But excellence in deliberation is a certain correctness of deliberation; hence we must first inquire what deliberation is and what it is about. And, there being more than one kind of correctness, plainly excellence in deliberation is not any and every kind; for (1) the incontinent man and the bad man, if he is clever, will reach as a result of his calculation what he sets before himself, so that he will have deliberated correctly, but he will have got for himself a great evil. Now to have deliberated well is thought to be a good thing; for it is this kind of correctness of deliberation that is excellence in deliberation, viz. that which tends to attain what is good. But (2) it is possible to attain even good by a false syllogism, and to attain what one ought to do but not by the right means, the middle term being false; so that this too is not yet excellence in deliberation—this state in virtue of which one attains what one ought but not by the right means. Again (3) it is possible to attain it by long deliberation while another man attains it quickly. Therefore in the former case we have not yet got excellence in deliberation, which is rightness with regard to the expedient—rightness in respect both of the end, the manner, and the time. (4) Further it is possible to have deliberated well either in the unqualified sense or with reference to a particular end. Excellence in deliberation in the unqualified sense, then, is that which succeeds with reference to what is the end in the unqualified sense, and excellence in deliberation in a particular sense is that which succeeds relatively to a particular end. If, then, it is characteristic of men of practical wisdom to have deliberated well, excellence in deliberation will be correctness with regard to what conduces to the end of which practical wisdom is the true apprehension.

[Understanding]

10. Understanding, also, and goodness of understanding, in virtue of which men are said to be men of understanding or of good understanding, are neither entirely the same as opinion or scientific knowledge (for at that rate all men would have been men of understanding), nor are they one of the particular sciences, such as medicine, the science of things connected with health, or geometry, the science of spatial magnitudes. For understanding is neither about things that are always and are unchangeable, nor about any and every one of the things that come into being, but about things which may become subjects of questioning and deliberation. Hence it is about the same objects as practical wisdom; but understanding and practical wisdom are not the same. For practical wisdom issues commands, since its end is what ought to be done or not to be done; but understanding only judges. (Understanding is identical with goodness of understanding, men of understanding with men of good understanding.) Now understanding is neither the having nor the acquiring of practical wisdom; but as learning is called understanding when it means the exercise of the faculty of knowledge, so 'understanding' is applicable to the exercise of the faculty of opinion for the purpose of judging of what someone else says about matters with which practical wisdom is concerned—and of judging soundly; for 'well' and 'soundly' are the same thing. And from this has come the use of the name 'understanding', viz. from the application of the word to the grasping of scientific truth; for we often call such grasping understanding.

[Intuitive Reason, Judgement and Experience]

11. What is called judgement, in virtue of which men are said to 'be sympathetic judges' and to 'have judgement', is the right discrimination of the equitable. This is shown by the fact that we say the equitable man

is above all others a man of sympathetic judgement, and identify equity with sympathetic judgement about certain facts. And sympathetic judgement is judgement which discriminates what is equitable and does so correctly; and correct judgement is that which judges what is true.

Now all the states we have considered converge, as might be expected, to the same point; for when we speak of judgement and understanding and practical wisdom and intuitive reason we credit the same people with possessing judgement and having reached years of reason and with having practical wisdom and understanding. For all these faculties deal with ultimates, i.e. with particulars; and being a man of understanding and of good or sympathetic judgement consists in being able to judge about the things with which practical wisdom is concerned; for the equities are common to all good men in relation to other men. Now all things which have to be done are included among particulars or ultimates; for not only must the man of practical wisdom know particular facts, but understanding and judgement are also concerned with things to be done, and these are ultimates. And intuitive reason is concerned with the ultimates in both directions; for both the first terms and the last are objects of intuitive reason and not of argument, and the intuitive reason which is presupposed by demonstrations grasps the unchangeable and first terms, while the intuitive reason involved in practical reasonings grasps the last and variable fact, i.e. the minor premiss. For these variable facts are the starting-points for the apprehension of the end, since the universals are reached from the particulars; of these therefore we must have perception, and this perception is intuitive reason.

This is why these states are thought to be natural endowments—why, while no one is thought to be a philosopher by nature, people are thought to have by nature judgement, understanding, and intuitive reason. This is shown by the fact that we think our powers correspond to our time of life, and that a particular age brings with it intuitive reason and judgement; this implies that nature is the cause. [Hence intuitive reason is both beginning and end; for demonstrations are from these and about these.] Therefore we ought to attend to the undemonstrated sayings and opinions of experienced and older people or of people of practical wisdom not less than to demonstrations; for because experience has given them an eye they see aright.

We have stated, then, what practical and philosophic wisdom are, and with what each of them is concerned, and we have said that each is the virtue if a different part of the soul.

[Practical Wisdom is Essential to Moral Virtue and Philosophic Wisdom]

13. We must therefore consider virtue also once more; for virtue too is similarly related; as practical wisdom is to cleverness—not the same, but like it—so is natural virtue to virtue in the strict sense. For all men think that each type of character belongs to its possessors in some sense by nature; for from the very moment of birth we are just or fitted for self-control or brave or have the other moral qualities; but yet we seek something else as that which is good in the strict sense—we seek for the presence of such qualities in another way. For both children and brutes have the natural dispositions to these qualities, but without reason these are evidently hurtful. Only we seem to see this much, that, while one may be led astray by them, as a strong body which moves without sight may stumble badly because of its lack of sight, still, if a man once acquires reason, that makes a difference in action; and his state, while still like what it was, will then be virtue in the strict sense. Therefore, as in the part of us which forms opinions there are two types, cleverness and practical wisdom, so too in the moral part there are two types, natural virtue and virtue in the strict sense, and of these the latter involves practical wisdom. This is why some say that all the virtues are forms of practical wisdom, and why Socrates in one respect was on the right track while in another he went astray; in thinking that all the virtues were forms of practical wisdom he was wrong, but in saying they implied practical wisdom he was right. This is confirmed by the fact that even now all men, when they define virtue, after naming the state of character and its objects add 'that (state) which is in accordance with the right rule'; now the right rule is that which is in accordance with practical wisdom. All men, then, seem somehow to divine that this kind of state is virtue, viz. that which is in accordance with practical wisdom. But we must go a little further. For it is not merely the state in accordance with the right rule, but the state that implies the *presence* of the right rule, that is virtue; and practical wisdom is a right rule about such matters. Socrates, then, thought the virtues were rules or rational principles (for he thought they were, all of them, forms of scientific knowledge), while we think they *involve* a rational principle.

It is clear, then, from what has been said, that it is not possible to be good in the strict sense without practical wisdom, nor practically wise without moral virtue. But in this way we may also refute the dialectical argument whereby it might be contended that the virtues exist in separation from each other; the same man, it might be said, is not best equipped by nature for all the virtues, so that he will have already acquired one when he has not yet acquired another. This is possible in respect of the natural virtues, but not in respect of those in respect of which a man is called without qualification good; for with the presence of the one quality, practical wisdom, will be given all the virtues. And it is plain that, even if it were of no practical value, we should have needed it because it is the virtue of the part of us in question; plain too that the choice will not be right without practical wisdom any more than without virtue; for the one determines the end and the other makes us do the things that lead to the end.

But again it is not *supreme* over philosophic wisdom, i.e. over the superior part of us, any more than the art of medicine is over health; for it does not use it but provides for its coming into being; it issues orders, then, for its sake, but not to it. Further, to maintain its supremacy would be like saying that the art of politics rules the gods because it issues orders about all the affairs of the state.

Book X

[The Happy Life]

6. . . . What remains is to discuss in outline the nature of happiness, since this is what we state the end of human nature to be. Our discussion will be the more concise if we first sum up what we have said already. We said, then, that it is not a disposition; for if it were it might belong to some one who was asleep throughout his life, living the life of a plant, or, again, to some one who was suffering the greatest misfortunes. If these implications are unacceptable, and we must rather class happiness as an activity, as we have said before and if some activities are necessary, and desirable for the sake of something else, while others are so in themselves, evidently happiness must be placed among those desirable in themselves, not among those desirable for the sake of something else; for happiness does not lack anything, but is self-sufficient. Now those activities are desirable in themselves from which nothing is sought beyond the activity. And of this nature virtuous actions are thought to be; for to do noble and good deeds is a thing desirable for its own sake.

Pleasant amusements also are thought to be of this nature; we choose them not for the sake of other things; for we are injured rather than benefited by them, since we are led to neglect our bodies and our property. But most of the people who are deemed happy take refuge in such pastimes. . . . Now, as we have often maintained, those things are both valuable and pleasant which are such to the good man; and to each man the activity in accordance with his own disposition is most desirable, and, therefore, to the good man that which is in accordance with virtue. Happiness, therefore, does not lie in amusement; it would, indeed, be strange if the end were amusement, and one were to take trouble and suffer hardship all one's life in order to amuse oneself. For, in a word, everything that we choose we choose for the sake of something else—except happiness, which is an end. Now to exert oneself and work for the sake of amusement seems silly and utterly childish. But to amuse oneself in order that one may exert oneself, as Anacharsis puts it, seems right; for amusement is a sort of relaxation, and we need relaxation because we cannot work continuously. Relaxation, then, is not an end; for it is taken for the sake of activity.

The happy life is thought to be virtuous; now a virtuous life requires exertion, and does not consist in amusement. And we say that serious things are better than laughable things and those connected with amusement, and that the activity of the better of any two things—whether it be two elements of our being or two men—is the more serious; but the activity of the better is *ipso facto* superior and more of the nature of happiness. And any chance person—even a slave—can enjoy the bodily pleasures no less than the best man; but no one assigns to a slave a share in happiness—unless he assigns to him also a share in human life. For happiness does not lie in such occupations, but, as we have said before, in virtuous activities.

[Happiness and Virtue]

7. If happiness is activity in accordance with virtue, it is reasonable that is should be in accordance with the highest virtue; and this will be that of the best thing in us. Whether it be reason or something else that is this element which is thought to be our natural ruler and guide and to take thought of things noble and divine, whether it be itself also divine or only the most divine element in us, the activity of this in accordance with its proper virtue will be perfect happiness. That this activity is contemplative we have already said.

Now this would seem to be in agreement both with what we said before and with the truth. For, firstly, this activity is the best (since not only is reason the best thing in us, but the objects of reason are the best of knowable objects); and, secondly, it is the most continuous, since we can contemplate truth more continuously than we can *do* anything. And we think happiness has pleasure mingled with it, but the activity of philosophic wisdom is admittedly the pleasantest of virtuous activities;

at all events the pursuit of it is thought to offer pleasures marvellous for their purity and their enduringness, and it is to be expected that those who know will pass their time more pleasantly than those who inquire. And the self-sufficiency that is spoken of must belong most to the contemplative activity. For while a philosopher, as well as a just man or one possessing any other virtue, needs the necessaries of life, when they are sufficiently equipped with things of that sort the just man needs people towards whom and with whom he shall act justly, and the temperate man, the brave man, and each of the others is in the same case, but the philosopher, even when by himself, can contemplate truth, and the better the wiser he is; he can perhaps do so better if he has fellow-workers, but still he is the most self-sufficient. And this activity alone would seem to be loved for its own sake; for nothing arises from it apart from the contemplating, while from practical activities we gain more or less apart from the action. And happiness is thought to depend on leisure; for we are busy that we may have leisure, and make war that we may live in peace. Now the activity of the practical virtues is exhibited in political or military affairs, but the actions concerned with these seem to be unleisurely. Warlike actions are completely so (for no one chooses to be at war, or provokes war, for the sake of being at war; any one would seem absolutely murderous if he were to make enemies of his friends in order to bring about battle and slaughter); but the action of the statesman is also unleisurely, and—apart from the political action itself—aims at despotic power and honours, or at all events happiness, for him and his fellow citizens—a happiness different from political action, and evidently sought as being different. So if among virtuous actions political and military actions are distinguished by nobility and greatness, and these are unleisurely and aim at an end and are not desirable for their own sake, but the activity of reason, which is contemplative, seems both to be superior in serious worth and to aim at no end beyond itself, and to have its pleasure proper to itself (and this augments the activity), and the self-sufficiency, leisureliness, unweariedness (so far as this is possible for man), and all the other attributes ascribed to the supremely happy man are evidently those connected with this activity, it follows that this will be the complete happiness of man, if it be allowed a complete term of life (for none of the attributes of happiness is *in*complete).

But such a life would be too high for man; for it is not in so far as he is man that he will live so, but in so far as something divine is present to him; and by so much as this is superior to our composite nature is its activity superior to that which is the exercise of the other kind of virtue.

If reason is divine, then, in comparison with man, the life according to it is divine in comparison with human life. But we must not follow those who advise us, being men, to think of human things, and, being mortal, of mortal things, but must, so far as we can, make ourselves immortal, and strain every nerve to live in accordance with the best thing to us; for even if it be small in bulk, much more does it in power and worth surpass everything. This would seem, too, to be each man himself, since it is the authoritative and better part of him. It would be strange, then, if he were to choose not the life of his self but that of something else. And what we said before will apply now; that which is proper to each thing is by nature best and most pleasant for each thing; for man, therefore, the life according to reason is best and pleasantest, since reason more than anything else *is* man. This life therefore is also the happiest.

[Happiness and the Philosopher]

8. But in a secondary degree the life in accordance with the other kind of virtue is happy; for the activities in accordance with this befit our human estate. Just and brave acts, and other virtuous acts, we do in relation to each other, observing our respective duties with regard to contracts and services and all manner of actions and with regard to passions; and all of these seem to be typically human. Some of them seem even to arise from the body, and virtue of character to be in many ways bound up with the passions. Practical wisdom, too, is linked to virtue of character, and this to practical wisdom, since the principles of practical wisdom are in accordance with practical wisdom. Being connected with the passions also, the moral virtues must belong to our composite nature; and the virtues of our composite nature are human; so, therefore, are the life and the happiness which correspond to these. The excellence of the reason is a thing apart; we must be content to say this much about it, for to describe it precisely is a task greater than our purpose requires. It would seem, however, also to need external equipment but little, or less than moral virtue does. Grant that both need the necessaries, and do so equally, even if the statesman's work is the more concerned with the body and things of that sort; for there will be little difference there; but in what they need for the exercise of their activities there will be much difference. The liberal man will need money for the doing of his liberal deeds, and the just man too will need it for the returning of services (for wishes are hard to discern, and even people who are not just pretend to wish to act justly); and the brave man will need power if he is to accomplish any of the acts that correspond to his

virtue, and the temperate man will need opportunity; for how else is either he or any of the others to be recognized? It is debated, too, whether the will or the deed is more essential to virtue, which is assumed to involve both; it is surely clear that its perfection involves both; but for deeds many things are needed, and more, the greater and nobler the deeds are. But the man who is contemplating the truth needs no such thing, at least with a view to the exercise of his activity; indeed they are, one may say, even hindrances, at all events to his contemplation; but in so far as he is a man and lives with a number of people, he chooses to do virtuous acts; he will therefore need such aids to living a human life.

But that perfect happiness is a contemplative activity will appear from the following consideration as well. We assume the gods to be above all other beings blessed and happy; but what sort of actions must we assign to them? Acts of justice? Will not the gods seem absurd if they make contracts and return deposits, and so on? Acts of a brave man, then, confronting dangers and running risks because it is noble to do so? Or liberal acts? To whom will they give? It will be strange if they are really to have money or anything of the kind. And what would their temperate acts be? Is not such praise tasteless, since they have no bad appetites? If we were to run through them all, the circumstances of action would be found trivial and unworthy of gods. Still, every one supposes that they *live* and therefore that they are active; we cannot suppose them to sleep like Endymion. Now if you take away from a living being action, and still more production, what is left but contemplation? Therefore the activity of God, which surpasses all others in blessedness, must be contemplative; and of human activities, therefore, that which is most akin to this must be most of the nature of happiness.

This is indicated, too, by the fact that the other animals have no share in happiness, being completely deprived of such activity. For while the whole life of the gods is blessed, and that of men too in so far as some likeness of such activity belongs to them, none of the other animals is happy, since they in no way share in contemplation. Happiness extends, then, just so far as contemplation does, and those to whom contemplation more fully belongs are more truly happy, not as a mere concomitant but in virtue of the contemplation; for this is in itself precious. Happiness, therefore, must be some form of contemplation.

But, being a man, one will also need external prosperity; for our nature is not self-sufficient for the purpose of contemplation, but our body also must be healthy and must have food and other attention. Still, we must not think that the man who is to be happy will need many things or great things, merely because he cannot be supremely happy without external goods; for self-sufficiency and action do not involve excess, and we can do noble acts without ruling earth and sea; for even with moderate advantages one can act virtuously (this is manifest enough; for private persons are thought to do worthy acts no less than despots—indeed even more); and it is enough that we should have so much as that; for the life of the man who is active in accordance with virtue will be happy. Solon, too, was perhaps sketching well the happy man when he described him as moderately furnished with externals but as having done (as Solon thought) the noblest acts, and lived temperately; for one can with but moderate possessions do what one ought. Anaxagoras also seems to have supposed the happy man not to be rich nor a despot, when he said that he would not be surprised if the happy man were to seem to most people a strange person; for they judge by externals, since these are all they perceive. The opinions of the wise seem, then, to harmonize with our arguments. But while even such things carry some conviction, the truth in practical matters is discerned from the facts of life; for these are the decisive factor. We must therefore survey what we have already said, bringing it to the test of the facts of life, and if it harmonizes with the facts we must accept it, but if it clashes with them we must suppose it to be mere theory. Now he who exercises his reason and cultivates it seems to be both in the best state of mind and most dear to the gods. For if the gods have any care for human affairs, as they are thought to have, it would be reasonable both that they should delight in that which was best and most akin to them (i.e. reason) and that they should reward those who love and honour this most, as caring for the things that are dear to them and acting both rightly and nobly. And that all these attributes belong most of all to the philosopher is manifest. He, therefore, is the dearest to the gods. And he who is that will presumably be also the happiest; so that in this way too the philosopher will more than any other be happy.

STUDIES IN MORAL PHILOSOPHY

This is a newly established book series to be published by Peter Lang Publishing, Inc., under the editorship of John Kekes. The editor invites proposals for original book-length manuscripts whose primary focus is on the nature of good lives, character and its development, virtues and vices; the consideration of these and related topics in the light of literary works is particularly welcome. Manuscripts should be written in plain English, readily accessible to non-specialists. Proposals, inquiries, and other correspondence should be sent to Professor John Kekes, Department of Philosophy, SUNY at Albany, Albany, NY 12222.